CLEMATIS
An essential guide

CLEMATIS
An essential guide

Ruth and Jonathan Gooch

THE CROWOOD PRESS

First published in 1996
Revised edition published in 2011 by
The Crowood Press Ltd
Ramsbury, Marlborough
Wiltshire SN8 2HR

www.crowood.com

British Library Cataloguing-in-Publication Data
A catalogue record for this book is available from the British Library.

ISBN 978 1 84797 251 4

The authors are aware that they are not fully informed on plant breeders' rights, trade
names, trade marks and so on; therefore, no legal rights can be extracted from this
book.

Picture credits
All pictures copyright to Tolver Gooch Ltd., except the following: 'Celebration' (Sussex
Plants); *C. integrifolia* 'Alba', 'W.E. Gladstone', 'Königskind', *C. ladakhiana* and
'Warszawska Olga' (Clematis on the Web); JOLLY GOOD and MIENIE BELLE (J. van
Zoest); 'Jackmanii Superba' (Photos Horticultural); 'Hakuree' (Szczepan Marczyński);
C. florida and 'Miss Bateman' (Anne Green-Armytage).

Frontispiece: 'Minister'.

Typeset by Jean Cussons Typesetting, Diss, Norfolk

Printed and bound in China by Everbest Printing Co. Ltd.

Contents

'Dorothy Tolver'
(TOP) and
'Geoffrey Tolver'
(BOTTOM), named
after Ruth's
parents.

Dedication

To our parents, who taught us the joys of gardening, and especially Dorothy and Geoffrey who helped us make our dream of a clematis nursery come true.

Acknowledgements

We are indebted to Wim Snoeijer for his opinions, guidance and proof reading; also to Victoria Matthews and Duncan Donald for their work with the International Clematis Register and their guidance over the years; and to Mike Brown and Val Le May Neville-Parry, National Collection Holders of Herbaceous and Montana Clematis respectively, for all the help they have given us.

We are grateful to many people for allowing us access to their gardens and nurseries for photography, including: Jan van Zoest; Marco de Wit; Val Le May Neville-Parry; Aili, Taavi and Aime Kivistik; Roy and Angela Nunn; East Ruston Old Vicarage; and to Gillian Skeggs for her floristry skills.

We are also immensely grateful to our youngest son, Peter, whose help has been invaluable!

Introduction

We both grew up with gardening in our blood. Both our fathers were keen amateur gardeners who grew almost anything, from vegetables and 'cutting flowers' for the house to tender summer bedding plants. Jon's father also grew dahlias to exhibit at the village flower show, and Ruth's father propagated shrubs and clematis. When first married and gardening together we became increasingly aware of the diversity of clematis. Until then we, like many people, were unaware there were any clematis beyond 'The President' and 'Nelly Moser' or that clematis did not have to climb.

Amongst the almost bewildering number of clematis there are to choose from, there is something for everyone. The majority are deciduous, although some are evergreen. Most are hardy in Britain, whilst a few require protection from extreme cold or wet during the winter. Clematis flowers vary in size considerably, from the size of dinner plates down to tiny scented, star-like flowers. Not only does the size of the bloom vary but also the length of stem. There are some very short, low-growing clematis and in the other extreme there is the very rampant Montana Group. One thing that makes clematis quite unique is that it is possible to have one in flower in our gardens almost all year round.

As clematis are generally thought of as climbers, these versatile plants can be used to clothe walls and fences, adorn pergolas and beautify containers. They can also enhance other climbers such as roses or honeysuckle, or clamber through shrubs and up trees. In our own garden we much prefer to see the clematis scrambling into and over other plants; they look so much more 'at home' growing with a living host, in fact, just as they do in the wild. And talking of wild, there is a range of species, or 'wild', clematis many of which make excellent garden plants.

This is a fully revised edition of the book written by Ruth, originally published by The Crowood Press in 1996. While much factual information has remained the same there have been important additions and updates, including a significant revision to the topic of Nomenclature. The Clematis Profiles A–Z have also been totally reviewed and significantly enlarged. Most exciting perhaps, has been the opportunity to include numerous photographs in this more modern style of layout and production.

This book has been compiled from experience gleaned over the years from growing and admiring these plants. It is written for gardeners – not botanists. The information given about the plants is to aid the gardener in their plant selection, so for many years in our nursery (Thorncroft Clematis) and website we have classified them in 'Groups'. Whilst updating the Clematis Profiles, we have sometimes adopted more recent cultivation information such as some new Cultivar Groups, defined by the actual appearance of the plant rather than its history. In other cases we have retained the use of Pruning Groups (Early Large Flowered and Late Large Flowered) as these are well known and we feel they reflect the more relevant aspect of allocating Groups. So we have listed the clematis under their commonly known name but have added either the Cultivar Group or Pruning Group associated with that plant as this will offer cultural guidance. We welcome feedback and further discussion on this.

We prefer not to take sides in the lasting dispute about the correct pronunciation of 'clematis'. In numerous parts of the British Isles, the pronunciation of clem-*ay*-tis has stood many a gardener in good stead. Probably the most common pronunciation and that favoured by dictionaries, is *clem*-ah-tis. Usage indicates they are both understood and accepted. You can take your choice and still be given the plant you want! Indeed in some parts of the UK and further afield the most common pronunciation is 'cle-*matt*-is', so we feel it best to leave regional preferences unchallenged.

To those readers seeking, or wishing to share their knowledge of clematis we would recommend joining the British Clematis Society or the International Clematis Society. Both have a comprehensive website, annual journal, newsletters and meetings for their members. The contact details for these two organizations can be found at the back of the book.

Our sincere hope with writing this book is that we may be able to inspire other gardeners to 'open their eyes', not only to the vast range of clematis available today, but also to the many different ways there are to grow them. Gardening ourselves has taught us a lot! Clematis are extremely labour-intensive plants to produce on a nursery, and we occasionally wish we grew something easier, if less beautiful! But when we see the result of our labours and talk to other clematis enthusiasts we then remember why we do it.

The 'companionable clematis' is justifiably fast becoming as popular as it was in its Victorian heyday. We hope that this book will encourage you to begin, or add to, a collection of clematis so that you too can experience the joys of these unique and versatile plants.

CHAPTER 2

Plant Hunters and Breeders

For centuries the rose has been immortalized by poets, artists and sculptors, but not so the clematis. The word clematis comes from the Greek *klema* meaning 'vine like', and while this makes the flower seem ancient, little was written about this 'vine' until the 1500s.

Clematis vitalba is our only native clematis in the British Isles. In 1548 in *The Names of Herbes*, William (physician to the Duke of Somerset, Lord Protector at Syon House) referred to *C. vitalba* as Hedge-Vine, possibly due to its growing habit. The name John Gerard, an apothecary and surgeon, gave it in his *Herball* of 1597 was Traveller's Joy, and it still carries that name today, as well as Old Man's Beard.

HOMEOPATHIC CLEMATIS

For years the clematis has been used world-wide for its medicinal properties, to cure such things as headaches and fever, as a laxative and diuretic, as well as for raising blisters! Our native *Clematis vitalba* (also known as Old Man's Beard and Traveller's Joy) was one of thirty-eight different plants discovered to possess healing properties by Dr Edward Bach during the 1930s. He used the individual plant remedies to treat the patient's emotional outlook rather than the physical condition they were suffering from. These 'Bach Flower Remedies' are still available today from health stores, as licensed homoeopathic medicines.

OPPOSITE: 'Paul Farges'.

THE FIRST INTRODUCTIONS

The first clematis introduced to Britain from abroad, the purple flowered *C. viticella*, came from Spain in 1569. This was during the reign of Queen Elizabeth I. At that time our native *Clematis vitalba* was known as Virgin's Bower in recognition of the fact, it is thought, that Elizabeth liked to be called The Virgin Queen. The new introduction *C. viticella* therefore became known as the Purple Virgin's Bower.

During Elizabeth's reign and onwards interest in plants gradually developed, and increasingly new clematis species were introduced to Britain from abroad. By the end of the 1500s four clematis had been introduced which are still grown today: *C. cirrhosa* and *C. flammula* in 1590 from Southern Europe, together with *C. integrifolia* in 1573 and *C. recta* in 1597 from Eastern Europe.

There was then a spell during the 1600s when clematis introductions ceased, until the early part of the 1700s when once again new species were brought to Britain. *C. crispa* and *C. viorna* came from America in 1726 and *C. orientalis* or Yellow Indian Virgin's Bower from Northern Asia in 1727.

Probably one of the most significant clematis discoveries was introduced to Britain from China in 1776. This was *C. florida* and it was to become one of the four main parents of our modern day hybrids. Two more valuable introductions were made in the late 1700s: that of *C. alpina* or Alpine Virgin's Bower from the mountain ranges of N.E. Asia and Central Europe in 1792, and *C. cirrhosa* var. *balearica* from the Mediterranean in 1783.

In the 1800s many other clematis species were

introduced to the British Isles. In 1820 *C. campaniflora* came from Portugal. Then *C. montana*, which was to become one of the most popular clematis species ever, was introduced from the Himalaya by Lady Amherst in 1831. *C. heracleifolia*, an herbaceous clematis which bears clusters of hyacinth-shaped flowers, was introduced from China in 1837, while three years later *C. paniculata*, a species from New Zealand, came to Britain.

Two rather unusual species were introduced about that time and are still grown today. *C. fusca*, brought from N.E. Asia in 1860, has hairy brown urn-shaped flowers which in some respects look more like a seed pod than a flower. *C. aethusifolia*, with carrot-like foliage and clusters of the prettiest little creamy-yellow bell-shaped flowers, was brought from northern China in 1875.

A very significant introduction was made from America in 1868: *C. texensis*, the species which was eventually hybridized to produce 'Gravetye Beauty', 'Duchess of Albany' and others. In the 1800s and 1900s, other American clematis species were introduced to Britain: *C. addisonii*, *C. columbiana*, *C. douglasii*, *C. fremontii*, *C. occidentalis*, *C. pitcheri*, *C. tenuiloba*, *C. versicolor*, *C. verticillaris*, and *C. virginiana*.

In 1898 another of today's popular species, *C. tangutica*, was introduced from Central Asia via Russia.

In fact, many of the original species of clematis are still being grown, although over the years some have been re-named or re-classified. This re-naming has caused great debates in the plant world and has often led to confusion.

THE PLANT HUNTERS

Plant hunting expeditions became more common during the 1800s. As travel became easier, while commercial and missionary work opened up the Far East, more and more expeditions set forth in a bid to satisfy the voracious appetites of plant collectors and botanists back home. Many of these expeditions were fraught with danger, and some plant hunters even lost their lives in the course of their adventures.

David Douglas (1799–1834), a plant hunter from Scotland, was sent to America in 1824 by the Horticultural Society. Amongst the 240 plant species he discovered was *Clematis douglasii*, a native of the Rocky Mountain states, which was named to commemorate his work. His life ended prematurely on the Sandwich Islands when he fell into a pit-trap used by natives to catch wild bulls; he was plant hunting alone and unfortunately the trap had already caught a bull.

Philipp F. von Siebold (1796–1866), a German medical man and naturalist, was employed as a doctor by the Dutch community in Japan, from where he introduced numerous trees and shrubs as well as clematis.

Robert Fortune (1812–1880) was born in Berwickshire and spent some time at the Botanic Gardens in Edinburgh until, in 1841, he moved on to the Horticultural Society's garden at Chiswick as superintendent of its 'hothouse' department. Following the opening of China to westerners, in 1843 the Society sent Fortune there to collect plants for them. He returned to England in 1846 and was appointed curator of the Chelsea Physic Garden, but he stayed for only two years before returning to China to introduce the tea plant to the hill regions of India. It was largely as a result of his work that the tea industry in India flourished. Fortune continued to visit China and later on Japan, collecting and studying their native plants, including a number of clematis.

Ernest Henry Wilson (1876–1930) was one of Britain's most famous plant hunters. Born in Gloucestershire, he worked first of all at the Botanic Gardens in Birmingham, and in 1897 he moved to work at Kew. He visited China a number of times collecting on behalf of subscribers, the first two being Messrs. Veitch and Harvard University. While in China in 1910, he had an unfortunate accident; he and his party were caught in an avalanche of stones, breaking his leg, and he had to be carried for three days before any medical help was obtained. Following his accident Wilson returned to America, from where he was later sent to Japan and the Far East, and in 1927, he was appointed Keeper of the Arnold Arboretum at Harvard. Tragically both he and his wife were

LEGACIES OF THE PLANT HUNTERS

Clematis	Now Named	Named After
C. armandii		Père Armand David, French missionary and plant collector
C. douglasii	*C. hirsutissima*	David Douglas
C. potaninii var. *fargesii*		Paul Farges
C. forrestii	*C. napaulensis*	George Forrest
C. fortunei		Robert Fortune
C. florida 'Sieboldiana'		von Siebold
C. tibetana var. *vernayi* L&S 13342	'Orange Peel'	F. Ludlow and G. Sherriff
C. montana var. *wilsonii*		E.H. Wilson

killed in a motoring accident in America in 1930 – a sad end for one of the world's most famous plant collectors. It has been said that Wilson's services to horticulture were probably greater than any other collector. He introduced some 1,200 species of trees and shrubs and collected over 65,000 sheets of herbarium specimens, many of which were clematis.

George Forrest (1873–1932) was born in Falkirk. During his twenty-eight year career as a plant collector he made seven expeditions to China and Tibet. Once, he recorded in 1910, while on the border of Tibet and China he was hunted for over a week by 'bloodthirsty bands of Lamas'. Hiding from them by day and travelling by night, he eventually managed to get to the city of Talifu in China, only to learn that two French missionaries from the same expedition had not been so lucky and had faced a horrific death at the hands of the Lamas.

Each of these famous men – there were of course many others – made a tremendous contribution to our plant collections in Britain and around the world. Without them we would not have had anything like the number of plants we now take for granted in our gardens, nor would we have our wonderful collection of clematis.

Many species clematis take their name from famous plant hunters, in recognition of their work.

THE EARLY HYBRIDIZERS

During the 1800s, while this frenzy of plant hunt-

ing was taking place abroad, in the countries to which the newly collected species had been introduced nurserymen began hybridizing them.

One of the first ever clematis crosses was made around 1835 by Mr Henderson of the Pine-Apple Nursery, St. John's Wood – a cross between *C. viticella* and *C. integrifolia* which resulted in the plant then known as *C. hendersoni*. We still grow this plant 180 years later, now known as 'Hendersonii' (Diversifolia Group).

As well as the aforementioned *C. viticella* (1569) and *C. florida* (1776) there had been other particularly important clematis introductions: the large flowered *C. patens* (1836) and *C. lanuginosa* (1851) from China, together with 'Fortunei' and 'Standishii'. 'Fortunei' and 'Standishii' were introduced from Japan by Robert Fortune during the mid 1800s and were widely used in hybridizing, but their origin has always remained in question. 'Fortunei' was described as being creamy-white

C. patens growing 'wild' in Japan.

and semi-double; both this and 'Standishii' are now widely thought to be cultivars of *C. patens*.

Both *C. patens* and *C. lanuginosa*, as well as the aforementioned *C. florida*, had large flowers. This no doubt created great excitement, and plantsmen back home became increasingly keen to experiment with hybridizing. Isaac Anderson-Henry of Edinburgh was one of the first to achieve success in hybridizing a beautiful large flowered clematis. During the 1850s he crossed *C. patens* with *C. lanuginosa* and produced two large flowered clematis: a white which he called *C.* x *henryi* (now 'Henryi') and a mauve named *C.* x *lawsoniana* (now 'Lawsoniana'), both of which we still grow today.

Meanwhile, George Jackman and Sons of Woking, Surrey, were also busy crossbreeding clematis.

ORIGINAL HYBRIDS STILL AVAILABLE		
'Belle of Woking'	Jackman	1875
'Countess of Lovelace'	Jackman	1871
'Duchess of Albany'	Jackman	1890
'Duchess of Edinburgh'	Jackman	1875
'Durandii'	Frères	1870
'Étoile Violette'	Morel	1885
'Fair Rosamond'	Jackman	1871
'Gipsy Queen'	Cripps	1877
hendersoni ('Hendersonii')	Henderson	1835
'Henryi'	Anderson-Henry	1855
'Jackmanii'	Jackman	1858
'Jackmanii Alba'	Noble	1878
'Jackmanii Superba'	Jackman	1878
'Lady Caroline Nevill'	Cripps	1866
'Lady Londesborough'	Noble	1869
'Lawsoniana'	Anderson-Henry	1855
'Lord Nevill'	Cripps	1878
'Madame Baron Veillard'	Veillard	1885
'Madame Édouard André'	Veillard	1893
'Madame Grangé'	Grangé	1875
'Miss Bateman'	Noble	1869
'Mrs Cholmondeley'	Noble	1873
'Mrs George Jackman'	Jackman	1873
'Nelly Moser'	Moser	1897
'Perle d'Azur'	Morel	1884
'Proteus'	Noble	1876
'Sir Trevor Lawrence'	Jackman	1890
'Star of India'	Cripps	1867
'The President'	Noble	1876
'Triternata Rubromarginata'	Jackman	1863
'Victoria'	Cripps	1870
'Ville de Lyon'	Morel	1897
'W.E. Gladstone'	Noble	1881
'William Kennett'	Cobbett	1874

'Jackmanii', one of the first hybrid clematis.

One of their first and certainly one of their most famous crosses was 'Jackmanni' (now 'Jackmanii'). This was the result of crossing *C. lanuginosa* with *C. hendersoni* and *C. viticella atrorubens* during 1858, and the first blooms of this cross were seen in 1862. Two plants were selected for naming, one 'Jackmanni', the other *C. rubro-violacea*, and they both received 'certificates of merit of the first class' when shown in 1863. 'Jackmanii' is probably one of the best known clematis in the world, despite the fact many people seem to have difficulty in pronouncing it – we have been asked many times for a Jackiamarny, and we have also been asked for a Jackanory – try Jack-man-ee-i!

Two other nurseries in Britain were also hybridizing clematis at this time. Cripps & Sons of Tunbridge Wells produced 'Lady Caroline Nevill' in 1866 and 'Star of India' in 1867, while Charles Noble of Sunningdale introduced 'Miss Bateman' and 'Lady Londesborough' in 1869. All four of these clematis are still grown today.

It was not just in Britain where clematis were being hybridized. There were famous nurseries throughout Europe also producing excellent crosses. The names of some of the clematis they produced are still familiar to us today.

Initially for our own interest, we decided to note all the old clematis we could find recorded which were hybridized during the nineteenth century yet are still being grown and sold today. The list turned out to be far longer than we had anticipated, and it is quite possible more could be added. Many of these old clematis are still favourites today; 'Victoria' and 'Durandii' are the two we would take to our desert island. Bearing in mind the majority of these cultivars are over a hundred years old, we are sure you will also find the list to be of interest.

By 1877 Jackman's Nursery listed 343 cultivars of clematis. This reflected the popular appeal of clematis at the time and the response to the hybridization boom in the wake of the finds of the plant hunters.

The almost fanatic plant collecting persisted until the outbreak of the First World War, with both Wilson and Forrest bringing numerous treasures back from China. Between the beginning of the twentieth century and the first weeks of war, many more new species were introduced. Among the most important were *C. armandii* and *C. montana* 'Rubens' (1900), *C. rehderiana* (1908), *C. spooneri* (1909), *C. chrysocoma* and *C. macropetala* (1910), and *C. fargesii* (1911), all from China, while the unusual 'rush-stemmed' *C. afoliata* (1908) came from New Zealand.

Although there have been some new species introduced since 1918, the onset of Clematis Wilt caused a fall-off in clematis interest between the two world wars. Despite this, the twentieth century saw many beautiful hybrid clematis produced.

We feel William Robinson and his head gardener Ernest Markham, at Gravetye Manor, Sussex, were between them largely responsible for the re-awakening of interest in clematis. In 1914 at Gravetye, Markham planted clematis seedlings which had been raised by Morel of Lyons. Markham also raised many seedlings himself, one of which was originally called *C. macropetala* var. 'Markhamii' (now 'Markham's Pink'). Two *C. viticella* cultivars were also raised by Markham, 'Blue Belle' and 'Little Nell'. The well-known Texensis Group cultivar 'Gravetye Beauty' is also a tribute to these two gentlemen. Robinson died in 1935, and following Ernest Markham's death two years later, his remaining seedlings were given to Jackman's Nursery in Woking, who named a magenta seedling from that batch, 'Ernest Markham'. These are all cultivars you will currently find available.

In the early 1800s American gardeners grew few clematis and were largely confined to growing their native species. This developed further with the introduction of some large flowered species from China and Japan, which were exhibited in Boston and Philadelphia in the mid 1800s.

As in England, American nurserymen began producing clematis during the late 1800s to satisfy the eager gardeners who were keen to grow these plants. By the early 1890s Parson's Nursery of Flushing, Long Island listed seventy-three cultivars.

However, it was J.E. Spingarn who, following a visit to England in 1927, and his enthusiasm to grow clematis, encouraged American gardeners. He believed that every garden should contain ten or twelve specimens – he aimed to make America 'clematis-conscious'. By the mid 1930s, Spingarn had collected and planted around 250 species and cultivars of clematis in his garden in Amenia, New York, and was considered at the time to be America's only clematis specialist. Spingarn's enthusiasm for these plants led him to write a chapter called *Clematis in America*, in Ernest Markham's book *Clematis* (1935).

In 1895 Frank L. Skinner moved with his family to Canada from Scotland. His keen interest in horticulture led him to breed hardy clematis suitable for coping with Canadian weather conditions. Among his many crosses he used *C. macropetala* and *C. alpina* to provide hardiness, and produced 'Blue Bird', 'Rosy O'Grady' and 'White Swan'. His clematis 'Blue Boy' raised in 1947 was a cross between *C. integrifolia* and *C. viticella* and is said to be extremely hardy. One of his first crosses was thought, for many years, to be lost to cultivation, but 'Grace' was found alive and well in Holland in the 1990s and is now in general production. This dedicated plant hybridizer was honoured in 1943 with an MBE.

Many of the clematis we grow today were produced back in the late nineteenth and early twentieth century by various enthusiastic French nurserymen. The names of Boisselot, Frères, Grangé, Lemoine, Morel, Moser and Veillard will go down in the history of clematis for producing some of the most beautiful of our large flowered hybrids. 'Marie Boisselot', 'Durandii', 'Madame Grangé', 'Étoile Rose', 'Perle d'Azur', 'Nelly Moser' and 'Madame Baron Veillard' are but a few of the 'famous names' produced by these nurserymen.

Elsewhere in Europe clematis also proved very popular; in fact two of today's favoured cultivars 'Lasurstern' (1905) and 'Elsa Späth' (1891) were hybridized in Germany.

POST WWII BREEDERS

It was not until after the Second World War, with the availability of new fungicides to combat the dreaded 'wilt', that interest in clematis was renewed. With new awareness created by magazines and gardening programmes, clematis received a new lease of life. Nurseries again began to specialize in clematis, and once more new cultivars and species were introduced from around the world by enthusiastic growers.

Mr Jan Fopma of Boskoop in the Netherlands was one of Europe's largest exporters of clematis in the late twentieth century, sending plants to Canada, Sweden, the United Kingdom and countries behind the 'iron curtain'. He specialized in producing and introducing clematis which would withstand their extremes of climate.

Other countries with comparable, equally dramatic weather conditions are those of the former Soviet Union such as Latvia, Estonia, Poland and also Sweden. In these countries clematis breeders were, and still are, busy working to produce clematis that will withstand temperatures down to -30°C, which they regularly cope with during the winter months. To enable clematis to overwinter in such a harsh climate, it is normal for them to be hard pruned down to one or two buds during the late autumn, then mulched with peat, bracken, or such like, to insulate against the frost. Snow cover also helps to insulate the crowns of the plants from the most severe frosts. In the spring the mulch is removed and the clematis are once again ready for their summer blooming.

Japan and New Zealand are countries from which we have also seen some stunning clematis introduced in recent years. Of particular note from New Zealand are 'Allanah', 'Prince Charles' and 'Snow Queen', and from Japan 'Frau Susanne', 'Fujimusume', 'Kaen' and 'Tae'.

America was home to one of the largest specialist clematis nurseries in the world in the second half of the last century. Arthur Steffen Senior became interested in clematis in the late 1950s, having previously grown geraniums for the wholesale market. His son Arthur Steffen Jr ('Bing') joined his father in the late 1960s after graduating from Cornell, followed by six years in the army. Bing Steffen was instrumental in promoting clematis throughout America. The nursery at Fairport, New York, produced around one million clematis plants a year, until disaster befell in 1990 following the use of a defective fungicide. The nursery was closed for almost three years while the devastating problems were resolved but, like the phoenix, it rose from the ashes, only to close finally a few years later. Some of their own hybrids introduced in the later years were 'Perrin's Pride' (1987), 'Sunset' (1988), 'The First Lady' (1989), 'Cotton Candy' (1991) and 'Juliette' (1992).

In England, Walter Pennell from Lincoln did much in hybridizing and increasing the numbers of large flowered clematis. Many of his introductions remain some of the most popular available today. They include 'Vyvyan Pennell', 'Richard Pennell', 'Walter Pennell' and 'Veronica's Choice'; also 'Charissima', 'H.F. Young', and 'Mrs N. Thompson', to name but a few.

John Treasure, another great clematarian of the last century, was also responsible for introducing and popularizing clematis. Tom Bennett wrote about John Treasure in the 1994 volume of *The Clematis*, the journal of the British Clematis Society: 'In the years when clematis were in the doldrums, John established, with foresight and determination and entirely from scratch (and, initially, in collaboration with Christopher Lloyd), Treasures of Tenbury, a nursery which was soon to become a mecca for all clematis devotees.'

Jim Fisk MBE, from Westleton in Suffolk, was for many years one of the 'famous names' in the clematis world. Not only did he raise and introduce his own plants, but he was instrumental in bringing to Britain clematis from all over the world. Without his influence we would quite possibly be lacking many of the best clematis we have today. 'Dr Ruppel' which Jim Fisk introduced from Argentina in 1975 and 'Prince Charles' from New Zealand are two of his best 'discoveries'. Another strong connection Jim Fisk had was with Poland, from whence came such beautiful flowers as 'Niobe' (1975), 'Generał Sikorski' (1980), 'Jan Paweł II' (1982), and 'Warszawska Nike' (1986). He also introduced 'Hakuookan' from Japan (1971). Many other 'English' clematis were introduced by Jim Fisk. Among them the ever popular 'Hagley Hybrid' (1956) and 'Alice Fisk', named after his mother (1967). There followed 'Margaret Hunt' (1969), 'Gillian Blades' (1975), 'Louise Rowe' (1984), and 'Freda' (1985). Jim Fisk died in 2004, but many of us remember his generosity and the great influence he had on so many gardeners, including ourselves.

There have been many other notable breeders in recent history. We have seen some excellent cultivars bred by Barry Fretwell in Devon. Probably his best known introduction was the stunning 'Princess Diana' (Texensis Group); also 'Rhapsody', 'Arabella' and 'Kiri Te Kanawa', to name but a few.

Vince and Sylvia Denny from Lancashire were avid collectors and breeders who were also keen to encourage other 'would be' hybridizers to 'have a go'. Their own introductions included 'Sylvia Denny', a double white which has become very popular and is widely grown, and a fantastic montana cultivar called 'Broughton Star', a semi-double, deep dusky pink which is probably the best of this group currently available. Other introductions of theirs we particularly admire are 'Laura Denny', a stunning white and 'Denny's Double', a very neat and tidy powder blue double with flowers in profusion.

Many other amateur growers also produced some wonderful new clematis. Ken Pyne in Chingford, Essex was one whose breeding and careful selection led to excellent cultivars such as 'Andromeda', 'Mercury', 'The Vagabond' and 'June Pyne' being introduced. All are a fitting tribute to an enthusiast and his attention to detail.

Amongst the greatest names of the last century, in many people's eyes, was the Swedish nurseryman and researcher, Dr Magnus Johnson. Magnus not only collected, grew and bred clematis, but he researched and recorded every detail of every clematis he could find. He studied herbarium specimens and travelled widely collecting seed and knowledge. This culminated in the first great encyclopaedic book on clematis: *Släktet Klematis* [The Genus Clematis], published in 1997. It took fifteen years to produce and despite the fact that it was published in Swedish, soon became an essential reference book for serious clematis enthusiasts. Over the following years it was translated into English and became an even more useful and admired source of precise detail.

As well as his great book, Magnus also left us with many good clematis suitable for most gardens, including those in severe cold climates. He made new crosses using the spring flowering Atragene Group, and his attempts to introduce the repeat flowering and scent of the koreana species has widened the appeal of this group of clematis greatly; good examples are 'Propertius', 'Columella' and 'Brunette'. Amongst many awards conferred on Magnus Johnson is the RHS Gold Veitch Memorial Medal in 2001, for his contribution to gardening and especially for research and hybridization of clematis.

In Warsaw, Poland, Brother Stefan Franczak, a Jesuit monk, earned a well-deserved reputation for patiently trialling and selecting clematis that thrived in the continental climate of central Europe. Many of his introductions commemorated great Polish victories or battles; hence we enjoy 'Monte Cassino' and 'Westerplatte'. His many hybrids include 'Kardynał Wyszyński', 'Warszawska Nike', 'Jan Paweł II', 'Błękitny Anioł', 'Kacper', 'Polish Spirit' and 'Emilia Plater'.

Uno Kivistik, together with his wife Aili, worked with roses and fruit trees on a collective farm in Estonia during the communist era. Their hobby of growing and breeding clematis eventually became a business and, as the Soviet Bloc opened up, those of us in 'the west' suddenly found a wealth of excellent clematis cultivars that were ideal for most gardens. From their impressive collection we have to mention 'Rüütel', 'Romantika', 'Semu', 'Piilu' and 'Roko-Kolla'. The nursery is continued by their son Taavi and his wife Aime.

From the severe cold north of Europe in the Crimea we have benefited from the work of Alexander Volosenko-Valenis, who worked at the Nikitsky State Botanic Garden and during the course of his work bred very hardy examples such as 'Alionushka'. Professor M.A. Beskaravainaya worked with Volosenko-Valenis and continued with breeding and research on clematis. Her work has also produced a number of very hardy cultivars.

RECENT INNOVATIONS

New Zealand has contributed to the world of clematis in two important ways. Firstly, Alister Keay, a nurseryman from Christchurch, has exchanged plants with many around the world and thereby introduced to us 'Aotearoa', 'Allanah', 'Snow Queen' and 'Jenny Keay'. Secondly, the indigenous species of *C. paniculata*, *C. forsteri* and *C. marmoraria* have given us a whole new range of evergreen, scented clematis that are quite novel in their habit and appearance. Many of these have been introduced via the experienced English plantsman Graham Hutchins and his contact with Joe Cartman in New Zealand.

In Japan there have been many clematis breeders. However, as they either worked as amateurs for their own pleasure, or were professionals supplying their own local market, they were seldom known to those of us in Europe. Over the latter part of the twentieth century though, there has been an increasing frequency of exchange of new cultivars both to and from Japan. Many of their best cultivars are the early large flowered types that grow so well in their climate. They also select those that are compact and well suited to growing in pots, so have been increasingly popular in Europe, as the trend is to smaller gardens and more container culture. For us, as a retail nursery, these new introductions are of huge importance. We have been very privileged to be allowed to introduce many new Japanese clematis to Europe on behalf of our Japanese friends.

The Japanese also grow many of their clematis for their cut flower trade, and this has given rise to a host of new clematis that have exquisite flowers with long flower stalks and extended flowering periods. Many of these cultivars are also excellent garden plants.

One of the best known breeders in recent years was Mr Kazushige Ozawa, who introduced many beautiful clematis largely for the cut flower trade in Japan. Two of his beautiful cultivars are 'Rooguchi' and 'Odoriba' which not only make very good cut flowers, but are also excellent planted in our gardens.

Other notable Japanese clematis growers and breeders of recent times are Mr Hiroshi and Mrs Masako Takeuchi, Mr Hiroshi Hayakawa, Mr Tetsuya Hirota and Dr Kozo Sugimoto. Many more will no doubt become known to us over the years to come.

Hybridizing is also still thriving in Europe today. Raymond Evison, based in Guernsey, continues his distinguished career introducing new clematis from abroad and also, increasingly, breeding his own cultivars. One of his many introductions, which is very well known, is 'Freckles'. Of those hybridized at his own nursery, the most recent cultivars have been chosen specially for today's modern gardens where very compact, free flowering clematis are required. Some of the best known are ARCTIC QUEEN, JOSEPHINE and REBECCA.

In Holland, Wim Snoeijer has spent several years concentrating his hybridizing efforts on the herbaceous types of clematis. Long flowering periods and scent are the most popular features of this group as well as their ability to blend into the garden as scramblers in herbaceous beds. But Wim also has new clematis in other groups in mind and this should keep us well supplied with a useful range of new clematis in coming years. FOREVER FRIENDS, INSPIRATION and 'Jan Fopma' are amongst the best known from his already long list of introductions.

In Germany, Manfred Westphal runs another large nursery of significant importance. From here we have been pleased to receive, amongst others, 'Königskind' and 'Rosa Königskind'. Also from Germany, Willem Straver has bred TEMPTATION, 'Maria Cornelia' and 'Dark Eyes' and we know that there are many more exciting cultivars waiting 'in the wings'!

Many of those clematis bred in Poland by Brother Stefan Franczak, mentioned earlier, were introduced to the clematis world by Dr Szczepan Marczyński, who himself is a breeder and wholesale grower of clematis. From his impressively efficient nursery in Poland, Szczepan has embarked on a breeding programme of his own and no has many good introductions to his name. Some are named after family members, such as his wife 'Barbara', mother 'Hania' and daughter 'Julka'; others continue the theme of marking notable people or events in Polish history, for example 'Solidarność', 'Lech Wałęsa' and 'Jerzy Popiełuszko'.

As well as those mentioned, there are many others who may only breed – or discover – one or two clematis. We find that at our nursery we are often asked if we can grow and introduce a new clematis that someone has 'discovered'. In some cases they are not sufficiently different or better than those already available and are not commercially worth introducing. But now and then there is a good, novel flower, and if the plant proves itself after a few years of trials then it can be well worth production and introduction. By this route we have introduced 'Pat Coleman', a chance seedling found by our friend (and plantswoman) of that name. 'Sheila Thacker' was named after the wife of Mr Charles Thacker, a former head gardener and respected clematarian for whom we introduced this wonderful large flowered pale mauvy-blue clematis. Our own breeding includes 'Dorothy Tolver' and 'Geoffrey Tolver' (Ruth's parents) and 'Fond Memories', which is our most significant and impressive cultivar to date.

So, from the very old to the very new, we have looked at many different clematis. Just for a moment we would like to reflect back on the 'old' clematis books, particularly the clematis in Moore and Jackman's *The Clematis as a Garden Flower* (1872), and wonder 'where are they now?' – some of the clematis they mentioned, as far as we are aware, are no longer around. Their names conjure up wonderful pictures. So who were 'Annie Wood' and 'Clara'? We also wonder who might have inspired the naming of 'Maiden's Blush'? Perhaps we will never know.

Clematis are clearly very much back in favour with gardeners and therefore nurserymen. This genus of lovely versatile plants again captivates the imagination and senses of all keen horticulturists, just as it did in the nineteenth century. The continued production of new cultivars can be anticipated with excitement throughout the twenty-first century.

CLEMATIS
BLUE RIVER

CLEMATIS
JACKMANII PURPUREA

CLEMAT

Omoshiro

CHAPTER 3

Selecting Your Clematis

Selecting and planting are probably the most important aspects of clematis cultivation. There are several vital questions to be taken into consideration.

- **Which** plant do I buy?
- **Where** do I site it?
- **When** do I plant it?
- **Why** do I want it?

The selection of the correct plant for the position chosen is so important with clematis because of the wide variety of types. The range of heights, flowering times, pruning needs, colours and so on give both scope for good planting design but, by the same measure, scope for mistakes. We hope that the following guidance will help you to avoid too many of the mistakes!

PURCHASING A PLANT

When selecting a plant always choose a mature clematis from a reputable source. By a mature plant we mean one that is probably eighteen months to two years old. It will have at *least* two good strong stems, although if it has more, so much the better. Check also to make sure it looks healthy; one infested with greenfly, whitefly, spider mite or mildew would be best avoided.

Try to make sure the plant is not terribly pot-bound. Do be careful though if you decide to

upturn the pot, not to tip compost all over the place. Even the most kind-hearted nurseryman may take exception to that. If you pick up a pot and find a few roots coming out of the drainage holes at the bottom, do not be too alarmed. When plants are grown on gravel or sand beds they will send roots down to find moisture and will quickly root into whatever is underneath.

However, if there is a large mass of root grown out of the pot then this could indicate an old or pot-bound plant. There may be times when this is unavoidable if you are looking for a particular cultivar, but it is useful to avoid these potential problems if you can. The plant to reject would be one where the roots can be seen on the surface of the compost as this would indicate, in all probability, that it was badly pot bound.

It is also advisable to make sure there are no damaged stems on the clematis above the soil, as this could be a possible site for the Clematis Wilt fungus to enter the plant.

Other plants we would try to avoid, unless you are happy to re-pot and grow on, are what are known in the trade as 'liners'. These are nothing more than rooted cuttings, potted and pruned down. Liners are small pots about 3in (7cm) across, and are designed to be potted on into larger pots, usually two or three litres, and grown on under cover until saleable. This can take another year. Occasionally you will find nurseries and garden centres offering liners to the unknowing public at very reduced prices. They are a good bargain *if* you are prepared to pot on and wait for them to grow until they are strong enough to be planted out. Unfortunately many people are not aware of this and plant liners straight out into the

OPPOSITE: Selecting your Clematis.

Pot sizes – 2, 2.5 and 3 litre pots.

garden where their chance of survival is governed largely by luck.

Other clematis to be wary of are some of those found on supermarket shelves and market stalls. Again if you are tempted, do take it home, but if it is small and weak be prepared to pot on, prune it back hard and wait for some months before you risk planting it out in the garden.

A well-grown mature clematis will, of course, be more expensive to buy in the first place, but it is well worth paying the extra to get a quality plant and be more sure of success in the long run. As is often said, 'you get what you pay for'.

You should also find that buying a clematis from a specialist grower who can give you all the advice you need regarding selecting, planting, pruning and aftercare will be well worthwhile. An awful lot can be gleaned from their knowledge and experience.

POSITIONING THE PLANT

The aspect of your chosen planting position is an important consideration when selecting your clematis. For instance if you have a chain-link fence between you and your neighbour and this is exposed on all quarters to the wind and the weather, then do avoid the evergreen clematis which require a sheltered south/southwest aspect in which to flourish. Instead, choose a cultivar which will cope with an exposed site and you will have that live green barrier in no time at all.

Also, if the situation is very shady, take into account the fact that the very deep, dark colours will just not show up. The dark blues and purples will be lost completely in a shady position, so choose instead one of the lighter, brighter colours – perhaps a pink, light blue or white. These will really cheer up a dull wall or corner of the garden. If your shady site is a very open, exposed north-facing aspect, careful selection will again be needed to find a cultivar which is not only the right colour but will also cope with an exposed situation.

Another site you need to be very careful with when it comes to selecting a clematis is a south-facing aspect which is in full sun all day long, or for the greater part of the day. You will need to bear in mind that some of the very pale-coloured flowers will lose their colour almost completely if exposed for many hours each day to the sun. Taking 'Nelly Moser' as an example, if you grow this clematis in full sun the colour will bleach out very quickly, whereas if she is grown in full- or semi-shade the colour will last and give a magnificent, colourful display.

Whilst considering the most suitable position for your new plant, bear in mind the need to provide them with a cool root system. Clematis do like to have cool, moist roots, and therefore very open sunny sites can be a problem. The sun will dry out the soil very quickly, leaving the roots to bake. Providing shade is at least as easy as regular watering, so you may like to choose a spot in the shadow of another plant or a wall or fence. Careful consideration of the exact location will often enable you to provide your clematis with ideal growing conditions.

It is wise to be aware of the fact that the later-flowering clematis need a good deal of sun to encourage flowering before the frosts halt them prematurely. Some late flowering cultivars that are best grown in full sun are *C. rehderiana*, 'Allanah', 'Huldine', 'Ernest Markham' and 'Lady Betty Balfour'.

Selecting the colour of your plant to suit the background against which it will be growing is also an important matter for deliberation. Walls are often a problem; we once planted 'Freda', which has deep carmine-coloured flowers and bronze foliage, on a red brick wall – it looked awful. We then moved the plant along to where the wall was cream, and the effect was amazing. Freda's bronze foliage and carmine flowers took on a whole new appearance; instead of looking drab merging into dull brickwork, she is now radiant in her new position. Another mistake we made was when planting against the wall of our dog shed, which is black. Again we did not take everything into consideration. The clematis we chose was a very deep dusky pink, and of course we should have realized that this combination of a black wall and dark clematis just did not complement one another.

When you have decided where to plant, another matter requiring your attention is the height and type of growth the clematis will eventually make. One day we overheard a lady saying to her friend that the *C. integrifolia* she was looking at, which was in full flower at the time, would look lovely growing up her wall. We then had to explain that the Integrifolia Group cultivars usually only make around 2ft (60cm) of growth and are not climbers. It is this sort of information that is so easily overlooked. Another mistake that is often made is planting a very tall or very rampant clematis in a confined space. Montana Group cultivars, which can grow thirty or forty feet (ten or twelve metres), will be unsuitable on a bungalow's walls unless careful training and pruning are carried out.

WHAT TIME OF YEAR TO PLANT?

Clematis can be planted almost all year round, providing the ground is not frozen solid.

The best times to plant are late winter to early or mid spring, and early to mid autumn. During the late winter and spring the ground will be moist and the soil will be starting to warm up as the days get longer and we see more sun. This is a good time to plant and will allow your clematis a chance to establish before the heat of the summer. Do remember though, that later on in the spring it can be very dry, so keep your new plant watered. If the soil dries out completely and the summer winds bake the foliage, your clematis will be far from happy.

During early to mid autumn the soil will, again, be moist and will still be quite warm following the summer sun. Provided you can plant at this time your clematis will have the best possible chance to establish before the worst of the winter comes along. We do feel, however, that clematis which can be a little on the tender side, such as the Armandii, Cirrhosa and Florida Group cultivars, would be far better planted in the spring. This allows them maximum opportunity to settle into their new position and time for the armandiis and cirrhosas to establish a good framework of ripened growth before winter sets in. Planting these clematis in autumn would not allow this essential ripening to take place. The same applies to those that dislike too much wet, such as the Tangutica and Heracleifolia Groups, where again spring planting will give the best conditions for the young plant.

Planting clematis during the heat of summer is of course possible, and many of us do just that. You must, however, realize that not only will the sun bake the earth but the warm winds will dry the foliage, so be prepared to give copious watering.

Alternatively, planting in the middle of winter, providing the ground is not frozen and is workable, is quite acceptable. It will mean, however, that you will need to be particularly sure that the clematis you are purchasing is alive and thriving. During the rest of the year your new plant will be in leaf and possibly in flower, but in winter there will be no leaves to see unless it is one of the few evergreen cultivars. Accordingly, attention must be paid to the buds in the leaf joints. By checking these you should be able to tell the state of the plant. If no healthy viable buds can be found in any of the leaf joints we would leave well alone and look for a plant showing some signs that spring is on its way. To check the newly formed buds in the leaf joints, *carefully* brush them with a finger-tip. If they feel papery and 'give' to the touch they are most likely not viable, but if the buds look fat and feel firm then they will sprout forth in spring, producing a good plant. Having checked the buds in the leaf joints, look down at the base of the plant near the compost. Very often during the winter and early spring you will see new shoots coming from low down, sometimes from below the soil level, sometimes from just above. These will give another indication as to how well your new clematis will grow on. Do not worry though if these shoots are not apparent, providing the buds in the leaf joints are viable.

PURPOSE BEHIND THE PURCHASE

Is your new plant to be a companion plant to add to an established shrub, tree or rose? Is it to become a screen from your neighbours or to hide an ugly building? Or is it perhaps to add extra colour to a part of the garden that needs brightening at that time of the year? It may even perform a mixture of these tasks.

You may be thinking of using clematis as companion plants in the garden. Over the years they tend to have been grown on their own as a specimen plant on a piece of trellis against the wall of the house. While they can look very attractive grown in this way we need to remember that there are many alternative ways to grow clematis, 'companion planting' being one. There are almost endless opportunities to use clematis to enhance the plants already in our gardens. We will suggest a few ideas to you here and these may help to stimulate your interest in this aspect of clematis growing. (There are more ideas in Chapters 7 and 8.)

Planting in association with other plants can work extremely well. We have a particular passion for old roses and grow many different cultivars in our own garden. Each has a clematis running up through it and this helps to provide additional interest in that part of the garden. Further opportunities can be found by using clematis to enhance another shrub which is between flowering and berries and is lacking interest. For example, a summer-flowering clematis grown through a pyracantha or cotoneaster will provide extra colour for either of these shrubs. Having first flowered in the spring, they later produce a spectacular autumnal display of coloured berries. Some friends have a *Cotoneaster watereri*, grown as a single-stemmed tree, and this is host to a clematis which flowers during mid to late summer, called 'Star of India'. The cotoneaster is an ideal host, showing the clematis flowers off to near perfection. Later in the season when the clematis has finally finished flow-

'Avalanche' growing into wisteria.

ering, the cotoneaster comes into its own with a glorious display of red berries.

Clematis can also be considered suitable candidates for use as screens, or perhaps for disguising an unsightly outbuilding. As was mentioned earlier in the section on where to plant, the evergreen cultivars can make an excellent screen, particularly the Armandii Group cultivars which can form quite dense growth. But do remember that evergreen clematis dislike cold biting winds. If you require a screen therefore in a very open, exposed area it would be wise to avoid these cultivars. Where there is harsh exposure to the elements, we would instead use one of the Atragene Group for screening purposes. Although these are not evergreen, they will hold their leaves well into the winter and in no time at all the spring is here and they will be in leaf again, together with a wonderful display of flowers. During the winter the old vines alone provide a surprisingly effective screen.

Where the screen just has to be evergreen and the site is exposed, you could try, as we have done, growing a selection of decorative ivies up livestock netting. This will soon form a dense, practically windproof screen, up which you could then grow a selection of clematis to add colour throughout the spring, summer and autumn months.

The cultivars of the Montana Group really do come into their own when you need to disguise an outbuilding. Beware though – a small garden shed could be totally buried under a montana! So for smaller areas, choose instead a cultivar from the Atragene Group. Neither of these will require much pruning other than a tidy-up when flowering has finished. We use Montana Group cultivars to camouflage our large, open-fronted car shelter which was made out of old electricity poles and floor boards. It was quite a transformation, from an unsightly wooden structure to a rounded, green and altogether more subtle shape with just enough space to drive the cars in and out. In the spring it is once again transformed into a pink and white flowering mass.

CONCLUSION

The choice of clematis can be an extremely difficult one to make. By now you have probably narrowed it down slightly after taking into account the site, flowering period, ultimate height and so on. Now comes the fun part: buying your plant. If you are lucky enough to have a well-stocked garden centre locally or a specialist clematis grower nearby, all is well and good. If you have neither, do not despair. Nowadays plant hunting can be done from the comfort of your armchair or study desk.

Traditionally, it was popular to search out a copy of the modern plant-hunter's bible, entitled *The Plant Finder*. Published each spring by the RHS, it lists literally thousands of plants and where to buy them, including, of course, clematis. *The Plant Finder* is also available on the internet, but for those with no computer, or no wish to 'surf the net', the book is invaluable for finding who stocks the clematis you are seeking.

Some specialist nurseries produce a comprehensive printed catalogue that gives all the details you will require. However, for an increasingly large proportion of people the internet provides the ideal way to find a supplier. Websites can provide a wealth of information about the plants, the supplier and their service. They can also provide many hundreds of photographs and up to date information on availability. There is, however, no substitute for personal recommendation or visiting the nursery in person, as this gives the maximum opportunity to seek advice and inspect the quality of the plants on offer.

Planting against a
wall.

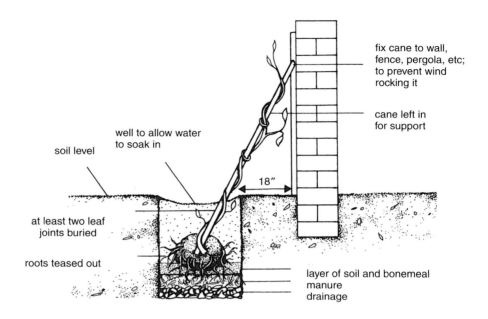

well to allow water
to soak in

soil level

fix cane to wall,
fence, pergola, etc;
to prevent wind
rocking it

cane left in
for support

18″

at least two leaf
joints buried

roots teased out

layer of soil and bonemeal
manure
drainage

root ball. This is a procedure that needs to be done
extremely carefully because it is possible for the
clematis stems to detach themselves from the
roots.

Having removed the pot, make sure to check the
roots before putting the plant into the ground. If
the roots spiral round very tightly together, tease a
few of them out very carefully so that, when placed
in the hole, some roots will be free from the mass
and be better able to grow down into the loosened
soil.

After carefully placing your plant in the hole,
check to make sure the roots are spread out a little.
Then be sure to remove any ties from around the
clematis and cane which will be below soil level,
otherwise the plant will strangle itself. The ties
above the soil can be dealt with at pruning time.
Now replace the soil which you dug out of the hole
and firm this down very carefully, making sure not
to damage the stems.

ENSURING ADEQUATE WATER

When replacing the soil into the hole it is a good
idea to leave a slight well around the base of the
plant (*see* diagram above) which, when the plant is
watered, will allow the moisture to seep straight
down to the roots where it is needed. Water the
plant in well, as this will make sure the soil has
settled around the root ball and that there are no
air pockets left.

Some people sink a pipe, or perhaps a bottle
with the bottom cut out, beside the clematis and
then water into this so that the moisture gets down
to the roots. We are not keen on seeing bits of pipe
or plastic bottles planted in the garden; they really
are not terribly attractive and are quite unnecessary if you adopt the method we suggested.

You will find that a newly planted clematis will
require fairly regular watering if planted during
late spring or summer, especially if the soil is free

draining. Make absolutely sure you water a new clematis if there is a prolonged period of drought. Often during these conditions clematis can suffer terribly, as they will lose a great deal of moisture from the foliage in the warm, drying winds. Even well-established plants suffer in droughts and, while it may be impractical to water often, do try to give it a watering can full now and again just to keep it 'ticking over'.

Planting against Walls

It is a good idea, when planting a clematis against a wall, to plant as far out from the wall as you are able – if possible plant about 18in (45cm) away, leaning the clematis towards the wall on its cane (*see* diagram, page 35). The soil close to a wall is always very dry, partly because the brickwork soaks up an awful lot of moisture, and also, depending on the prevailing wind direction, the wall will keep the rain off the soil up to about 2ft (60cm) away.

Planting near Mature Trees and Shrubs

When planting a clematis to grow into trees or over large, mature shrubs, remember that the host plant may have totally drained the surrounding soil of nutrients. It is essential, in this sort of situation, to improve the soil before planting, as previously described, and also to be aware that regular watering will be necessary until your clematis is well established.

If at all possible, when planting against a tree, position your clematis on the north side of its host, as this will enable the host plant to shade the root system of the clematis. The clematis will then naturally grow towards the light. It can be quite difficult planting near mature trees, as they can have a vast root system. This can make it difficult to dig a hole large enough to accommodate the clematis with a good layer of manure in the bottom of the hole. Therefore it is often necessary to site your clematis several feet out from the trunk of the tree, just to find sufficient ground, free from roots, to plant into (*see* diagram).

When planting a clematis to grow over a shrub,

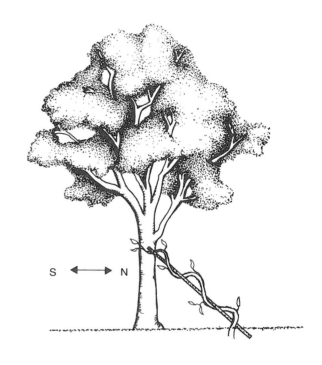

Planting on the north side of a tree.

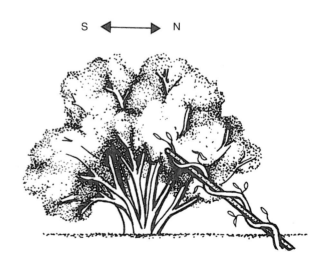

Planting on the north side of a shrub.

again plant on the north side if possible and also out on the 'drip line' of its host (*see* diagram, page 36). Bear in mind that if the shrub has dense foliage, when it rains the water will run off the leaves and down to the ground at the outer edges of the shrub, leaving the ground underneath it bone dry. If you plant out on this drip line, however, the clematis will be well watered when it rains.

Protecting the Roots

When planting a clematis in a position which is exposed to full sun for most of the day, it is advisable to shade its root system from the worst of the baking heat. You can do this by using some stones, gravel, bark chippings or perhaps a small paving slab or roof tile. These can be placed at the base of the clematis and will provide the plant with a cool root run.

Alternatively, you may prefer, as we do, to plant something else in front of the clematis. Depending on the space available, you could use lavender, cistus, ornamental sage (either bronze or variegated) or ground cover plants such as helianthemums, artemisia, diacia and so on. Many of the hardy geraniums or pinks would also be suitable. There are many different plants you could use for this purpose, but check that they can cope with a hot sunny position.

DEAD-HEADING FOR NEW GROWTH

If the clematis you purchased was full of flowers at the time of planting but seems to spend the summer sitting there with no intention of growing, in order to encourage it to start making new growth you can dead-head it as the flowers die off; otherwise the plant will use all its energy to develop and ripen the seed heads rather than produce fresh growth. Dead-heading is not always necessary, or practical, on a mature clematis, but it will help a very young plant to concentrate on the important task of producing strong stems. It is always tempting to buy the plant with lots of flowers on, but it

---

QUICK PLANTING GUIDE

1. **Prepare soil** with manure, garden compost and so on.
2. **Dig deep hole** (check depth before removing pot).
3. **Add stones** for drainage if waterlogging may occur.
4. **Loosen soil** in bottom of hole.
5. Add one big single handful of **bonemeal**.
6. **Remove plant ties** low down.
7. Tease out **roots**.
8. Bury at least one, preferably two **leaf joints below soil level**.
9. Firm down soil, leaving a **well**.
10. Water in and **keep watered** during dry weather.

---

will need this extra attention after you have finished enjoying its flowers.

TO SUMMARIZE

Clematis generally prefer a rich, well-drained soil with plenty of moisture. They also require a cool root system and deep planting. Thoughtful pruning and additional feeding really are well worth the trouble.

MOVING CLEMATIS

There can be a number of reasons why a clematis requires moving from its original planting position. The aspect may be too sunny, too shady, or too exposed. You may be moving house and wish to take a favourite clematis with you. Or there may be colour clashes in your planting schemes that need correction.

Transplanting a clematis needs to be carried out with forethought and care. The best time to move a clematis is when it is dormant, during the late winter or early spring, but while the ground is open and workable. In fact, pruning time is ideal.

First prepare the new situation well, with manure, compost, bonemeal etc, exactly as you did when first planting the clematis. A larger hole will be required this time to allow for deeper planting. The root-ball needs to be deeper than it was originally, to allow for the burying of at least two leaf joints below the surface of the soil. A hole 18in–2ft (45–60cm) across and deep must be prepared.

Before digging out the plant, reduce the top growth in size to make the job more manageable. Hard prune the clematis down to about 2ft (60cm) above the soil. This need not be done too exactly, as final pruning will be carried out when replanting has been completed. Ensure that the vines remaining on the plant are cut free from their original support.

Dig out the root-ball no less than 1ft (30cm) square and 1ft deep, to allow for minimum root disturbance, which in turn should ensure the operation is successful. Once loosened, the root-ball can be lifted out onto a piece of thick plastic or sacking which can then be carried or dragged to the new planting position.

The plant can then be slid into the new hole and bedded down into place with fresh compost. Use your heel to firm around the hole, and then drench it with a can of water. Once this has been completed final pruning can be carried out. Starting at soil level, work up each stem and prune off just above a good set of buds in the leaf-joints.

If moving house, the clematis can be placed in a large plastic flower pot, where it can remain until you can plant it in the new garden.

During the first year following its move do not allow the transplanted clematis to dry out completely. Treat it as you would a new clematis, and it will recover and flourish.

A word of warning when moving certain clematis – the Montana and Armandii Group cultivars, for instance, do not take kindly to moving after having been planted for several years. They make a very woody base in their early years and will not readily respond to the required pruning and interference of transplanting. However, if the move is judged essential, it is a risk worth taking. The same goes for transplanting a clematis at the wrong time of the year, rather than the late winter or early spring. If you do have to move a clematis during the height of summer, then frequent watering will

be essential. Again, if the move is essential it is worth the risk.

CULTIVATING CLEMATIS AROUND THE WORLD

As mentioned in earlier chapters, wild clematis are found in all parts of the world, and it is always tempting to try to grow as many types as possible in our gardens, including those from other countries. In Britain and much of Europe we are very fortunate that our climate allows us to grow a very wide range of plants, including many clematis.

Gardeners in other parts of the world can have difficulty providing the right conditions for some of the clematis we grow regularly. As an initial guide we will give some thoughts on growing clematis in the more extreme conditions, although local knowledge and experience has to be the best guide. Membership of organizations such as the *Royal Horticultural Society*, the *International Clematis Society* and the *British Clematis Society* can also provide a great deal of helpful information.

Clematis gardening in parts of America, Canada and Northern Europe is somewhat different to the British Isles. In the UK, the temperature between winter and summer varies only marginally compared to the extremes witnessed in other countries, where gardeners have to cope with severe climatic changes from dry heat in summer to -30° or -40°C in winter.

Extreme Cold

Some clematis will cope better than others with this severe cold, particularly if planted deep to protect the crown.

The Viticella Group cultivars cope admirably, as do many other hard prune types which can be cut down and thickly mulched in autumn to insulate against the frost. Final pruning can be carried out at the onset of better weather when the mulch can be removed.

The Atragene Group (macropetalas, alpinas etc.) are quite robust and will survive harsh climatic conditions and are well suited to northern latitudes, where their early flowering on mature wood means they do not require long summer days to produce their flowers. Their display of blooms in the spring must be a welcome sight after a long hard winter.

Extreme Heat

Generally, most of the clematis that are commonly grown as garden plants can survive severe cold better than tropical heat. So the gardener in very warm climates may have less choice than those who cope with long harsh winters.

High humidity is one reason why the Atragene Group cultivars do not flourish in much of Japan, and therefore these types are not recommended for any sub-tropical climate.

High temperatures can also be associated with lack of rainfall, and therefore many clematis will only thrive in hotter regions if they are given frequent supplies of moisture. It is not enough to give occasional irrigation if this leaves the clematis with very dry conditions in between times. Even one day of very dry roots can stunt the growth of a clematis and, although it can be revived with water to live another day, it is unlikely to flower or grow so well for many weeks after that setback.

In these conditions we have found that those gardeners who have the greatest success are those who grow their clematis in containers where they can be given a steady supply of water. Certainly our contacts in South Africa find that this works very well, and it also helps to overcome any problems of poor soil, as a good compost can be used. This enables a wide range of large flowered hybrids to be grown in dryer and hotter regions of both the northern and southern hemispheres.

For those who wish to grow clematis in warmer climates there are certain species that are more tolerant of higher temperatures and in some cases dryer soils. The *C. florida* species and its cultivars are generally comfortable with high temperatures, and in England they are well suited to growing in conservatories where high summer temperatures are tolerated and warmer winter conditions are preferable.

Tangutica Group cultivars are generally found to be more tolerant of dryer sites and will stand high temperatures. The winter flowering *C. cirrhosa* originates from the Mediterranean region where it survives the summer heat and drought by dying back to a dormant state in mid-summer and re-growing with the autumn rains. Another species that we know grows well in the hotter parts of America is *C. terniflora*, which has a wonderful perfume; in those parts it is called the 'Sweet Scented Autumn Clematis'.

The herbaceous groups related to *C. heracleifolia* and *C. integrifolia* can be successful in warm climates; their more compact nature helps to reduce their need for moisture. The Viticella Group cultivars are generally more tolerant of a wide range of growing conditions, but some in this group are only distantly related to the original European species and therefore it is best to keep to the smaller flowered cultivars or the species itself.

Finally it is worth mentioning that the more your climate varies from our gentle mid-European, maritime conditions, the more likely it is that flowering times, flower size, colour and habit will be quite different to those described in this book or some specialist catalogues. It may be that you will be more successful, or have earlier flowers or more of them, but experimenting may be the only way to find out.

CHAPTER 5

Feeding

Providing additional feed for your clematis can be as simple or as complicated as you, the gardener, wish to make it. Feeding is essential for the growth of the plant – a healthy plant is better able to resist disease and attack by pests.

Let us assume you planted your clematis in well-prepared soil, with plenty of nutrients added, to enable the plant to have the best start possible. If you now give up thinking about feed, after two or three years, when the clematis has exhausted the early supply of food, it will survive only by luck. If it does survive, it will probably not be as floriferous as it would have been if you had encouraged it to a better performance with the addition of extra feed.

The busy gardener may not be able to afford what can add up to a considerable amount of time to provide additional feed. Regular liquid feeding particularly can be most time consuming. The solution we use in our garden, where time is limited, is a handful of bonemeal, worked in around the base of each clematis, with either a small hand fork or fingers. If done at pruning time, this will allow the plant to tick over gently. This is a slow acting feed that will provide nourishment over a long period. Bonemeal in spring, followed by a mulch with manure during the autumn, will be quite adequate for most clematis – and this is work enough for most gardeners. It may not produce the most abundant growth but should maintain most clematis well enough to produce a good display.

OPPOSITE: 'Louise Rowe'.

FERTILIZERS

If you do have the time, interest and inclination to provide further food for your clematis, then the subject of feeding will need to be researched. Additional fertilizers need to be checked as to their suitability for clematis and the time of year to apply them. For instance it would be unwise to use a feed that would encourage the clematis to put on an enormous amount of lush, tender growth too early in the year, before the worst of the frosts have finished.

You therefore need to look at the individual feeds to see exactly how your plants will react to them. On the fertilizer packaging you will find an indication of its chemical formula, which is a guide to its uses. This will be expressed in terms of N, P and K, where N is Nitrogen (this puts on leafy growth), P is Phosphorus (which is a root feed), and K is Potassium, or potash (this promotes flowers and fruit). The relative quantities of these nutrients are expressed as numbers, for example, 10:5:10. By looking at this information on the labels of different feeds, you can decide which would be best to use and when.

Bonemeal

Bonemeal contains 3.5 per cent N and 7.4 per cent P (or 3.5:7.4:0).

A small amount of nitrogen is best early in the spring to encourage the plant gently into growth, but not too quickly. Water it in if there is no rain forecast. The extra phosphorus will benefit the roots, which of course are an essential part of the plant – without strong, healthy roots, the rest of the plant has a poor future. But note that bone-meal has no potassium to help with the production of flowers; this can be remedied with Sulphate of Potash.

Sulphate of Potash

Sulphate of Potash (Potassium Sulphate) improves the flowers, not only in terms of quantity but also their size and depth of colour. This can be used in addition to bonemeal, but we would suggest about one month later, during mid-spring. Again, one single handful worked in around the base of the plant will be adequate. Like bonemeal, do water it in if there is no rain forecast.

An excellent natural source of potash is wood ash, or bonfire ash. Do remember though that anything other than wood will usually produce an ash that can be very toxic to plants. A reliable supply of bonfire ash would be useful when mulching, which is described later in this chapter.

Other Fertilizers

Some other fertilizers are: fish, blood and bone (6:7:6), Growmore (7:7:7), Phostrogen (10:10:27 + trace elements), Osmacote (14:13:13), and Osmacote tablets (10:11:18 + trace elements). One application during late spring or early summer of any of these should be sufficient.

All these fertilizers have a high rate of nitrogen. We would therefore recommend using any of these on your clematis from late spring onwards when the chance of severe frosts is reduced. Fish, blood and bone and Growmore are excellent, well balanced feeds for use during late spring and early summer if you wish. Phostrogen can be used either as a granular feed, sprinkled onto the ground, or as a liquid feed. Either way, wait until late spring to use this.

Liquid Feeds

Again, we would only recommend liquid-feeding clematis from late spring onwards, once the weather has improved. If you have the time to do this your clematis will most certainly benefit.

The best liquid feeds for clematis are those with a high potash content. This helps produce an abundance of flowers and enriches their colour. The liquid tomato feeds are very good, such as Tomato Maxicrop or Tomorite. Phostrogen is another liquid feed which has a high potash content and is an excellent alternative to the tomato feeds.

When liquid-feeding, do be careful not to overfeed. A fortnightly liquid feed from late spring onwards is adequate for most clematis. It is far more important to keep your plant regularly watered than to add liberal amounts of liquid feed. So concentrate your efforts on watering with the occasional addition of liquid feed. If you overfeed clematis, the outcome will be a clematis with incredibly healthy, lush foliage and few, or no, flowers.

There are those who recommend not using liquid feeds once the clematis have budded up or are in flower. This is because it is feared that the liquid feed boosts the plant and pushes it on; therefore if liquid feeding is continued, instead of the flowers lasting for eight weeks, they may well be over in four. However, we feel that it is unlikely that the plant reacts quite so immediately, and as long as the guideline of fortnightly feeding is followed it is not necessary to complicate the matter any further!

It is necessary for the plant to slow down and begin a period of dormancy during the autumn. So we would suggest you stop liquid feeding by early autumn, thus allowing the plant the rest it needs.

Liquid feeding in many gardens is hardly necessary if the soil is in good condition and well maintained. There is one time in the year however when liquid feeding in the garden is always beneficial, if you grow any of the large-flowered clematis which have a double flowering period – that is, they flower in late spring and again in early autumn. We would suggest that after the early flowers have died, you dead-head the plant. Then apply one or perhaps two doses of liquid feed about a week apart, to encourage the plant to grow and produce better flowering wood. This dead-heading prevents the clematis making unnecessary seed-heads.

Feed well for an impressive display – this was the authors' award-winning exhibit at the Chelsea Flower Show.

These seed-heads can be very attractive, but we prefer a better second crop of flowers. We would certainly recommend this treatment.

Hoof and Horn

Although not a liquid feed, hoof and horn also has a very high nitrogen content, so if you are particularly keen to use it, wait until early summer and then a single application will be sufficient.

FOLIAR FEEDING

The liquid feeds are also excellent to use as foliar feeds, particularly if you have a type of clematis that is prone to chlorosis (yellow leaves). For plants that are suffering from yellowing leaves the application of a liquid feed containing the trace elements, (micro-nutrients) magnesium and iron (written as Mg and Fe on the packets) will improve the leaf colour to a healthy green. Remember a healthy plant is much more capable of overcoming pest and disease attack.

Mix the feed, as recommended, in a hand sprayer and liberally cover all the leaves once a week after sundown for perhaps three or four weeks, and you should see a great improvement.

Foliar feeding is especially useful if you are growing clematis permanently in conservatories. This application will not only keep the foliage in good condition, but it also seems to help keep down the 'bugs' which can be such a nuisance under glass. This reduces the need to use insecticides (*see* Chapter 11).

MULCHING

Having prepared the soil well and given your clematis a really good start, you will find the nutrients which were incorporated when planting will soon be spent. It is then a good idea to mulch clematis to top up the nutrients in the soil, which in turn will revitalize your plants.

Mulching is an excellent means of providing several important things for clematis. It will help to

hold in moisture, provide additional feed and also shade the root system from the baking sun, all of which are equally important. There are many different materials you can use for mulching, but the one which we consider by far the best is manure, as this will provide all three of the important aspects of mulching. If you use manure, do make sure it is well rotted.

Other mulches you could use are good garden compost, leaf mould or potting compost. They will not help quite as much regarding the provision of food, but will help to retain moisture and provide shade for the roots. Leaf mould is the mulch nature provides for itself, and if you are able to collect leaf sweepings in autumn, you can easily make your own. Composting leaves for a few months in a black dustbin liner works very well.

Mulching is best done during late autumn when the soil is already moist from the autumnal rains. First of all, add a good single handful of bonemeal to the soil around the base of your clematis. Work this in using your fingers, or if you prefer, a short hand-fork. A thick layer of mulch can then be added on top to a depth of about 3in (7 cm). When using manure, leave a gap of about 3in (7 cm) between the clematis stems and the mulch, as it could cause the stems to rot. Spread the mulch over an area of about 12in (30cm) around the stems.

When pruning in the spring, you can gently fork the mulch into the soil surrounding your clematis, at the same time adding another good single handful of bonemeal.

Mulching was referred to in Moore and Jackman's book of 1872, *The Clematis as a Garden Flower*, where they recommended annual manurings with horse or cow manure, to keep up the vigour of clematis. They also recommended a dressing of leaf-mould to be beneficial on heavy soils. This advice, although almost 140 years old, is still relevant today. We tend to think of cocoa-fibre as a modern development in the horticultural world, but Moore and Jackman suggested the fibre of the 'cocoa-nut', would be a suitable substitute where mulching with manure would be objectionable.

POTS AND CONTAINERS

Feeding plants that are kept permanently in pots and containers is absolutely essential, as the feed which was in the compost at planting time will quickly be exhausted. We would therefore recommend you apply one good single handful bonemeal at pruning time, then wait until the frosts have finished to begin liquid feeding. Obviously plants kept in containers will have to be watered, so a fortnightly addition of liquid feed is simple to incorporate into this routine. Stop feeding by early autumn.

Instead of using liquid feeds in your containers you can apply the new 'plug' feeds, which slowly release fertilizer over a period of months. The plugs we have seen are about the size of a large thimble and look similar to the honey-coated seed sticks you feed to budgerigars and canaries. You will need to work out the quantity of compost your container holds and from that, you will be able to calculate the number of plugs to use, as recommended on the packet.

BASIC FEEDING PROGRAMME

- **Bonemeal** at pruning time, late winter to early spring (one good single handful worked in around base of the clematis).
- **Mulch** in autumn, preferably manure.

COMPLETE FEEDING PROGRAMME

- **Bonemeal** at pruning time.
- **Sulphate of Potash** mid to late spring.
- **Dead-head** early large-flowered cultivars, and apply one or two doses of liquid feed one week apart.
- **Mulch** in autumn, preferably manure.
- For **container** grown clematis, regular liquid feed or slow release pellets.

spring and early summer, single flowers will be produced from the new wood later in the year.

Having produced a strong base to your clematis by hard pruning the young plant in its first year, you can begin light pruning each spring.

Light pruning consists mainly of removing the dead wood and making the plant tidy, but to do a really good job more is required. Light pruning requires some patience, so pick the right day!

When you begin pruning, first of all carefully remove all the dead material. You will be amazed at the amount of dead wood you will get off a mature clematis, so have a wheelbarrow ready. Start at the top of the plant – a step-ladder may be needed for some of the taller growing cultivars – and taking each stem in turn, trace it from the very top of the growth down to where there is a noticeably good set of buds in the leaf joints. This may be as much as 3ft (1m) back along each stem. Having reduced the height considerably and got rid of all the old dead tangled top growth, the plant will start to look better.

Continue to work down the whole plant taking each stem in turn. You will find that each stem that produced a flower the previous year will be dead about 12–18in (30–45cm) from the tip, so work down from each tip and prune off again just above a good set of buds.

This is the part which will really test your patience. It is very often the case that having pruned one stem carefully you will then later accidentally cut through it lower down. Do not despair; there is usually another set of buds you can prune down to. You may also find that however careful you are untangling your plant, inevitably at some point a good stem will be damaged. Do not leave a damaged stem on the plant; it will be much better to prune down to a good set of buds below where the damage occurred.

Having removed all the dead wood, now look to see if there are any weak, spindly stems. These will be best removed right down to soil level. This will encourage new stronger stems to grow low down.

After several years of light pruning a plant, do consider at pruning time removing one or two of the very old stems right down, almost to soil level. This sounds drastic, but it will help ensure a continual re-growth of stems from below the soil. Having taken the plunge and pruned through an old stem, you will then need to remove all the attached growth, which is a very tedious task to perform, but the result will be well worth it.

You may well feel inclined, having read this, to avoid buying any clematis which require light pruning, but what we have tried to describe would be the ultimate in light pruning. Of course, this type of pruning can be adjusted to the amount of time available, but try to find time to remove the dead tangled growth from the top of the plant. If you can do no more than that, your plant will still look better than if you had ignored it completely.

The clematis in this group will also benefit from dead-heading after the first display of flowers has finished each year. This was described earlier, but generally it is the same procedure repeated in summer, carried out to encourage a second flush of flowers in autumn. (*See* Liquid Feeding, page 42.)

Group 3: Hard Pruning

This group includes both climbing and herbaceous scrambling cultivars.

Climbing Cultivars
(including Late Large-Flowered, Florida, Tangutica, Vitalba and Viticella Groups)

Hard pruning is more or less as previously described for young clematis, but will change slightly as your plant matures. Pruning should be carried out around late winter to early spring.

These cultivars begin flowering sometime after midsummer and flower from the top of the current season's growth. This means that if the ultimate height of the plant is 8ft (2.5m), following its hard prune in the spring, the plant will grow around 8ft before flowering.

With the 'hard prune' cultivars it is a good idea to prune down as hard as possible, bearing in mind these clematis normally only flower on the current season's growth. Consequently if you fail to hard prune, the old wood will start to send shoots out from about 3–4ft (1–1.2m) off the ground. The

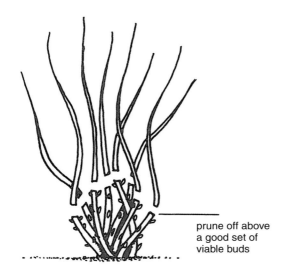

prune off above
a good set of
viable buds

Hard pruning – group 3.

plant will then grow another 6–12ft (2–4m), depending on the cultivar, before it begins to flower. If the plant is not pruned again, the same thing will happen the next year, until the only local inhabitant able to enjoy the flowers will be the sparrow sitting on the guttering.

To begin hard pruning, start at soil level and work up each stem, leaving at least two good sets of buds in the leaf joints, and prune off just above the second set (*see* diagram above). On an old clematis make sure the buds in the leaf joints are viable. If the buds are green or a good healthy-looking reddy-brown, it should be fairly obvious. If, however, you cannot be sure of their state of health, touch the buds carefully: if they feel firm they will be viable, whereas if they feel papery or soft, they are not healthy and you will need to work further up the stem until a good set of buds is found. Take each stem in turn and prune it off, and when all the stems have been cut through you can enjoy pulling down all the old growth and consign it to the bonfire.

There are, as always, alternatives to the basic rules. After pruning as hard as possible for at least

two or three years you can adjust your hard pruning to get the plant to grow and flower to even better effect. If some stems are not pruned down as hard as others, the clematis will have stems of varying length – some pruned to 6, 12, 18 or 24in (15, 30, 45 or 60cm) and so on. By doing this, when the plant flowers it will produce blooms over a greater area, hence giving you a far better display of flowers overall.

We would suggest however that each year you lower the stems which were not pruned so hard the previous year. This will encourage new shoots to grow from low down, so that the plant will always have new wood to replace the old.

Because they require hard pruning, when growing Group 3 clematis into trees it is a good idea to hard prune in the first two or three years, to enable the plant to make a good number of stems low down. After this has been achieved, we would only hard prune down as far as the lowest set of branches on the tree. By doing this you will save yourself the trouble of having to train the clematis up the trunk of the tree each year. Once the clematis is able to grow into the branches of the tree it will wind around them and grow in the most natural way.

One day a customer was enquiring why his clematis was not flowering. He had hard pruned it correctly and had fed and watered it well. This had me really puzzled until he explained that the fence on which his clematis was growing was 6ft (2m) high and his plant was just growing too tall. Each time the plant reached the top of the fence he pruned it 'to keep it tidy'. Of course, what he was doing each time he 'tidied' it was to remove the flowering growth. Had he instead trained the stems sideways as they grew throughout the year, or else when they reached the top of the fence, trained them back down again, the plant would have had a wonderful display of flowers. The lesson to be learnt from this is that once you have hard pruned your clematis in the spring, do not prune it any more until the flowers have finished; then you can tidy it up if you feel it is necessary.

Many of the Tangutica Group cultivars are some of the most rampant clematis which require hard pruning each year. They not only grow very tall, but make very deep, dense growth, smothering anything and everything which gets in their way. We would not recommend growing these clematis if space is limited in the garden. However, if space is not a problem, these are enchanting plants to grow, with their hundreds of bright yellow lantern-shaped flowers displayed all summer long. These, in turn, leave a host of silvery seed heads, adored by the birds in winter and spring for nest building.

During the early years, prune these cultivars really hard, down to about 12–18in (30–45cm), then after that, if space really is unlimited, prune back to the framework of old stems. This can be done quite easily with shears, especially as there is no need to prune just above a good set of buds. The Tangutica Group cultivars in our garden are growing quite close to other clematis and climbing roses; therefore, because space is limited, we need to prune down very hard every year. Again we use the shears and prune all stems down to approximately 18in (45cm). All that is left is a collection of dead sticks. After a session like this you might think you have killed your clematis, but after several weeks its new growth will prove you wrong.

Herbaceous scrambling, erect and climbing cultivars
(Diversifolia, Flammula, Heracleifolia, Integrifolia, Texensis and Viorna Groups)

The pruning of these herbaceous cultivars is very simple. They tend to grow in two different ways. The Flammula, Integrifolia, Texensis and Viorna Group cultivars normally die right down in winter, while the Diversifolia and Heracleifolia Group cultivars make quite woody growth and leave some viable buds low down on the stem.

For those groups that die back to ground level, their old stems can be pruned right back during late winter or early spring. This growth can be pruned off, as close to the ground as is practical, being careful not to prune so low that you cut off the tips of the new season's shoots as they are emerging through the ground.

With the others, you will find that the majority of the old growth will be dead with just a few viable buds showing low down on their stems.

Therefore, start at the base of the plant and work up each stem pruning off just above the second set of leaf joints. If the clematis was planted deeply enough, the new season will see fresh shoots appearing from below ground.

When you are tidying herbaceous beds during late autumn and early winter you could prune off about half the previous season's growth, leaving the final pruning until late winter or early spring.

In recent years we have found it wise to delay the hard pruning of the Heracleifolia Group for about a month, until mid spring, as their stems can die back after late hard frosts or wet spring weather.

A member of the Integrifolia Group after hard pruning.

OPTIONAL PRUNING

For some clematis you can adjust your pruning technique, depending very much on where they are growing and when you want them to flower.

For instance, a few of the very late flowering clematis may not make sufficient flowering wood, when hard pruned, to bloom before the frosts. Whereas if they are lightly pruned, just enough to remove most of the previous season's flowering

A member of the Diversifolia Group before pruning …   … and after pruning.

stems, you will find that the plant manages to flower a few weeks earlier, thus allowing them the chance to display their flowers before the frost brings a premature end to your enjoyment.

And conversely, there are opportunities to hard prune clematis that are in Group 2 (Light Prune). This will delay flowering by six to eight weeks, but will keep the plant more compact. This is a useful technique to use for container grown clematis in particular and is explained in detail in Chapter 9.

Basically, some 'Hard Prune' clematis can benefit from light pruning and some 'Light Prune' clematis will benefit from hard pruning. Experimentation with your secateurs can bring excellent results.

PREPARING FOR WINTER (ALL CLEMATIS)

During the autumn, before the weather turns wintry, inspect your clematis. If there is a great deal of very heavy top growth which is likely to be knocked around in high winds, this could cause unnecessary damage to the plant and possibly its support as well. Damaged stems can be a source of infection, which can also cause the stems to rot.

Whether the clematis is normally lightly or hard pruned, it is therefore a good idea to remove any large mass of tangled growth from the top of the plant. Do, however, leave alone the main stems which are tied into the support, and complete the pruning in the normal way during late winter or early spring.

MILD WINTERS: ADDITIONAL PRUNING

During a mild winter some clematis will be encouraged to put out lush new shoots far too early, long before the worst of the winter weather can be declared over. While we strongly feel the main pruning of clematis should wait until late winter or early spring, it would do no harm to 'check' this sudden surge of boisterous spring behaviour during mid winter. Simply reduce each stem which has put out a long new shoot back to a more dormant set of buds. This should help to discourage the clematis from premature growth, preserving its strength for when spring arrives.

PRUNING UNKNOWN CULTIVARS OF CLEMATIS

If you have the misfortune to lose a name label, or move house and inherit an unknown clematis and therefore do not know the pruning required, give the plant a simple light prune in late winter or early spring and then sit back and wait for it to flower. A very rough guide, but one well worth remembering, is that if it begins flowering before the longest day then lightly prune it. If, on the other hand it begins flowering after the longest day then in future springs hard prune it.

PRUNE AND FEED

Always give a good single handful of bonemeal when you have pruned your clematis. Work it into the soil around the base of the plant, and if the spring is very dry, water it in. We would recommend that you use only bonemeal at pruning time as it works nice and slowly. Leave the other fertilizers until after the frosts have finished as you do not want to encourage too much fresh growth too early in the season.

A good rule to use when pruning is: secateurs in one hand, bucket of bonemeal in the other!

BASIC PRUNING GUIDE

1. When planting, make sure to plant deep – bury at least two leaf joints.
2. Lightly Prune – start at the top and work down.
3. Hard Prune – start at the bottom and work up.
4. Feed with bonemeal.

FINAL THOUGHTS ON PRUNING

We hope this pruning guide will be of use to you and has given you confidence to experiment with your pruning techniques. If you are new to clematis growing, and pruning still seems a mystery, try starting with the hard prune cultivars. This is a relatively simple procedure and should give you the confidence, in future years, to try a clematis from one of the other groups.

Since our nursery has been open to the public we have found that the biggest question mark over the cultivation of clematis is the pruning. We decided, because of this, to hold clematis pruning demonstrations each spring. These have proved extremely popular with our customers. It would be worth enquiring at your nearest specialist clematis nursery if you are interested in seeing a pruning demonstration, or contact the British Clematis Society (www.britishclematis.org.uk) who should be able to give you the relevant details.

CHAPTER 7

Growing with Artificial Supports

To grow clematis as climbers in certain positions in the garden it will be necessary to provide them with some support. They will climb, but they need something to climb up or over.

The majority of clematis are climbers and will cling onto the stem, twig or branch of another plant as they do in the wild. The way they do this is to wrap their petiole (leaf-stalk) around whatever is available. Unlike ivies, which can attach themselves directly on to brickwork, clematis require a support of some kind before being able to climb. Clematis will indeed happily clothe walls, fences, screens or pergolas, providing this additional support is given for the clematis to attach itself to.

You can also use clematis to cover arbours, gazeboes, obelisks and arches, perhaps in conjunction with other climbing plants such as roses, honeysuckle and wisteria. They can also be grown as festoons, pillars or as standards. More than one plant of a particular cultivar could be grown, or several clematis of differing colours could be grown together to form a free-standing pillar of colour.

Another interesting way to grow clematis is as 'trained' groundcover. Instead of allowing the plants to scramble freely, they are given support and trained horizontally. The ideas are almost endless, but we should first look at those already suggested, in greater detail.

WALLS AND FENCES

These can be considered together, as the methods of support are applicable to both. Clematis, being unable to cling directly onto brickwork or wood, need trellis or wires around which they can wrap their leaf stems. A variety of these supports is commercially available as fancy wooden or plastic

'Prince Charles' adorning a house.

OPPOSITE: 'Perle d'Azur'.

trellises, and they come in an array of shapes, sizes and designs. The wooden trellises are usually made of hardwood and will last for many years. Plastic trellis, although good at the outset, will gradually break down after a few years of scorching heat in summer and freezing temperatures in winter. We prefer wood to plastic. The wood can quite easily be treated with 'plant friendly' preservative, and will last a very long time. Trellis can be bought in many sizes, from long narrow rectangles to large squares and fan shapes. For ease of transport, you can even buy trellis that expands. It can even be bought ready shaped to cover a drain pipe!

When fitting trellis ensure that a gap of about ¾in (2cm) or more, is left between the wall and the trellis. This will allow the clematis room to scramble up and be trained and tied in whilst also

'Veitch', one of the more compact montanas that is suitable to grow on the wall of a bungalow.

giving the leaf stems anchorage points. Small blocks of treated wood can be fixed onto the wall to which the trellis can then be screwed. When fixing we would recommend using screws rather than nails as they can more easily be removed if necessary. If the wall is colour-washed for instance, then every few years the clematis and trellis will need removing for essential maintenance to the wall. This is best done either at pruning time, when the clematis could be hard pruned, or later in the season, after the clematis has flowered, when the plant can be cut down and the trellis removed for painting. The occasional hard prune during early autumn for this purpose will not do a clematis any harm. It may, depending on the cultivar, simply mean a less impressive display of blooms the following year.

Whilst ready-made hardwood trellises can be attractive, they can also be expensive. You could try making trellis, using bamboo canes, to your own design. We have seen fan-shaped trellises made of canes and also a large, oblong design with 'windows'. Both were very attractive, making effective use of natural material.

Clematis netting is also available for use on walls and fences as support. This is usually plastic-covered wire mesh and can be bought by the metre/yard. This is very useful, quite cheap to buy, and comes in a range of colours, usually brown, green, or white. Care is needed to match the wire colour with the intended site: brown against a red brick wall would be fine, as would white against a pale colour washed wall; without this consideration the netting would detract from the beauty of the plant.

The method we prefer to use for training a clematis on a wall or fence is simply to use nails and wire. Nails with a large head are ideal. For brick walls use masonry nails or 'vine eyes', whereas for fences, almost any large headed nail will do. You can then train your clematis wherever you wish. Knock in a few nails, leaving about a ¾in (2cm) gap between the head and the wall, then, using a reel of training wire, twist the wire around the first nail to anchor it, and stretch it tightly to the next nail and twist, and so on. You can make diamonds, squares, rectangles or you

Clematis used to screen a shed.

could train your clematis around a window or a door – there are endless possibilities. As the plant grows, if it runs out of space, knock in another nail, twist another piece of wire and the clematis will continue its growth. This is a simple and cheap method of support, which will quickly be covered by the clematis. If you do not like nails driven into the brickwork of a house, use only a sufficient number to support the outer edges of the plant.

When there is a low wall or fence in need of softening by clematis, its 'height' can be trained sideways to grow horizontally. With a few nails and some wire, even a rampant montana can be trained along, rather than up. Near our nursery is a low boundary wall in a front garden. In the spring the wall is completely covered with montana flowers and is a really wonderful sight. Then during the summer, the appearance of the brickwork is 'softened' by the foliage. With the additional planting of summer flowering cultivars of clematis into the montana, the season of blooms could be extended right through the summer. The montana may not grow to 30ft (10m) in height, but travels as far horizontally.

SCREENS AND PERGOLAS

These are effective means of displaying clematis and, providing the site is not too exposed to the wind and weather, many different types can be grown.

Usually a screen is built to hide or disguise something unsightly from the house or sitting-out area of the garden. Often these are used to hide fuel tanks, compost bins and garden storage areas, or used as a dividing screen between the flower and vegetable gardens.

When building a screen or pergola with wooden posts, treat the timber with wood preservative. You can buy poles ready treated, or it is quite simple to treat them yourself. The bottom 2ft (60cm) of the upright posts is best treated with a suitable long life preservative, as this will be in the ground and therefore vulnerable to rotting. The rest of the pole should be treated with a 'plant friendly' product.

Dig a hole about 18in (45cm) square and 2ft (60cm) deep, and stand the pole in the middle, wedging it with some large stones around the base or a few inches of concrete to stop the pole 'giving' in a high wind. The hole can then be filled in with a mixture of good top-soil, manure, garden compost, leaf-mould and so on, ready for planting.

The poles of our pergolas and screens are not sunk into the soil at all. To prevent rotting, each pole has been stood on a house brick and then bolted to a piece of iron from our scrap metal merchant. The iron has been driven into the ground to a depth of 2–3ft (60–90cm) leaving the remainder approximately 18in (45cm) above ground, to which the pole can be bolted or wired. This works well for our pergola because, although it stands exposed to the prevailing wind, the two long sides are bolted or wired together by poles across the top and with diagonal poles to brace the structure.

Another alternative to burying the poles in the ground is to buy metal 'post holes'. These are available from fencing suppliers and are basically a metal tube into which the pole is slotted. Beneath the tube is a long metal spike, which is driven down into the ground and the post then inserted. The pole and the metal tube can then be bolted together to make the structure more rigid.

If evergreen growth is required on a screen or pergola, then the Armandii or Cirrhosa Group cultivars are ideal for this purpose, providing the position is not open to the biting cold winds. These clematis will only flourish in a sheltered position. Where a screen or pergola is in a very exposed position and evergreen plants are required, we would recommend using ivies or other robust evergreens as a base of foliage and, when they are established, interplanting with clematis for added colour. Montana Group cultivars, although not evergreen, do keep their foliage into the start of winter, and new leaves soon appear in the spring. It could mean putting up with a few 'bare' weeks, but this is a minor drawback set against the advantages.

Pergolas tend to be sited in the middle of gardens, rather than tucked away in sheltered areas. If the position is open and windy, avoid tender clematis and choose from the vast number of 'toughies' (those clematis which specialist growers will recommend for any aspect). From this range of clematis you can have a succession of blooms from early spring right through to early winter. Our pergola stands exposed to the south-westerly winds, and some clematis have not thrived. We are now replanting using cultivars that should cope better with this situation. Early and late flowerers are planted alternately, approximately a yard (a metre) apart and we will endeavour to train the stems, preventing them from intertwining with one another, to facilitate pruning. It is not impossible to prune one clematis out of another, but it is a fiddly, time-consuming occupation requiring a great deal of patience.

ARBOURS, BOWERS AND GAZEBOS

These decorative structures are popular in many gardens, and afford numerous opportunities to grow climbing plants and form a shelter in which to sit and admire the garden. *The Oxford English Dictionary's* definition of an arbour is: 'Bower, shady retreat with sides and roof, formed by trees or lattice-work covered with climbing plants.' All three structures comply with this definition despite their differing romantic names.

The arbour when positioned in a sheltered part of the garden can be adorned with almost any clematis. If however, it is situated in an open windy site, it would be better to use the tougher clematis. In a windy aspect the plants may be required to form a wind-break, keeping the seats sheltered. For this purpose we recommend using the Montana or Atragene Group cultivars to form a permanent dense backdrop and then, once they are established, inter-planting some summer flowering clematis. This will give maximum colour and coverage to the arbour and should give months of pleasure.

If the arbour is in a sheltered position it would be an opportunity to use any of the evergreen Armandii Group cultivars as the main backdrop, so on mild spring days, when the sun encourages sitting out, the perfume from the clusters of flowers could be appreciated.

USING SCENTED CLEMATIS

Perfume is an essential ingredient in a garden, and it is particularly pleasing when scented flowers are placed near a seat. We have mentioned the scented Armandii Group cultivars as being suitable for a sheltered position, but for a windy aspect, try one of the scented *C. montana* cultivars – such as 'Elizabeth' or 'Odorata'. For later perfume in the summer, try growing *C. flammula* or 'Triternata Rubromarginata' near a seat. *C. flammula* has clouds of tiny, white star-shaped flowers, with a very pleasant hawthorn-like fragrance. 'Triternata Rubromarginata' has the most wonderful almond-like perfume, and has to be our favourite amongst the scented clematis. Again, like *C. flammula*, it has small, white star-shaped flowers, but those of 'Triternata Rubromarginata' have deep red tips – very pretty flowers, as well as being highly scented. Further scented clematis can be identified via the Plant Profiles.

An arbour covered with a mixture of perfumed clematis, fragrant old-fashioned climbing roses, and honeysuckle, is our idea of a perfect place to sit and rest when the weeding is finished.

ARCHES

Arches are also splendid structures on which to display clematis. Again, scented cultivars are a welcome bonus, especially when the arch spans a pathway. Avoid choosing clematis of rampant growth should the arch be small or narrow. We know of a gentleman who planted 'Bill MacKenzie' to grow over a small arch. Once the clematis was established, he was unable to walk through the arch for half of the year, because the plant completely filled the gap! On the other hand 'Bill MacKenzie' would be marvellous planted against the pillar of a large arch.

Two or more different cultivars of clematis can be grown together, depending on the size of the arch, and these can be selected to complement a colour scheme. A combination of white with light or dark blue such as 'Mercury' with 'H.F. Young', or 'Laura Denny' with 'Elsa Späth', would make a pleasing spectacle when grown in tandem against an arch. Alternatively, combinations of colours can be selected through shades of pink, red or purple. If a real impact of colour is desirable at a specific time of the year, then growing more than one plant of the same cultivar together would establish the effect more quickly.

Our preference for an arch is to grow a highly scented climbing rose with a clematis, whose colours compliment each other. Some roses have very few or no thorns, which is an asset close to a path. A few suggestions are on page 62.

FESTOONS, OBELISKS, PILLARS AND POLES

Each of these give structure to the garden, and their height readily accommodates clematis as climbers. Festoons can be used to divide the garden into smaller sections, or beside a path as an alternative to a pergola. Obelisks, pillars and poles are attractive additions almost anywhere in the garden and provide tall columns of colour in flower beds and borders. They add a new dimension to areas of low planting.

Rose	Clematis
'Zéphirine Drouhin' (cerise pink)	'Alba Luxurians' (white) or 'John Huxtable' (white)
'Kathleen Harrop' (soft shell-pink)	'Elsa Späth' (deep violet-blue) or 'Venosa Violacea' (white/purple)
'Madame Alfred Carrière' (pinky-white)	'H.F.Young' (blue) or 'Lasurstern' (blue)
'Goldfinch' (golden yellow to primrose)	'Royal Velours' (reddy-purple) or 'Jackmanii' (bluish-purple)
'Alchymist' (eggy-yellow)	'Gipsy Queen' (purple) or 'The President' (purply-blue)

Each of these will require treated poles placed in the ground as supports.

Festoons are built using a row of poles, each 6–8ft (2–2.5m) tall, placed about 8–10ft (2.5–3m) apart. Between each pole is slung a length of sturdy rope, wire or linked chain which should be allowed to hang slack. The taller growing clematis can then be trained up each pole on wires, and tied in along the chain to form garlands (*see* diagram, below).

If the festoon is placed at the back of a border, the base of the poles will be discreetly hidden by other plants and you can use clematis cultivars that will grow to 12–15ft (4–5m) tall. Cultivars such as 'Henryi', 'Marie Boisselot', 'Mrs Cholmondeley', or 'William Kennett' would be ideal in this situation. If, however, the base of the poles is visible, plant two clematis at each pole, one taller growing cultivar with one which will flower low down. A combination of 'William Kennett' with 'Miss Bateman' or 'Asao' for example, would look splendid. If you prefer hard prune cultivars, try the taller growing 'Victoria' or 'Star of India', twinned with 'Prince Charles', 'Pink Fantasy' or 'Carnaby'.

Ornate obelisks made from metal can make an impressive feature in a garden. If placed where they are likely to catch the prevailing wind, it would be advisable to cement the structures into

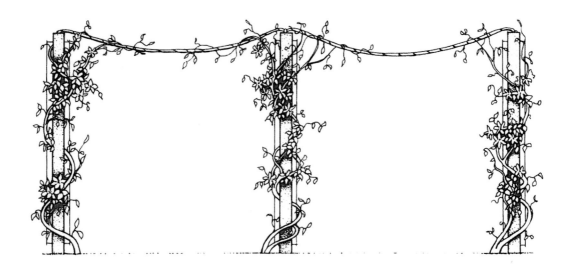

Festoons.

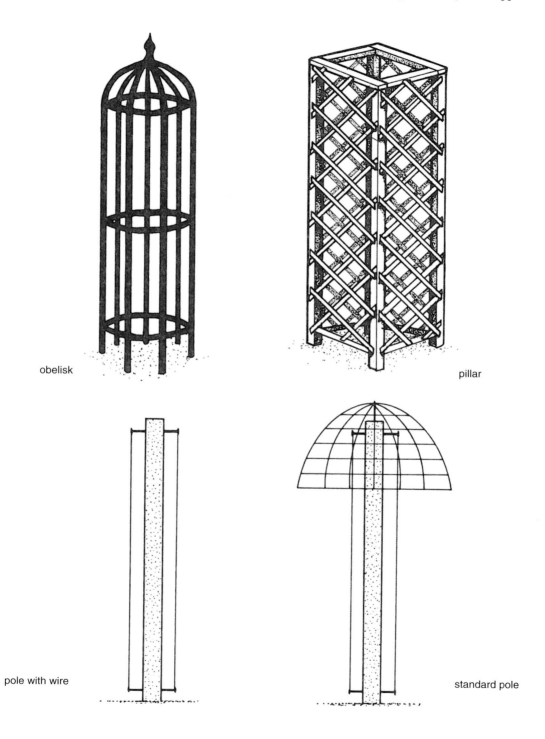

obelisk

pillar

pole with wire

standard pole

Obelisks, pillars and poles.

Clematis	Rose
'Lady Caroline Nevill' (double and single, mauve)	'Surpassing Beauty' (dark red)
'Will Goodwin' (pale blue)	'Ghislaine de Féligonde' (light orangey-yellow
'Sylvia Denny' (double & single, white)	EDEN ROSE '88 (white/lavender/pink)
'Rouge Cardinal' (dark red)	'Sombreuil' (white)

the ground. Once in position an assortment of clematis can be grown through them (*see* diagram, page 63). On the obelisks in our sunken garden we have used a combination of roses and clematis, trying to find complimentary colours, textures and flowering seasons.

Wooden pillars can be constructed using four

'Rouge Cardinal' with rose 'Sombreuil' on an obelisk.

treated poles and four pieces of diamond trellis 6ft × 2ft (2m × 60cm). Erect the poles in a square 2ft (60cm) apart, leaving 6ft (2m) out of the ground. The trellis can then be nailed onto the poles to form a tall square column. Before planting with clematis, fill the central square with several inches of bark chippings or gravel to prevent weed growth (*see* diagram, page 63).

Four clematis can then be planted, one along each side. If you have a special colour scheme in that area of the garden, your choice of clematis can blend with it. In a white border you could use 'White Columbine' for spring colour, ARCTIC QUEEN for early and late summer blooms, FOREVER FRIENDS and 'Roko Kolla' for mid-summer to early autumn flowers. In a mauve/purple border, try 'Helsingborg' for spring colour, 'Kinju Atarashi' and 'Louise Rowe' for early/mid-summer blooms followed by 'Étoile Violette' for mid-late colour. For a pink-red colour scheme try 'Ruby', 'Bees' Jubilee', 'Rüütel' and 'Little Nell'. Experimenting with colour schemes and planting ideas can be great fun, and it is exciting waiting for the plants to flower.

If space is limited in a bed or a border, which excludes the use of anything as large as a pillar, you could instead erect a single pole to give height. Having placed the pole in position drive in eight nails, four near the top and four close to the soil. Nails 2in (5cm) long with large heads are ideal. Knock them into the pole so that about (1in (2.5cm) is left protruding. Each top nail should be directly above a bottom nail. A piece of training wire can then be twisted tightly around the top nail and stretched down and twisted around the bottom nail. Continue to do this with the other six nails. These four wires will then provide the necessary support for the clematis to wrap its leaf stems around (*see* diagram, page 63).

Another option would be to grow clematis as a standard to form a weeping mop-head. Use a single pole, wired as previously described, to which can be added a rose trainer. The latter looks similar to a large upturned hanging basket or the frame of an umbrella. Nail this firmly to the top of the post to make a solid structure. When the clematis has climbed the wires of the pole and reached the top, the growth can be trained over and around the frame. This will allow the blooms to cascade down in a fountain of colour. Again, as with the festoons, you could use more than one cultivar of clematis. Choose one to give flowers low down (one of the clematis recommended for a container would be ideal), and the other could be a taller-growing cultivar, but one with the same pruning requirements (*see* page 63).

BEDDING OUT

Bedding out clematis was used by Victorian gardeners in the late 1800s. Some think of 'bedding plants' as those tender summer flowering salvias, alyssum and lobelia, which are not planted out until the risk of frost has passed and are removed in early winter as the first frosts kill them off.

Clematis, however, can be treated differently and used as a permanent bedding display, unlike the annuals which are changed each year. Planting clematis in a flower bed without support and allowing them to ramble where they please would be fine. But we have one or two ideas of ways to make the planting much more interesting which will also help to give some year round colour. An island flower bed of almost any shape can be trans-

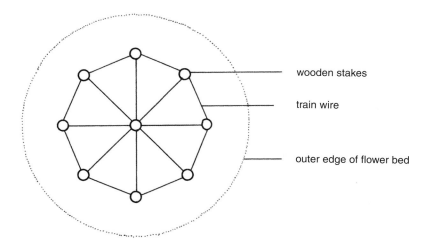

wooden stakes

train wire

outer edge of flower bed

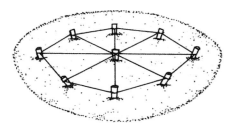

Bedding out.

Whites	Blues	Purples
ARCTIC QUEEN	'Ascotiensis'	'Daniel Deronda'
'Gillian Blades'	'Ivan Olsson'	'Fukuzono'
FOREVER FRIENDS	'Lasurstern'	'Night Veil'
'John Huxtable'	'Semu'	'Jackmanii'
'Mercury'	'Błękitny Anioł'	'Star of India'
'White Magic'	'Tie Dye'	'Dark Eyes'

formed this way. The use of a circular bed is shown on page 65.

To get the best from clematis in this situation some form of support is necessary to prevent their blooms lying on the bare earth and spoiling. The design shown uses nine wooden stakes, each 18in (45cm) long, and a reel of strong wire. Decide where you want the centre of the circle to be and drive a wooden stake into the ground. From this central stake, measure out approximately 3ft (1m) and drive in another stake. Continue this with the other stakes so that they form a circle around the first peg. Each of the surrounding stakes should be driven into the ground at least 12in (30cm) and at a slight angle away from the centre. The distances of the stakes from the centre and from the perimeter can be adjusted to suit the size of your bed. The outer pegs should not be too close to the edge of the bed. The wire can be put in place, twisting it tightly around each stake. Start at one of the outer stakes, twisting the wire firmly around it about 2in (5cm) from the top, then stretching the wire across the bed, twist it around the central peg and then out to the one opposite the first. Do each opposite pair in turn, and then finally take the wire around all the outer stakes to make a circle of wire. By driving the stakes into the ground at an angle, leaning away from the centre of the circle, you can draw the wires tight enough to prevent them from hanging slack without the risk of pulling the stakes out of the ground (*see* diagram, page 65).

This task may take time to complete thoroughly, and because it involves tramping about on the soil itself, leave forking in manure and compost until after the supports are erected and wired. Then the whole bed can be manured and forked over.

This basic structure offers scope to indulge in a range of planting ideas. Place the outer ring of stakes about 2ft (60cm) in from the edge of the bed to allow room for planting 'edging' or 'front of border' plants around the perimeter. In our plan, we have used a colour scheme based on white and various shades of blue and purple. Select the clematis, first choosing four or more different cultivars to match the size of bed. Clematis can be chosen from both Group 2 and Group 3 – that is, they could be 'light pruned' or 'hard pruned', but here all should be hard pruned. By hard pruning the Group 2 clematis, you lose the early display of flowers from the old wood but promote a massive display of flowers in mid-summer. By doing this you will have a far greater range of colour, size and form of blooms from which to choose. Avoid choosing a double flowered clematis which only produces double flowers on old wood, because if this is pruned away, the double flowers will be lost. There are exceptions such as: 'Denny's Double', 'Kiri Te Kanawa', 'Purpurea Plena Elegans' and 'Mary Rose'; these will all flower double from new growth, and can be used in this type of planting scheme. We have selected a few cultivars to give you some ideas.

We would choose six clematis – two whites, two blues and two purples – from our suggested list. Mix large- and small-flowered cultivars together and also star- and round-shaped flowers to make a massed collage of shapes and sizes.

Whilst this planting will give a glorious display of flowers throughout the summer months, winter and spring could look rather empty when the clematis are pruned down. This is when other plants can compensate and take over.

In our design we would use one of the silvery-blue grasses – the low growing *Festuca glauca*

'Azurit' is ideal as an edging plant, but requires splitting every other year to remove dead stems. Between the grasses small groups of purple crocuses, snowdrops and grape hyacinth could be planted alternately. The grass would give year-round interest, with the bulbs adding to the display during the winter and spring. Within this outer edging plant an inner circle of dwarf lavender: 'Hidcote' makes a good compact plant and has rich, purple flowers with a strong perfume. This planting complements the colour scheme, with its silvery-grey foliage and purple flowers, providing interest throughout the year with varying colour, shape and texture.

When the outer edge of the circular bed has been planted for year round interest, the centre of the bed could look particularly bare during the spring once the clematis have been pruned. This gives more scope for further interplanting with spring bulbs, this time perhaps using something taller, such as tulips. Lily-flowered tulips are a favourite of mine and for this colour scheme we would use 'White Triumphator'.

Other variations to this theme could include the use of box hedging or the gold and green varie-gated grass, *Carex* 'Evergold', which makes an unusual edging plant. Using these 'permanent' plants as edging gives structure to the whole

'Margaret Hunt' trained against a wall.

'Margaret Hunt' scrambling over heathers.

design, and by planting various bulbs, colour can be added during a season when the clematis are not in flower.

Imaginative use of artificial supports in the garden can thus provide another dimension to growing clematis. The ideas given can be adapted to suit your own gardening style. Whilst some are elaborate and quite expensive, others can be simple to create and not a drain on the gardening budget, yet still achieve the desired effect.

Artificial supports are in keeping with a formal gardening style, whereas for more informal planting schemes the use of natural supports for clematis is more appropriate.

CHAPTER 8

Growing with Natural Supports

Having used all the hard landscaping features, the walls and fences, the pillars, posts and pergolas in the garden to support clematis and felt the uses of these plants has been exhausted, stop and look again. Numerous opportunities still await for these under-used climbers to add their wonderful array of colourful blooms to the rest of the garden. A myriad of plants already in our gardens are crying out to be given the chance to host a clematis.

Moore and Jackman in their book suggested that clematis could be used to drape a mural ruin or to cover an unsightly bank or slope. While very few people have a 'ruin' in their garden on which to drape clematis, some readers may well have a bank or slope which could house a few clematis to great effect. Yet every one of us who has a garden must have some other plants through which to grow clematis. Roses, trees and tree stumps, shrubs, heathers and conifers, herbaceous beds and rockeries, are all waiting for you, the gardener, to have the necessary inspiration to transform, and enhance, their natural beauty.

When the predecessors of our modern clematis were growing in their wild state, there was no trellis for them to climb, nor walls, arbours or festoons of rope. Instead, all that they had to climb or scramble over was shrubby undergrowth, rocks and trees. In their natural habitat clematis will clamber up and drape themselves over their hosts in a most appealing fashion.

OPPOSITE: Montana Group cultivars clambering into a large tree.

CLIMBING HOSTS

Other climbers will be enhanced by the addition of a clematis – especially if the host plant has a relatively short flowering season, or has no flowers at all, as in the case of ivies.

We have had several climbing plants in our garden which have been hosts to a clematis; they include honeysuckle, pyracantha, wisteria, solanum, ivies and roses. Each plant should be allowed to have its own share of the limelight, whilst sharing the centre stage with another great performer.

One wall of the house is cream colour-washed, and there we grew 'Freda' (Montana Group) together with a bronze-leaved honeysuckle. 'Freda' also has bronze foliage, and the two together complemented one another. The montana would begin flowering almost before the leaves were fully open, during spring, and flower on almost to the beginning of summer, its cherry-red blooms showing up to good effect against the cream wall. There was then a short break before the honeysuckle began flowering during mid-summer, but it went on flowering until early autumn.

The east wall of the house is traditional Norfolk red brick and for many years was host to a wall-trained pyracantha. In about eight years the pyracantha grew almost to the eaves of the house and made a perfect situation in which to attempt to grow evergreen *C. armandii*. We say 'attempt', because our whole garden stands exposed to the elements, and this east-facing wall is the most sheltered wall of the house. *C. armandii*, being somewhat tender, prefers a more sheltered aspect in which to flourish, but we decided that the pyracantha could host the *C. armandii* using its own foliage to provide the clematis with some extra protection. This worked rather well, and although we are sure the *C. armandii*, given a choice, would have preferred to grow with more protection, it thrived for many years and flowered profusely for us each spring.

Our wisteria is trained on the south wall of the house and was planted close to the brickwork before the terrace was laid around its base. In the normal way we would have preferred to plant a clematis close to the trunk of the wisteria, but in this case the terrace was in place before we had considered the possibility of using the wisteria to host another plant. True, a paving slab could have been removed to allow enough room to plant a clematis, but the problem was solved another way.

We had used three terracotta pots to display clematis on our stand at the Royal Norfolk Show. The largest pot held 'Hendersonii' (Diversifolia Group), the middle sized pot contained 'Prince Charles' and the smallest held a *C. integrifolia*. After the flower show, the three pots were placed in a group on the terrace at the base of the wisteria. The vines of the two taller clematis were then allowed to clamber up into the trunks of their host where they provided a splash of colour for much of the summer. The low growing herbaceous *C. integrifolia* was given no support and was allowed to drape over the edge of its pot, providing a colourful display of flowers at the base of this arrangement. This made a good planting combination with the wisteria making a tremendous display of mauve blue flowers during the late spring and early summer. Then from mid-summer through to early autumn, the clematis took over, adding their display of flowers to a plant which would otherwise be devoid of interest until its own flowering period began again the following year.

In another part of the garden we used *Solanum crispum* 'Glasnevin' which has purplish-blue flowers, together with the deep maroon-red climbing rose 'Guinée' and the white clematis 'Snow Queen'. This was another group of climbers which, as individuals, are beautiful enough but when planted together made a stunning sight.

During 1994 we began a new piece of garden,

reclaimed from the end of a paddock; it is about the size of an average terraced-house garden. We wanted this garden enclosed, behind tall hedges, so one could sit in peace and solitude, shut away from the rest of the world. In such a relatively small, narrow area a large hedge would be totally impractical as it would take up most of the garden. Someone then had the idea of using ivies, grown up stock netting, to make a narrow hedge 6ft (2m) tall. This made an almost windproof screen, providing shelter for the plants in the garden and seclusion for those seeking peace and tranquillity.

On the outside of one of the long sides of this ivy hedge there is a grass path running the whole length. This was a useful place to display some of the species clematis whose small flowers would have been totally lost at the back of a border. They need closer inspection to appreciate their delicate charm. These were grown up through the ivies, enabling the onlooker to stand very close to study each individual flower, and their appeal was able to captivate everyone. Amongst the clematis planted here were 'Orange Peel', *C. pitcheri*, *C. ladakhiana* and the evergreen *C. cirrhosa*.

ROSES

For us, planting roses and clematis together is one of the best ways to display both of our favourite plants. Some of our best loved roses are the old fashioned cultivars, their blooms varying from open shaggy heads to those of tightly packed rosettes. Their colours are usually subtle shades, from creamy whites through shades of yellow, apricot and pink, to deep, almost purply-reds. Even the cerise shades are not harsh, but have a gentleness which is very pleasing to the eye, and most have an exquisite, heady perfume.

Many of these old roses have a much shorter flowering season than their modern counterparts, but by interplanting them with clematis, flowers can be enjoyed in that area of the garden for a longer period.

We grow both light and hard pruning cultivars of clematis with our roses and find neither are difficult when it comes to pruning. In fact, the pruning of clematis grown with roses can present a golden opportunity to the gardener who, by careful consideration, can manipulate nature to produce flowers at a desired time. The first time this happened in our garden was by sheer chance, but it made us realize there were further possibilities, simply by adjusting the pruning technique. We had a climbing rose, 'American Pillar', which is bright pink with a white eye and has a rather short flowering season during late spring and early summer. For many years this rose had been host to the later-flowering purple clematis 'Gipsy Queen'. The idea of the planting was that the clematis, having been hard pruned, would be flowering during the mid to late summer after the rose had finished. However, one year, on our annual pruning pilgrimage around the garden, we had overlooked the pruning of this clematis. Because of this the clematis flowered several weeks earlier than normal, at the same time as the rose. The dark purple flowers of the clematis with the bright pink blooms of the rose made a pleasing combination. From then on, when pruning the clematis, if it was not too 'leggy', we gave it a light prune to tidy it up and then it flowered with the rose. If however, it had become an unruly mess, it was hard pruned to keep it under control, and it then flowered when the rose was over.

We have planted together what might seem an odd combination of clematis with a rose. With the vigorous white rambling rose 'Bobbie James' we planted two white clematis, the large-flowered 'Marie Boisselot' and the medium-sized flowered 'John Huxtable'. This will seem an incredible feat

of pruning to perform due to the fact that one of the clematis is generally treated as requiring light pruning, the other hard. Having hard pruned both clematis in the early years, we then changed to only lightly prune both, sufficient to tidy them up. The effect was rather good – the all-white combination of flowers of varying sizes from the small blooms of the rose to the large flowers of the clematis.

The earlier flowering clematis which have two separate flowering periods are ideal grown with roses. We find in our garden that the early flowers of the clematis are out in bloom at the same time as the roses. When they have finished flowering both can be dead-headed which will encourage them to put on some new growth during the summer. We will then have another flush of flowers during the late summer and early autumn when both the roses and clematis are often back in flower together.

While dead-heading your roses after their early flush of flowers, it is well worth taking the time and trouble to also dead-head your clematis. We appreciate this is a very time-consuming occupation, but even if you can only do some, it would improve your chances of a better display of clematis flowers later in the year.

Below are some of the light-prune clematis and climbing roses we have grown together.

We also grow hard-prune cultivars of clematis with our roses. These will begin flowering during mid-summer while the roses are still in flower, and will go on flowering for many weeks through the summer and early autumn after the roses have

Light Prune Clematis	with	Rose
'Elsa Späth' (deep blue)		HÄNDEL (white/pink)
'Dr Ruppel' (mauve/carmine bars)		'Phyllis Bide' (pinky-peach)
'Proteus' (rosy-lilac)		'Albéric Barbier' (creamy-white)
'Lasurstern' (lavender blue)		'Albertine' (pink-gold)
'Vyvyan Pennell' (dark lavender)		'Gloire de Dijon' (buff/apricot)
'Will Goodwin' (light blue)		'Ghislaine de Féligonde' (orangey-yellow)
'Sylvia Denny' (white)		EDEN ROSE '88 (creamy-pale pink)
'H.F. Young' (bright-mid blue)		'Felicia' (pink)
'Fujimusume' (true blue)		'Alchymist' (pale orangey-yellow)
'Belle of Woking' (silvery-grey)		'Sophie's Perpetual' (cerise)

'Solidarność' and rose 'Alchymist'.

finished. This is a good way to extend the flowering period and provide colour in that part of the garden while the roses are taking a break.

There are one or two hard-prune clematis we would avoid when choosing a clematis to plant with a climbing rose. *C. terniflora*, *C. rehderiana*, 'Paul Farges' and 'Bill MacKenzie' for instance would completely swamp the majority of roses. The only roses which would probably stand up to their competition would be those such as R. 'Rambling Rector', 'Kiftsgate' and 'Sir Cedric Morris'. Even with these vigorous individuals, it would however be wise to allow the rose a few years to establish itself before adding the clematis.

Below are some of the hard-prune clematis and climbing roses that we have grown together.

The planting of roses and clematis together works very well, as both require similar treatment – that is, good well-manured soil, and pruning at a similar time of year. Do not be too concerned if you find it necessary to spray the roses against black-spot or greenfly, as any of the sprays available to the public should not harm your clematis.

We also have a few of the taller-growing, old fashioned bush roses in the garden and grow clematis through those. Some of our favourite plantings are in the box on page 73.

'Margot Koster' planted with the bush rose 'Auguste Seebauer' makes an interesting combination as the flowers are almost the same colour. The only real difference is the shape; 'Margot Koster' has open, rather gappy tepals that twist slightly as the flower opens and which, seen amongst the blooms of the rose, look very pretty.

'Grüss an Aachen' is a very beautiful old bush rose of flesh pink fading to cream and is rather short to host a clematis, growing to only about 2ft (60cm) tall. The clematis 'Margaret Hunt' grows close by this rose, scrambling across the ground. We allow just two or three stems to wind up through the rose; otherwise the poor thing would be swamped. 'Margaret Hunt' is a deep dusky pink with medium sized blooms, whose colour enhances the flesh-pink in the rose.

Although we are lucky enough to have quite a large garden, it is still not big enough to hold all the combinations of roses and clematis which we would like to grow together. We hope our suggestions will inspire you to try growing these two beautiful plants together.

Hard Prune Clematis	with	Rose
'Perle d'Azur' (azure blue)		'Zéphirine Drouhin' (cerise-pink)
'Étoile Violette' (purple)		CASINO (yellow)
'Rouge Cardinal' (ruby-red)		'Sombreuil' (white)
'Prince Charles' (light mauve-blue)		'Blairii No.1' (pale pink)
'Madame Grangé' (reddy-purple)		'Paul Lédé' (apricot pink)
'Little Nell' (white/mauve-pink)		'Paul's Scarlet' (scarlet red)
'Warszawska Nike' (purple)		'Compassion' (apricot/yellow/pink)
'Gipsy Queen' (purple)		'American Pillar' (cerise pink/white)
'Polish Spirit' (deep purple)		'Lady Hillingdon' (apricot-yellow)

Clematis	with	**Bush Rose**
'Prince Charles' (light mauve blue)		'Fantin-Latour' (blush pink)
'Margot Koster' (deep mauvy pink)		'Auguste Seebauer' (rich rose pink)
'Sylvia Denny' (white)		'Madame Isaac Pereire' (purply crimson)
'Margaret Hunt' (dusky mauve-pink)		'Grüss an Aachen' (flesh pink to cream)

'Julka' and rose 'Bonica'.

'Jackmanii' scrambling through a rose hedge.

TREES

Trees can take on a whole new appearance when clothed with a clematis. Depending on the size of the tree, many different clematis can be used for this purpose. For example, a very large holly of

about 30ft (10m) tall makes a perfect host to a scrambling pale pink montana which provides a magnificent display of flowers during the late spring.

Leylandii were very popular trees which, over the years, have been used extensively for hedging and windbreaks. This was probably due to the fact that they are so quick growing. Unfortunately, unless kept tightly clipped, they will eventually become far too large for the average garden. Even when kept under control a leylandii hedge can be rather boring so the additional planting of a montana will add some colour and interest. We have used some large conifers, including the golden leylandii and 'Harlequin', as a windbreak between the garden and the nursery. Close to one of these trees we stood a large half oak barrel in which we grew six different hard prune clematis. Each year, following their pruning, they clambered up into the leylandii adding a blaze of colour during the summer months.

Training into a tree.

'Giant Star' wending its way up a large mature tree.

The ornamental cherry tree, *Prunus* 'Amanog-awa', has an upright habit, like a column, pale pink semi-double flowers borne during late spring and leaves that turn to shades of red and orange in autumn. This alone provides interest through two different seasons and is a bonus in any garden. But if you plant beside this tree, as a friend of ours did in his garden, the clematis 'Jackmanii' whose lovely purple blooms can be seen high up in the prunus during late summer, this adds yet more to the visual pleasure of the garden.

We had an old plum tree which really had seen better days so it became host to two clematis; one was the species *C. tangutica* and the other 'Triternata Rubromarginata'. Having hard pruned both these clematis for two or three years, we later decided to leave them un-pruned to do their own thing. By doing this we found they began flowering early in the summer and continued until the first frosts, leaving the gorgeous fluffy seed heads that

C. flammula disguising a tree stump.

the *C. tangutica* produced, to be enjoyed all winter. After a few years, when they became very tatty looking, we pruned both clematis down very hard, thus allowing them a chance to rejuvenate.

When planting a clematis into a tree it is essential not to buy a cultivar which will out-grow and swamp the tree. A vigorous montana will only be suitable to grow into very substantial trees where a less vigorous clematis would be totally lost. It is also more appropriate to use such a strong growing clematis in a tree that is not of great value itself. If the tree has passed its best and is just to be used as a 'prop' then the montana is ideal.

It is most important to improve the soil near the tree before expecting a clematis to grow in these conditions. An established tree will have drained the soil of all nutrients and moisture, so regular watering through the early years until the clematis is also established will be essential. Further information on this aspect of growing clematis can be found in Chapter 4 under 'Planting Near Mature Trees and Shrubs' (page 36).

TREE STUMPS

The remains of once proud trees can be unsightly monstrosities if left in the garden with no adornment. They do, however, provide a perfect place to grow clematis to make an attractive feature.

If you have a very large tree in your garden that has to be taken down, it is unlikely the stump and root will be removed. This can be put to good use by covering with clematis. First of all you will need to wire the stump to provide some anchorage for the clematis. A piece of chicken or livestock netting nailed over the top would be the most convenient solution. Alternatively hammer in a few nails around the stump and twist some training wire round each nail head. A few pieces of wire crisscrossed like this would be fine.

When a tree has been felled, it will no longer hurt it to axe through one or two roots if necessary, to make a large hole in which to place some manure or good soil ready for planting. Almost any clematis could be used for this depending on the situation and your personal preferences.

'Romantika' adding contrast to a *Philadelphus*.

SHRUBS

Shrubs in the garden each play their own part in adding height or width, different coloured foliage, berries or catkins perhaps, and most have a character of their own. While it would be wrong to take away their individuality, their appearance could be enhanced with the addition of a clematis.

Early winter is the best season for the evergreen shrub *Garrya elliptica*, when it is 'dripping' with long, silvery, grey-green catkins, a visual treat to be enjoyed from the warmth of the house on a cold, damp day. During the summer months, when the catkins from the previous winter have long gone, the garrya is a rather boring-looking green bush. But it is a marvellous host for the tiny bluey-white, bell-shaped flowers of the native Portuguese clematis, *C. campaniflora*, which displays its flowers during the summer. In the autumn the clematis should be pruned down to about 2–3ft (60–90cm) to remove the old vines from the garrya, as they would detract from the beauty of the shrub's winter display. Then, during late winter or early spring when the worst of the winter weather has passed, the clematis can be pruned down to about 1ft (30cm) from the ground.

Other shrubs with winter interest such as cornus (dogwood), with its colourful bare stems of orange, red, fluorescent green and black, or the contorted hazel *Corylus* 'Contorta', whose cork-

screw like branches are seen to perfection once its leaves have been shed in autumn, all cry out to be adorned by colourful clematis during the summer. The majority of summer flowering clematis would be successful grown through these shrubs, but we would perhaps choose a cultivar that requires hard pruning and is not too rampant – a Viticella Group cultivar would be ideal. We have seen 'Kermesina' flowering in the variegated dogwood *Cornus alba* 'Elegantissima', the small, deep red flowers of the

'Victoria' clambering over a prostrate conifer.

clematis looking truly elegant amongst the white-edged grey-green leaves of the cornus. We would suggest that if you try this, you semi-hard prune the clematis when the dogwood begins to lose its leaves in autumn. This will allow the stems of the cornus to be seen during its finest months, without the old clematis vines distracting the eye. Final pruning of the clematis can again wait until late winter or early spring.

We have also used clematis in various cotoneasters in our garden. The aim is to use a cultivar which will flower during a period when its host will have little to offer. Ideal would be an early to mid-summer flowering clematis, whose display would be over by the time the cotoneaster berries were ready to take over the show. We have also grown a pyracantha as a free standing shrub which was host to a spring-flowering clematis called 'Ruby'; it looked fantastic during April and May when the whole shrub was hung with the pinky red bells of 'Ruby'. Fortunately, or unfortunately, this clematis usually has a second, almost equally magnificent display of flowers in the autumn, by which time the berries of the pyracantha had turned orange! It looked awful. If we had used a blue or a white alpina all would have been well.

The flowering season, or period of interest, has been extended for other trees and shrubs as well. Our *Magnolia × soulangeana* is host to the later flowering 'Jackmanii Superba', whose rich purple flowers show up well against the pale foliage of the magnolia. The more compact *Magnolia stellata* is host to 'Princess Diana' which makes a wonderful partnership.

Two weigelas in our garden each entertained a clematis. *Weigela florida* 'Foliis Purpureis', which has dull, purplish-green foliage, supported the large, pale silvery-pearl blooms of the clematis 'Peveril Pearl', which really helped to brighten up this rather dull shrub in summer, when its own display of flowers has finished. The variegated *Weigela florida* 'Variegata' played host to the Polish clematis 'Warszawska Nike', whose rich, reddy-purple flowers were displayed to near perfection amongst the cream and green leaves of the weigela.

There are simply endless combinations of

shrubs and clematis which you could try, but you don't have to have them spreading their periods of interest throughout the year – they could be in bloom together. Our ceanothus hosted the lovely pink clematis from Japan called 'Asao'. The large pink flowers of the clematis with the small fluffy-looking blue flowers of the ceanothus made a wonderful sight together during late spring and early summer.

We hope this has inspired you to try using clematis in your shrubs. Further advice on soil preparation and planting in shrubs can be found in Chapter 4.

HEATHERS AND CONIFERS

Some years ago, beds of mixed heathers and conifers became very fashionable and we planted up three – two island beds and a bank. The tremendous variations of shapes, sizes, colours and textures of conifers is amazing, and combined with heathers for groundcover they make very attractive features, with little maintenance required.

Our soil is on the limy side and not ideal for many types of heather. We found that with the addition of some peat or peat substitute at planting, the winter-flowering *Erica carnea* was the heather we could grow most successfully. They were in flower from early winter through to the spring and made a wonderful display, but had little value through the summer months. This is where clematis took over.

We used a mixture of hard and light prune clematis amongst our heathers and conifers, but *all* were hard pruned during late autumn. This allowed the heathers to have a spell free of clematis vines, so we could then enjoy their flowers over the winter.

There are many clematis that could be used for this purpose, but avoid choosing cultivars which only flower on old ripened wood, such as the Atragene and Montana Groups. Because of the need to hard prune each year, there would never be any old wood for them to flower from. Others to avoid would be the double flowering cultivars such as 'Vyvyan Pennell' which only flower double from the old wood. Their single flowers could be enjoyed, but there would never be any double blooms. One of the light prune types we grew through heathers was 'Mrs Cholmondeley'. In the normal way, with light pruning, this would begin flowering from early summer, semi-continuously to early autumn. Having been hard pruned, 'Mrs Cholmondeley' does not begin flowering until mid-summer, but will still flower well into late autumn. Therefore, by hard pruning these clematis, the early flowers normally produced from the old growth will have to be forfeited, but instead the blooms from the new growth are brought forward and enhanced.

Also much less suitable are the very rampant cultivars from Group 3, such as *C. terniflora* and 'Bill MacKenzie' which could completely smother heathers and conifers, causing them to brown-off and develop dead patches.

Apart from the few clematis we have suggested avoiding, there are many cultivars to choose from which would be suitable to enhance winter flowering heathers during their 'dull' season. Simply allowing the clematis to scramble over the heathers and conifers, going where nature takes them, will not only provide extra colour to that part of the garden but allow the clematis the freedom to take on a very natural appearance.

HERBACEOUS BORDERS

Wherever they are, herbaceous borders always give us the feeling they should be surrounding an English country cottage. Even the wide herbaceous borders in the gardens of large houses and halls try to have that typical 'laid-back' country feel about them. Yet they are very often laid out with swathes of colour, all planned and organized.

Oh how we would like to 'disorganize' a carefully constructed border by lacing a blue clematis through a group of pink lupins! Or perhaps allowing the Viticella Group cultivar 'Maria Cornelia' to clamber up tall blue delphiniums and hang its small white bells from those glorious towers of colour. 'Comtesse de Bouchaud' could creep her

light pink blooms through the silvery-blue ornamental thistle *Echinops ritro*. In fact, anywhere there is a gap in your herbaceous border where a hole can be dug, try a clematis. Does it really matter about your colour scheme? If it does, then choose a clematis within your chosen colour arrangement – there are so many cultivars to pick from.

As with the suggestions for clematis to grow with heathers, we would avoid those cultivars only flowering from their old wood as that would limit your ability to prune and tidy, which is essential in the herbaceous border. Also avoid the very vigorous cultivars from Group 3 which could swamp your other treasured plants.

A border would be the obvious place to grow all the herbaceous clematis, such as those in the Diversifolia, Heracleifolia and Integrifolia Groups, or the non-climbers in the Flammula Group. Perhaps at the back of the border you could grow the herbaceous 'Praecox' with some support. We have seen this done at Sissinghurst Castle at the tower end of the purple border – wonderful. Some of the self supporting members of the Heracleifolia Group can be planted mid-border to give height, to display their clusters of hyacinth-like flowers and add perfume too. Herbaceous clematis do not suffer from wilt, they can usually survive a dry spell better than many and they have a long flowering period.

Given some support, *C. recta* 'Purpurea', with its wonderful purply-bronze young foliage, makes a marvellous backdrop to other herbaceous plants. We have seen this used to good effect planted behind the hardy cerise flowered *Geranium psilostemon*. We have used 'Durandii' with its rich indigo-blue flowers draped through the silver foliage of the curry plant *Helichrysum italicum*. They make a wonderful combination especially when the curry plant flowers. Its broad clusters of bright yellow flowers held on erect stems seem to highlight the bright yellow stamens at the centre of the clematis blooms.

The little herbaceous *C. integrifolia*, or one of the many cultivars now available, could be used at the front of the border, either with a few pea-sticks for support or left to scramble at will. 'Alionushka', a

'Arabella' tumbling over the edge of a border.

scrambling, non-clinging pink herbaceous-type clematis could be put to good use growing through the blue spire-like flowers of *Caryopteris × clandonensis* which, with its silvery-grey foliage, makes an excellent border plant.

You don't have to use just the herbaceous clematis in a border; almost any clematis could be used. Any of the hard prune (Group 3) clematis would be suitable, apart from the rampant cultivars already mentioned. They could all be reduced by about two-thirds during the autumnal tidying of the border plants, with their final hard prune waiting until late winter or early spring. The clematis will also appreciate the annual mulch which is usually applied to a herbaceous border in the autumn, and will reward you with a glorious display the following summer.

GROUND COVER

Many plants can come under this heading when used by gardeners not only to provide colour and foliage but also to suppress weeds. There is one herbaceous clematis that is ideal for this purpose: 'Praecox'. Despite the fact that it requires hard pruning, it will be back in force, covering the ground by the time most of the weeds are becoming a problem. It will not stop the weeds altogether, but what few weeds do grow will be weakened by the lack of light under the foliage cover of the clematis and therefore be easier to pull out. The clematis could be under-planted with daffodils and tulips, which would provide some colour while the clematis is re-growing after pruning. 'Praecox' makes a particularly attractive display, with thousands of small, star-like flowers of white with bluey-mauve tips through the summer until late autumn.

ROCKERIES

Although these can be planted up with clematis, there are very few we would consider trying, due to the fact that the majority just grow too big. In a traditional rock garden, the plants are normally chosen because they are compact and low growing, which of course, most clematis are not.

There are now, however, a few clematis available which would be ideal in rock gardens. Three we have used were crosses between species from New Zealand. 'Joe' was the result of a cross between *C. marmoraria* and *C. paniculata*, whilst 'Moonman' and 'Lunar Lass' were the results of a cross between *C. marata* and *C. marmoraria*. These clematis are dioecious, which means that each plant carries flowers of only one sex; hence 'Moonman' carries male flowers, while 'Lunar Lass' has female flowers.

These plants would not be suitable for the 'faint-hearted' gardener to try. Because of their country of origin, where the climate is quite different to that here in the British Isles, they will require special conditions, lengths to which perhaps only the dedicated alpine gardener would go. On the rock garden, try growing them in a sunny, sheltered, free draining position, whilst not allowing the plants to dry out during a drought. You will then, we hope, be successful. They strike easily from cuttings, so it would be worth taking a few to have replacement plants ready if needed.

One group to try on a rockery would be the Integrifolia Group cultivars; they only grow to a height of 1–3ft (30–90cm) and they have a long flowering period from early-summer to autumn.

COLOUR COMBINATIONS

Careful planning can be used to design interesting combinations, although many of the best happen by pure chance! Our variegated holly tree was host to the pink summer flowering clematis 'Comtesse de Bouchaud', in front of which is the old purply-cerise rose 'Madame Isaac Pereire'. The three plants together make a glorious display of colour for many weeks through the summer, the rose adding another, unplanned, dimension to the effect, especially with a few of the clematis flowers mingled in with the blooms of the rose.

In our previous garden we had the light blue *C. macropetala* growing along a 6ft (2m) tall larch lap fence, in front of which was a large *Pieris* 'Forest

Flame'. During April and May the fence would be completely covered in the delightful double blue bells of the clematis, while in front, the pieris was ablaze with its orangey-red shoots of young growth – a gorgeous combination.

At Sissinghurst Castle gardens, well known for its clever colour combinations, the clematis 'Victoria', a deep pinky-mauve, can be seen in the rose garden beside a brilliant yellow day lily (hemerocallis) – another outstanding mixture of colours.

For anyone with a yearning to use their garden as a palate on which to paint, the use of clematis with other plants presents endless opportunities.

We hope that these suggestions of different ways to grow clematis, using other plants as hosts, will give you inspiration to try at least one or two. Begin by wandering around the garden during the spring, summer and autumn and discovering which plants you have already that look bare or uninteresting in that particular season. Then, bearing in mind the aspect, and the size of the host plant, careful selection can be made for the ideal clematis to accompany that plant.

CHAPTER 9

Growing in Containers

Not everyone has a garden with space in which to grow and enjoy a variety of trees, shrubs and clematis. However most people will have a small area in which a pot could stand. Whether it is on a patio or terrace, a concreted backyard or a paved courtyard, a conservatory or a balcony, or even a roof garden, a clematis will brighten up a dull spot with its colourful display.

Many clematis will do well in containers if given the right growing conditions. Some clematis look wonderful and do well in pots, others will do well but not look so good and a few just won't flourish at all. You need to be aware of all the varying needs of container cultivation to achieve success. This success will not come without time and effort.

The choice of pot or container is vital, as is the compost used. The training, support and pruning all need to be carefully considered, as do feeding and watering. When growing clematis in containers in conservatories, glasshouses or 'garden rooms', it will also be necessary to keep a watch out for pests and disease. It is essential to deal with such problems as and when they occur.

Before considering which clematis to buy for your pot, give thought to all of these aspects in turn, as they will help you to select an appropriate clematis for your needs.

CHOOSING A POT OR CONTAINER

Nowadays there is an almost endless array of decorative pots and containers available in most garden centres. To select one suitable for a clematis will require careful thought. A major factor is whether or not the pot is frost-proof. If it is to stand out all winter, this is essential or else it becomes a very costly error!

Pots and containers come in all shapes and sizes, and are made from a wide range of materials. They vary greatly in cost, from the elegant Grecian urn to the more humble plastic pot. They can all, however, be made to look beautiful once plants have been added.

Oak barrels, old chimney pots, terracotta, earthenware, concrete, plastic and wood – all can make good containers for clematis providing they are large enough and have adequate drainage.

The ideal size of container or pot will be one which is at least 18in (45cm) deep, as this will allow the clematis to be planted deep, which is so essential for success. The wider the pot, the better, as it will hold more compost for the plant to root into, more nutrients and more moisture, all of which are essential if the plant is to flourish.

Oak barrels, usually found cut in half, are excellent for clematis, and can be reasonably cheap to buy from a garden centre. Do check, before purchasing one, that it has sufficient drainage holes in the bottom.

Old chimney pots can look charming planted with a clematis. Check to see if a local reclamation yard has one at a suitable price. They can be very expensive, but they are of course weather-proof

OPPOSITE: 'Pat Coleman'.

and can be most attractive as visual 'full-stops' in garden design.

Terracotta is a favourite with many gardeners, and comes in all shapes and sizes. We would choose a fairly traditionally shaped pot rather than the 'Ali-Baba' type (which narrows at the top), as the latter can be difficult to extract a plant from when it comes to re-potting. Remember when purchasing terracotta to ask if it is frost-proof. Some pots can be left to over-winter out of doors, but with others it is necessary to move the pot under cover. Our terracotta pots stand out for most of the year, but with the onset of winter they are carefully removed by sack-barrow into a polythene tunnel where they stay until spring.

Decorative earthenware pots are readily available and are usually quite reasonably priced; again, choose one of the larger ones and check that it is frost-proof.

Many decorative plant containers are made from concrete and come in various shapes and sizes. Avoid buying a shallow trough or bowl. Instead, choose one that is at least 18in (45cm) deep – a traditional urn shape would be more suitable for a clematis.

Plastic flower pots have gradually taken over from terracotta for nursery production, largely because of the vast difference in price. If it is intended to keep several clematis in pots, this makes sense. Decorative plastic pots can now be bought in a range of sizes and colours to suit most peoples' needs. However, plastic containers will provide no protection for your clematis against the elements, especially in extremes of temperature. We would not recommend using plastic if the pot is to stand roasting in the sun all day during the summer, or if it is exposed to the worst of the cold during the winter. If it stands in a shaded position during summer and then is moved into a glasshouse or garden shed to over-winter then these pots would be adequate. In fact plastic pots can be a bonus when moving clematis in and out during the various seasons, as they are so much lighter and less liable to break than the more expensive pots.

There are also some very good wooden plant containers available now. Again, check on the drainage holes before purchasing, as some of these containers are designed only as decoration rather than to actually plant into.

With wooden planters, it is necessary every now and again to treat the wood with a preservative, checking first that the preservative is 'plant friendly'.

With expensive decorative plant pots it is unnecessary to plant them up permanently. You could have one or two of these good pots, but actually grow your clematis in large plastic flower pots, and then stand those into the decorative pots when the clematis are in flower and ready to go out on display. This aspect of growing clematis is dealt with in greater detail later in this chapter.

DRAINAGE AND COMPOST

Having selected a suitable pot, you will then need to decide what compost to use. You may prefer to mix your own using good garden compost or leaf-mould and a loamy top soil, but for most people it is easier to buy a bag of compost which is already mixed. Almost any standard potting compost will be suitable and most garden centres offer a wide range. The compost we prefer to use when potting clematis is John Innes No.3, a loam- rather than peat-based compost. The extra weight will help provide the pots with better stability.

Because of this loam mix the compost will pack down quite firmly in the pot, so we would suggest mixing a small bag of peat (or cocoa-fibre or other peat substitute if you prefer) into the compost beforehand. To one 25-litre bag of John Innes No.3 mix one 10-litre bag of peat or peat substitute. You will find that the peat (or substitute) will help to 'lighten' the loam and will also help to retain moisture which would otherwise drain through the compost quite quickly.

Before filling your pot or container with compost it is essential to put a few broken crocks

OPPOSITE: A medley of clematis with rose 'Evelyn May' in a pot.

or large stones into the bottom of the pot to cover the drainage holes, making sure the holes are not blocked completely. We also then add a layer of pea-shingle to a depth of 1–2in (2.5–5cm). Without this the compost will wash down and block the holes, thus preventing essential drainage. To aid drainage it is worthwhile standing the pot onto 'feet', thereby raising the pot off the ground. Most places which sell pots and containers also sell ornamental feet. While these look very nice, you may well have something else which will do the same job. We have used old house bricks, which work just as well.

Having completed this preparation you can now put a layer of compost into the pot, leaving enough room to allow the clematis to be planted deep. Check the depth before taking the clematis out of its pot, making sure it can be planted deep enough to bury the lowest one or two sets of leaf joints. Add a good single handful of bonemeal to the compost in the bottom of the pot and mix this in lightly.

Now you can remove the clematis from its pot and plant it firmly into its new compost. Do not forget to remove any ties which are around the plant and which would end up below soil level. Tease out some roots to encourage them to grow into the fresh compost. We would also recommend leaving a gap of at least 1in (2.5cm) between the top of the compost and the rim of the pot. This will allow plenty of room when watering and avoid compost washing out over the top. You may like to leave the compost low enough below the rim to add a layer of gravel or stones, which helps to shade the roots as well as providing a surface to break the flow of water when watering. This ensures the surface compost is not washed away, it looks attractive, and also discourages weeds. Choose the best colour of covering material to match your container and your clematis.

SUPPORTS

There are many different ways to support and train a clematis grown in a pot, depending on where and how you wish it to grow. A pot stood close to a wall or fence could have the clematis trained on wires or trellis fixed directly onto the wall. If you do decide to use this method, make sure the pot is frost-proof as it may have to stand out all winter with the clematis attached to the wall.

A free-standing method of support is generally far more appropriate. The pot can then be moved under cover for the winter if necessary. This also allows the plant's flowering position in the garden to be changed if desired. There are many decorative free-standing supports for clematis now available. While purpose made supports look attractive, a similar effect can be made using bamboo canes, which are considerably cheaper to buy. Canes can be made into fans or wigwams very easily, and will last for several years.

CHOOSING A SUITABLE CLEMATIS

When growing a clematis in a pot as a specimen plant you obviously want the very best display possible from it, so you need to choose the best cultivar for the situation.

Many clematis will grow well in containers, but some will look far more impressive than others. Those cultivars with a compact, free flowering habit will certainly be more pleasing to the eye than those which grow tall and 'leggy' and which would be better growing through a shrub rather than stood alone as a specimen. The clematis which have this bare, leggy look are generally those which require hard pruning each year, and make a substantial amount of growth before flowering. Cultivars such as 'Huldine', 'Perle d'Azur' and 'Gipsy Queen', for instance, are lovely clematis, and would grow equally as well as any others in a pot, but will not look so pleasing because of their leggy habit.

The other clematis that we would not recommend growing in containers because of their rampant nature are those which make an enormous amount of top growth and really do benefit from growing 'free' in the ground. Therefore, avoid the Montana and Armandii Groups and any of the

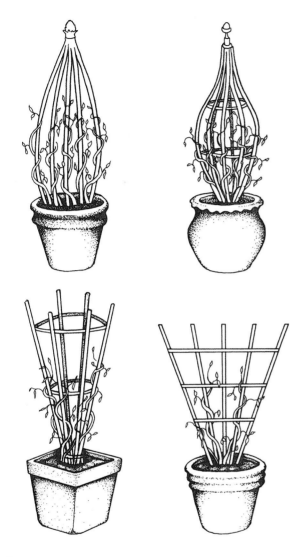

Decorative free-standing supports for pot-grown clematis.

CLEMATIS FOR POTS

Early to mid spring flowering: Any of the shorter growing cultivars in the Atragene Group. These will do well in almost any climate and any aspect.

Late spring and summer flowering: 'Ameshisuto', Bijou, 'Burma Star', Cezanne, Crystal Fountain, 'Frau Susanne', 'Fujimusume', 'Ivan Olsson', Jolly Good, 'Königskind', 'Lady Northcliffe', 'Louise Rowe', 'Mercury', 'Pat Coleman', 'Piilu', 'Rooran', 'Solidarność', 'Still Waters', 'Tae' and Temptation. Many of these cultivars have two flowering periods and will benefit from dead-heading once the early flowers have finished. They will then give a second glorious display of blooms later in the summer.

Flowering mid-summer onwards: 'Betty Corning', Cassis, Fleuri, Forever Friends, 'Hagley Hybrid', Jackmanii Purpurea, 'John Huxtable', 'Madame Julia Correvon', Mienie Belle, 'Niobe', 'Odoriba', 'Pink Fantasy', 'Rüütel', 'Tie Dye' and 'Westerplatte'.

Early or late flowering: 'Pink Fantasy' is ideal in a pot for early or late flowering, depending on whether it has been light or hard pruned.

Most of the summer: The little herbaceous integrifolias are super in pots.

other very vigorous growing clematis. If you are in any doubt at all when selecting a clematis to grow in a pot, ask a specialist grower who will advise you.

The ideal clematis for a pot is one which has a naturally compact habit and will flower very freely. We have selected a few of the very best clematis for containers and have listed them in the box, according to when they flower.

The herbaceous integrifolias which flower for most of the summer only need a relatively small pot. Following their hard prune during late winter or early spring, as they begin to grow, a few small pieces of twig can be pushed into the compost to hold the new growth upright, as you will find that once the plant is in full flower it may get top heavy and collapse, draping over the edge of the pot. On the other hand we like to grow integrifolias in pots with no support for their growth, standing the pots in front of larger pots holding clematis to provide interest lower down.

Doubling Up

Another way of growing clematis in pots is to grow two cultivars together. It is essential then to have a large container. It is also advisable to select two clematis which have identical pruning, for example, two hard prune or two light prune cultivars. Some very pleasing colour combinations can be made, either by use of contrast, perhaps having a light with a dark colour or, alternatively, by blending two pastel shades. When selecting two clematis for a contrast in colour the effect will be less harsh if the colours also complement one another. Some examples of effective combinations are given below.

PINK CHAMPAGNE with 'Elsa Späth': the deep pink and mauve of PINK CHAMPAGNE contrasts with the deep violet-blue of 'Elsa Späth', but they also complement one another with the dark, but slightly mauve blue of 'Elsa Späth' highlighting the mauve in PINK CHAMPAGNE.

'Gillian Blades' with 'Hakuookan': these offer a startling contrast of white with dark purple. However, the flowers have similar star shapes. The mauve white of 'Gillian Blades' is highlighted by the dark purple tepals of 'Hakuookan' whose crown of white stamens blends with the colour of 'Gillian Blades' tepals.

Other eye-catching combinations could be REFLECTIONS with KINGFISHER, or REBECCA which is a wonderful red with 'Pat Coleman' which is clear white with red anthers.

'Peveril Pearl' is a wonderful subtle mixture of pastel shades and in different lights during the day many colours are revealed: a pale, silvery mauve-grey with a hint of pink in its make-up. Put 'Peveril Pearl' with a deep rich purple such as 'Kacper' and the effect is beautiful.

If you prefer subtle, pastel shades together, try 'Pink Fantasy' with the light mauve-blue of 'Betty Corning', both hard pruned. Or perhaps the light pink 'Comtesse de Bouchaud' with the white 'John Huxtable'. These two clematis have flowers of an identical shape and size; only the colour varies.

Another interesting combination to try, and one we mentioned earlier, is the marrying of two completely different flower shapes. We have grown, in two separate pots, 'Hendersonii' (Diversifolia Group) and 'Prince Charles' at the base of our wisteria. Both clematis grew up through the foliage and stems of the wisteria and therefore needed no separate support. As they grew their stems inter-twined so that at flowering time they were well mixed together. The combination of the dark blue nodding, bell-shaped flowers of 'Hendersonii' with the open pale mauve-blue of 'Prince Charles' looked splendid.

A quite exotic look can be achieved by growing together a combination of clematis with colours that blend well but have flowers of a different shape. If you garden in a mild climate or can grow under cover try pairing 'Venosa Violacea' with *C. florida* 'Sieboldiana'. Their colouring is almost identical – 'Venosa Violacea' has a white centre with dark purple margins, whereas 'Sieboldiana' has a large crown of dark purple staminodes set off by creamy-white tepals. While their colours are the same they are displayed in reverse on the flowers. If you try this combination of clematis, but live in a cold climate and cannot move the pot under cover for the winter, try using several layers of garden fleece to protect 'Sieboldiana' from the worst of the winter weather.

The joy and satisfaction derived from growing clematis in containers comes from the fascinating opportunities they offer in terms of colour, seasonal flowering performance, habit of growth and potential for companionable contrast. Selection and use is a matter of individual taste, as is always the case in gardening. It is fun, and often rewarding, to experiment.

CONSERVATORIES

Some clematis that are tender or semi-tender require the controlled cultivation of indoor protection in glasshouses, conservatories or garden rooms. There is a select band of beautiful cultivars that flourish only when given the warmth and shelter from searing winds and frost that inside protection offers. For those who garden in colder climates, conservatories can also provide suitable conditions for growing many of the regular clematis already mentioned. Few clematis will object to the warmer conditions although some additional aspects, such as pests and diseases, will need to be addressed.

Those clematis ideal for growing in pots under

cover are the Florida and Forsteri Groups. *C. florida* 'Alba Plena' and *C. florida* 'Sieboldiana' are the classic floridas but also well worth growing are *C. florida* 'Thorncroft', 'Best Wishes' and Viennetta.

The Forsteri Group cultivars originating from New Zealand are evergreen, often very compact, and some have a gorgeous perfume – both attributes that are ideal for an indoor plant. These clematis are not always successful in many parts of Europe when grown in the open garden where winter wet is often the cause of their demise. So a conservatory gives the opportunity to enjoy these excellent plants. *C. forsteri* grows to 8–10ft (2.6–3m) so would benefit from a wall to spread its growth over. Many others, such as 'Joe', 'Lunar Lass' and 'Pixie' can be left as prostrate or very low growing specimens, and the latter two have a good scent.

Pests and diseases can be a problem when growing clematis indoors. The plants will need regular watering and humidity control, foliar feeding and protection from the risk of scorching. Checking for pests and diseases can be carried out at the same time as regular watering. Flying pests can be controlled to a certain extent under glass by the use of yellow sticky fly traps. These can be bought quite cheaply from most garden centres and are simply hung up near the plants. Pests such as greenfly and whitefly are drawn to the yellow colouring and will be held fast by the glue. (Pest control is covered in detail in Chapter 11.)

Because the atmosphere needs to be kept humid, you may have problems with botrytis. Dispose of any leaves as they die off, because if left hanging in healthy foliage or on the compost the botrytis spores will quickly multiply and cause the stems to rot. Botrytis can be recognized by

'Pixie' cascading over the edge of a pot.

remembering its common name – 'grey mould'. The humid atmosphere will help reduce the risk of infestation by spider mite. Good ventilation is also a requirement, so windows need to be kept open as much as possible.

The need for regular liquid feeding is greater when a clematis is confined to a pot, as we will look at shortly, but in a conservatory using liquid fertilizer as a foliar feed is also helpful as it will ensure the whole plant remains in a healthy state and is therefore better able to fend off attack by pests and disease. A weak solution used once or twice a week through the spring, summer and early autumn is sufficient. Avoid the use of foliar feed when the sun is full on the plant, as this would cause severe scorching of the foliage. Spray the leaves early in the morning, thus allowing them time to dry off before the sun gets too strong, or else wait until early evening when the sun is less powerful.

Strong sunlight is a problem for clematis grown under glass. Like many plants, clematis do not appreciate being baked in full sun, which is made worse by the effect of the glass. Where scorching becomes a problem, such as in mid-summer, pots are best stood in a sheltered position outside, or given shading inside.

Occasionally you may notice the new growing tips of the clematis dying back. The tip will go black and sometimes the top one or two sets of leaves will also be affected. This die-back is caused by stress which in turn has been caused by extremes of climate or irregular watering. Early in the year the weather can be very hot during the day with the temperature under glass rocketing. At night the temperature plummets. The high day-time temperature encourages the clematis into lush, tender growth which the cold nights will damage.

Allowing pots to dry out completely and then soaking the compost to rehydrate them will also cause damage, particularly to the growing tip. Whilst regular watering is essential to maintain a healthy plant do make sure the pot remains free-draining. If you are growing a potted clematis in a glasshouse, the pot will probably be standing on sand or gravel which will be free-draining. In a conservatory or garden room, however, the pot should stand in something waterproof to protect the flooring. Large plastic saucers are available in which a layer of gravel can be placed; your clematis pot can then be stood on this and will drain freely when watered. A little water in the bottom of the saucer will help provide extra humidity, but to avoid water-logging ensure that the bottom of the flower pot is not standing in water.

ACHIEVING A SUCCESSION OF FLOWERS

When clematis are grown in pots for a floral display it is essential to get the longest, most spectacular display of blooms possible, both in colour and quantity. The majority of clematis will flower for eight weeks, some even longer, and in a relatively small display area such as a patio or terrace, the longer the flowers last, the better. There are some clematis that really do flower continually for many weeks, in particular 'Fukuzono' and others in the Diversifolia Group, many of which we grow in pots with great success. These cultivars are non-clinging and also require hard pruning, so training has to be a top priority with these each year, tying in the stems as they grow. Our reward is weeks of glorious flowers throughout the summer months.

Other clematis which give a long flowering season in pots are the early large-flowered hybrids which offer two periods of interest – late spring to mid-summer and again from late summer to early autumn. In order to get the maximum flowering period from these clematis it is vital to carry out a summer pruning, as soon as the early flowers have finished. In a pot this pruning needs to be quite severe in order to keep the clematis compact. Roughly halve the size of the plant and start feeding regularly as described in Chapter 5. In about eight weeks you should have the second flush of flowers to enjoy.

It is very satisfying to get a spectacular display of clematis blooms for as much of the year as possible within the confines of a patio. One way of achieving this is to buy just one or two expensive large decorative pots. Instead of planting directly into these you may, as previously described, plant into cheap plastic flower pots which are almost the same size as their attractive counterparts. These planted pots can then be stood in the decorative pots when ready for display. The ideal situation would be to arrange a 'nursery area' where the clematis could be held until almost ready to burst into bloom, whereupon they can be moved into their display position and inserted into the decorative containers. The plants could be potted, pruned, fed and trained out of sight, only to go out on view when in flower. They can then be returned to the nursery area when the blooms have finished.

By growing clematis in pots in this way several plants can be grown, each flowering at different times of the year. The display could begin with one of the shorter growing Atragene cultivars, flowering during the spring. This can be followed by one of the early large-flowered clematis which blooms in late spring to the early summer. The pot could be changed again for one containing a clematis flowering in mid-summer. Finally, the early large flowered clematis should be back in flower again for late summer and autumn when it can be put out on display again in the 'posh pot'.

So with the help of three clematis and one decorative container, the floral display could last from early spring right through to autumn. We have tried this with great success. When a display of flowers is required in an important area of the garden, such as on a patio or terrace, it is advantageous only to see clematis which are in flower. As each finishes its display it can be changed for one about to bloom.

The changing-over of the pots is quite a simple procedure if the rim of the plastic pot is slightly higher than that of the decorative pot, as it can then be easily lifted out. We have one earthenware pot into which the plastic pot fits without leaving any rim to get hold of causing us considerable problems when it comes to changing the plants over – it takes two of us to do the job. The plant and pots are very carefully placed on their side on the ground. Then with the aid of a cane pushed up into a drainage hole, the inner pot can be gently pushed out. The other person can take some of the weight by holding the plant and its framework and

help to gently ease the two pots apart. This makes the task sound like quite a problem, but it is really simple and well worth the effort.

To achieve a really spectacular display of potted clematis requires time, effort and dedication, but many people will find it an interesting challenge to try at least one pot of clematis.

If you have insufficient time, and have space for only one pot, for maximum colour and minimum effort use half an oak barrel and plant together three clematis with identical pruning, perhaps 'Carnaby', 'Semu' and one of the Texensis Group cultivars. This should ensure flowers from late spring through to autumn. Around the base of these you could plant a few tulips, and as they finish flowering they could be removed to be replaced by a few summer bedding plants.

Plantings such as this will provide colour for many months, and yet not require too much space or time, other than that taken to prune, train, water and feed.

WATERING AND FEEDING

When keeping a clematis permanently confined to a pot, watering and feeding need to be kept up. It is wise to check your plant most days during the spring, summer and autumn to see if it needs water. In the spring your clematis will be growing rapidly, and attention needs to be paid most days to training and tying in the new growth; at the same time the need for water can also be assessed. During a really hot spell in summer, particularly if your pot or container stands in the sun, watering will need to be carried out every day. In the autumn, however, because the plant is not making fresh growth the need for water will be reduced, but still check regularly and prevent it from drying out.

During the winter, if the container is left outside, there will probably be no need to water, but if it is stood where it is sheltered from the rain, do check to make certain it does not dry out completely.

Clematis need a great deal of water for most of the year but resent standing saturated. When checking the need for water, if the top of the compost looks dry, and it feels dry 1in (2cm) or so below the surface, then water is required. The amount needed will depend on a number of things: the size of container, whether the clematis is in full growth or flower or whether it is dormant, the weather conditions and when it was last watered. It is always safer to water frequently rather than allowing the pot to dry out completely and then flooding it. Once compost has been allowed to dry out it takes some time and effort before it will again retain moisture. During very hot weather it may require watering every day.

Feeding a pot-grown clematis is essential to maintain the plant in a healthy, free-flowering state. Because its roots are confined to a relatively small area, they are unable to search for further nourishment as they would be able to if planted in open ground. Therefore additional feed must be provided.

Early in the growing season start the feeding programme at pruning time, during late winter and early spring. This will consist of one good single handful of bonemeal lightly worked into the soil. When the clematis has been in the pot for about two years, we would suggest removing the top 1–2in (2.5–5cm) of compost from the pot. Bonemeal can then be added and worked into the soil around the roots and the pot can be topped up with fresh compost, which should then be watered in.

As soon as the weather has improved in the spring and the risk of severe late frost has passed, then liquid feeding can begin. Obviously a clematis kept in a pot has to be watered, so the addition of liquid feed is quite simple. The liquid feeds we would recommend are Phostrogen or one of the tomato feeds such as Tomorite or Tomato Maxicrop – those which have a high potash content are best. (For further information on feeds refer to Chapter 5.) The feed can be diluted in the watering can and simply watered in. Avoid applying liquid feed if the pot has dried out, as this could damage the roots of the plant; therefore make sure the soil is slightly moist before applying liquid nutrients.

We would recommend using liquid feed once a fortnight if using it at full strength (as recommended on the packet or bottle.) Beware of overfeeding, which promotes lush foliage, but few flowers. Alternatively, the feed can be applied weekly at half the recommended dosage.

You may choose not to use liquid feed at full strength once the buds have really fattened up ready to flower, or while the plant is in bloom. This is because, some believe, the feed will continue to speed up performance and they fear the flowers will be over and finished too quickly. However, we do not feel this is too great a risk, and a weak dose of liquid feed will cause no harm. Liquid feeding needs to be stopped early in the autumn, to allow the plant a natural period of dormancy.

An alternative to liquid feeding container-grown clematis is to use a slow-release fertilizer. This can be bought in the form of thimble-sized plugs, using the recommended number for the volume of the container. These are simple to use and can save time whilst ensuring the plant receives the essential nutrients.

PRUNING AND TRAINING

Clematis grown in pots and containers require thoughtful pruning and training. This will allow the plants to grow and flower to their full potential, thus rewarding the gardener for their time and effort.

Clematis in containers are generally pruned as they would be if they were in the open garden (*see* Chapter 6). All clematis, including the spring flowering Atragene Group, are hard pruned the first year after planting, to encourage a strong root system and a generous supply of shoots from below soil level. This treatment gets the plants off to a good start, with a sound network of vines low down. Subsequent pruning, from the second year, is as for the clematis group classification.

To recap on pruning – *Hard Prune:* starting at soil level, work up each stem checking for healthy viable buds in the leaf joints; leave at least two good sets of buds and prune off immediately above the second set. *Light Prune:* starting at the top of the plant, work down each stem, pruning off

'Pat Coleman' pruned to keep her compact in a pot.

'Pat Coleman' in flower nine weeks later.

immediately above a good set of buds; then completely remove dead or weak stems.

With experience however, this basic pruning can be modified so that you can dictate the time you wish your clematis to flower. The examples below explain how to achieve this.

The early flowering large-flowered hybrids, such as 'H.F. Young' and 'Nelly Moser', normally have two periods of flowering: late spring to mid-summer, and again in late summer to early autumn. By altering the pruning of these you can change their flowering times. If you wish these types to have a mass of flowers from mid-summer through to early autumn, hard prune them during late winter or early spring. This will delay the flowering for some weeks. Instead of them having the early flush of flower from the old wood, they will

put all their vigour into providing one glorious display in late summer from the current season's growth.

Many of the more recent introductions that are designed to be good 'patio clematis' for growing in pots are best treated in this way. Therefore, even if they are really Group 2 Light Prune types in nature, they respond very well to hard pruning both in early spring and again after their first flush of flowers. This way you keep the plant compact and tidy, and you get more than one period of flowering.

If, however, you prefer to keep with the traditional double flowering periods of these clematis, but find they are growing too tall for the support in the pot, then when carrying out the spring pruning, cut them down lower than usual, to about 3ft

(1m), or half the height of the support they are to adorn. This will allow the clematis to retain some old wood to produce an early display of flowers. Once these first flowers have died, it is worthwhile dead-heading the plant. This, with the addition of some liquid feed, will encourage the clematis to put on sufficient new growth to provide an equally good display of flowers later in summer.

With the cultivars of clematis which require hard pruning – those that normally flower mid-summer onwards – the blooms can be delayed by a few weeks with additional pruning. Following their hard prune during late winter or early spring, they will begin to grow. Allow the young stems to make about 6–9in (15–22cm) of growth, then nip out the tips just above a leaf joint, which will encourage the stem to branch out again. Do this once only during the spring, otherwise the clematis will not have time to make flowering wood and bloom before the autumn frosts halt its progress. All our clematis which are pot-grown for display at flower shows are pruned in this way.

Following their initial hard prune in their first spring, the light prune cultivars of clematis should be trained to build a good framework of stems. This is done by tying in the vines as they grow, in a horizontal manner, gradually training them in a spiral around their support. Garden twine or plas-tic-covered wire can be used as ties, although the metal split-rings designed for sweet peas are quick and easy to use. This early training is most impor-tant and should last for many years.

The hard prune cultivars will need training each year as they grow. When training these carefully, on a weekly basis in the spring, you will realize just how much new growth they can produce in a short time.

As with children, clematis need control, supervi-sion and guidance in their early stages of growth. This helps to curb their impulse for unruly behav-iour!

PREPARING POTS FOR OVER-WINTERING

Sometimes, having enjoyed a fine display from our

flowering pots and containers during the summer, we neglect their care during the autumn and winter. It is worth giving them some attention at this time, in the hope they will repay you the following year.

To allow your clematis a period of dormancy, stop applying liquid feed early in the autumn. As the weeks progress and the weather deteriorates, necessary action will need to be taken to avoid disasters during inclement weather. If your container is exposed to severe wind and weather conditions, it would be advisable to secure it to prevent it from blowing over, or move it to a shel-tered position. This could be by a window in a garage or garden shed, or best of all in a cold glasshouse.

Where a pot has to be left out all winter, meas-ures can be taken to protect it where it stands.

A small single handful of bonemeal worked into the soil and lightly watered in will give the clematis some slow-acting feed to sustain it through the winter. A mulch can then be applied to help insu-late the plant from the worst of the cold – this could be peat, leaf-mould or garden compost. Or you could use bracken or perhaps a few pieces of conifer, such as leylandii, with the stems pushed into the soil around the edge of the pot and the tops bent over towards the clematis to form a blan-ket. It is worth sprinkling a few slug pellets onto the soil prior to this, as slugs and snails might well find this an ideal spot to over-winter.

If during the summer, your clematis has made a large amount of heavy top growth, cut some of this back to its support, thus pruning off the excess growth which could cause wind resistance. The pot will then be less likely to topple over if caught in a gale.

If you are growing one of the tender cultivars of clematis in a pot, such as one of the floridas, and are unable to move it under cover for the winter, we recommend you use some form of effective protection for your plant unless you enjoy a mild winter climate. Plastic bubble-wrap, used for pack-aging, is ideal for insulation and can be wrapped around the plant and fastened with string. In recent years garden fleece has become a popular method of giving plants winter protection. It is readily available and sold by the metre. Fleece reminds us of muslin, being a very fine white material that can be wrapped around the plant, using two or three layers. The ends can then be fastened together with clothes pegs.

In the late winter or early spring the protective cover will have to be removed to allow access for pruning, and then replaced until the weather has improved. As the days lengthen and warm up, the fleece or bubble-wrap can be removed on fine days and replaced if severe frost is forecast.

Whichever method you use to over-winter your pots, whether it is inside or out, do check them periodically to see if they need watering.

RE-POTTING AND ROOT PRUNING

The need to re-pot a clematis is inevitable, as after a few years, the plant will become pot-bound. The frequency of re-potting will depend on the size of the pot being used. The larger the pot, the less often re-potting will be needed.

You will find that, given ideal conditions and treatment, your clematis will remain healthy for several years. There will, however, come a time when, despite all the care given to it, the plant will look sick and the vigour will be gone. The flowers too may be smaller than they once were and the

Root pruning – slicing off side of root ball.

Root pruning – slice one third off bottom of root ball.

whole plant will lack its former glory, thus signalling the need for re-potting.

Pruning time affords an opportunity to check if the plant is pot bound. When removing the top layer of soil, ready to top dress with bonemeal and fresh compost, you can see whether the root growth has extended to the sides of the pot. If the roots are tightly packed against the sides, then the time has come to re-pot. This usually involves moving the plant into a larger container, but when a large pot is used in the first instance, it becomes difficult to re-pot into an even larger container. You therefore need to know how to use the same one again.

Pruning time is the best time to re-pot a clematis, as the plant will still be in a dormant state yet ready to burst into growth as the weather improves. Unlike pruning, which can be carried out regardless of the weather (we have pruned clematis in a snow storm!) it would be better to re-pot a clematis during a milder spell. Avoid re-potting while the pot and compost are frozen.

This can be a tricky operation to perform and may require two pairs of hands. The first thing to do is to prune the clematis down to a manageable height. There is no need to check for viable buds in the leaf joints on this occasion, as the final pruning will be done when the re-potting has been completed. Prune off all stems at approximately 2½–3ft (80–90cm) above the soil level and remove the old top growth. When removing the trellis or canes, remember to cut through any petioles (leaf stalks) attached to the lower part of your plant, and remove any ties that remain in place, because if the canes are pulled straight out, the stems in the pot may be damaged and may become a source of infection by fungus. The entire operation needs to be performed very carefully in order to avoid damage to the lower stems.

Having reduced the height of the plant, the next step is to remove it from its pot. This is a difficult process due to the size and weight of the pot, plant and compost. Prior to re-potting, the plant should be left un-watered and sheltered from any rain for about a month. This will not do the plant any harm at this time of year but will allow the compost and roots to dry out slightly, which should then allow it to be removed from the pot more easily. To ease the roots away from the sides of the pot, you will need to use an old carving knife, a stiff metal rule or similar aid. This can be run around the inside edge of the pot to loosen the roots and compost.

Now comes the very tricky stage when the root-ball has to be removed from the pot. You will find it easier to lay the container on its side and with the aid of a small hand fork ease the plant out. If the pot can't be laid down, slide a border fork down between the pot and the root-ball and prize the plant out of its container. Another pair of hands will come in useful to steady the pot or to use a second fork. Do not be tempted to pull the plant out by its stems as irreparable damage will be caused. If necessary a cane can be tapped into the drainage hole of the container to help push out the root-ball.

Having removed the plant from the pot you need to prepare the root-ball for re-potting. This will involve cutting the roots down to allow room for extra compost to be added. Taking a sharp border spade, a small hand saw, or possibly an old bread knife, gradually slice down the sides of the root-ball and cut off about 1–2in (2.5–5cm) of roots from the outer edges. Now lay the root-ball on its side and cut off the bottom third. If, when performing this task for the first time, you are concerned about this, only remove a relatively small amount of root, just sufficient to add some fresh compost. Having satisfied yourself that this method works, on later occasions you can be more severe! Once you have reduced the mass of roots the remaining root-ball can be re-potted into the original container, as there will now be room to add fresh compost. Before doing so, clean out the container, replacing the crock or stones over the drainage holes. Fresh compost can be similar to that used when first potting the plant, but this time add a double handful of bonemeal to the compost and mix well. Put a layer of compost into the bottom of the pot and test the depth with the plant, bearing in mind the plant needs re-potting 2–3in (5–7cm) deeper than it was originally. This should now be possible because the root-ball has been reduced in depth. Having established the right depth, fill in with compost around the root-

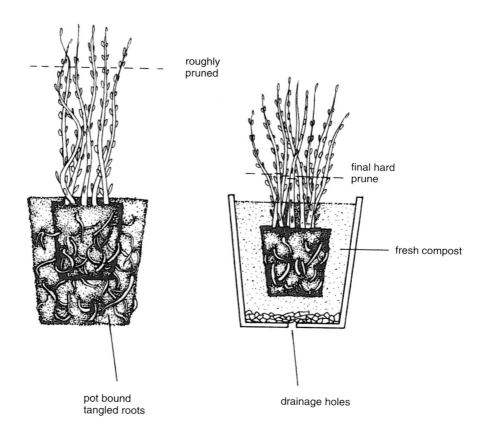

roughly
pruned

final hard
prune

fresh compost

pot bound
tangled roots

drainage holes

Reducing the root ball to re-pot in the original container.

ball, firming it as you go. Allow a gap near the rim of the pot for watering and water well, thus allowing the compost to settle around the roots.

Having completed the task of re-potting, give the clematis a final prune. The initial prune was only a rough one, to make the clematis easier to handle. Now a good, hard prune is needed, leaving only two sets of leaf-joints with viable buds above the soil. The supports can then be replaced and

within a few weeks the clematis will be back in full growth.

Growing clematis in containers can be very rewarding, especially if one does not have a garden in which to grow a large number of plants. Over the years we have come across many people who live in flats and manage to grow clematis in pots on their balconies. This proves how little space you need to grow these lovely plants.

CHAPTER 10

Propagation

Propagating clematis is, of course, a necessary task for the nurseryman to perform, but it can also be an enjoyable challenge for the keen gardener.

There are four main ways to propagate clematis: by layering, cuttings, division and seed. The first three will provide you with a new plant identical in every respect to its parent. The fourth method (seed) will provide a new plant which has similar characteristics to its parents but not identical. Tissue culture is also now used commercially by some large-scale producers but is still relatively rare in the reproduction of clematis and is not something the amateur can make use of.

Cuttings are the main commercially viable means a nurseryman has to reproduce clematis in a large enough quantity for the market. Layering would take far too long, and a great deal of space would be needed, while division would not be viable due to the vast number of stock plants required. Because nurseries are generally reproducing 'named' cultivars, the need to propagate them vegetatively is essential. The process of cross-pollination means that plants grown from seed would not be identical to the parent plants. Therefore, calling seedlings by their parents' names would be totally incorrect.

For the keen gardener, any of the main methods of propagation would be suitable as only a relatively small number of plants are needed.

Hybridizing and growing clematis from seed provides a fascinating pastime. The excitement felt when one's offspring finally flowers far outweighs

OPPOSITE: Clematis seedheads showing viable seed.

the disappointment of not always being able to produce a masterpiece. When a distinctive new clematis is eventually created, the thrill of having this reproduced by the thousand, and grown and loved by gardeners, makes all the time and effort involved well worthwhile.

For most though, the satisfaction of being able to produce just one new plant to pass on to a friend will be reward enough.

Please note: some plants, including some clematis, are covered by Plant Breeders' Rights, and therefore unlicensed propagation of these cultivars is prohibited in certain territories. This prohibition of propagation is legally enforceable and includes cuttings, layering and division. Where we are aware that this applies we have added PBR (Plant Breeders' Rights) to the individual clematis entry in the Profiles A–Z section.

LAYERING

This method of propagation is simple and reliable, and when only a few new plants are needed it is the most satisfactory method of propagation. In fact layering could not be simpler for, having prepared the vine, nature does the rest, apart from keeping it watered during a dry spell. Layering is quite a slow process and can take about a year. Because of this and the amount of space needed to layer many stems, this method of propagation is not commercially viable for nurserymen to use.

Method

The best time of year to attempt layering a clematis is during late spring and early summer, as the weather and soil begin to warm up. First of all select a good, strong stem at the side of your clematis plant which can be carefully untangled from the rest of the plant. This stem will be drawn down towards the ground very carefully, so as not to crack it, and it can then be pegged down into the soil while remaining attached to the parent plant. If the clematis you wish to layer is normally hard pruned during late winter or early spring, when pruning, leave un-pruned one or two stems which will be suitable for layering. Then, in the late spring these stems can be layered.

Bear in mind that where the stem is going to come down the soil will need preparing in readiness to accept it. This can be done in two ways: the stem can be pegged either direct into the ground or into a compost-filled flower pot which has been sunk into the ground.

When pegging directly into the ground, make a shallow trench about 3in (7cm) deep along where the stem will lie. Then fill this with cutting compost, or if your soil is in good condition, mix a little peat or peat substitute with the soil dug from the trench. Then add several handfuls of grit or sharp sand, mix well and replace in the trench. This open, gritty compost will be ideal for the layer to root into. If the trench is made long enough it will be possible to 'layer' as many as four or five joints.

Layering.

You may however prefer to use flower pots for your layering. This method has the advantage that once the young plants are well rooted they are already potted up. We would suggest using 4in (10cm) pots for this and to use as many pots as you have good leaf joints available. To ensure success it is always worth doing two or three, even if only one plant is required. Fill each pot with cutting compost and then sink it into the ground where the leaf joint can be pegged into it.

The procedure will be the same for pegging direct into the ground or into pots. Each leaf joint to be layered should have a ½in (1cm) cut made in it to aid rooting, as the stem will be quite woody and unlikely to produce roots without encouragement. With a very sharp knife, starting ½in (1cm) below the leaf joint, make a shallow cut up towards the joint, on the underside of the stem. The cut and leaf joint should then be dusted with hormone rooting powder. The prepared stem can then be buried, making sure the prepared leaf joint is about ¾–1in (2cm) below the surface of the compost and pegged in place with a piece of stiff wire. If you wish to make more than one layer, repeat this procedure along the stem at each leaf joint. The growing tip of the stem will be too soft to use and will not root, so at the last joint layered, insert a short cane or stick into the ground. The top 18in (45cm) or so of stem can then be tied up this rather than being left lying on the soil.

The most important thing now is to water well and not let the 'layers' dry out – a regular check will ensure this does not happen. The layers will not require feeding while they are still attached to the parent plant. As always, the parent will provide food for its young!

Be aware that where the soil has been disturbed in the garden could be an 'interesting spot' for a cat to dig. If this becomes a problem, the easy solution would be to cover the area with a piece of chicken or livestock netting, bent over to form a small tunnel. This should prevent disturbance by animals and also the unruly hoe!

About a year later check to see if you have had success. Gently brush away the compost so that the wire peg can be removed and carefully give the stem a gentle tug. If the young plant stays firm it is well rooted. If, however, it yields but it has small roots and the leaf and joint remain healthy-looking, it is worth replacing the peg and compost, leaving in place for a few more weeks. When it is rooted, you can cut the old stem off the parent plant and insert each of the rooted stem sections, if they were layered direct into the ground, into 4in (10cm) pots.

Keep your young plants in their pots for a further year to eighteen months to allow them a chance to establish a strong root system of their own before being planted into the garden. The method for growing on and pruning young plants is described under 'Potting up Cuttings', below. Use the same method to produce young layered plants.

CUTTINGS

Propagating clematis by means of cuttings is the method favoured by most nurserymen. It is certainly the most common, commercially viable method of propagation and is nowadays more widely used than grafting.

Many clematis cuttings strike quite easily, some within three to four weeks. Others are reluctant to send out roots and may take several months before doing so. There are a few cultivars which seem almost impossible to strike and defy even wily nurserymen.

Some of the easiest clematis to strike are the Montana Group cultivars. If you have never tried taking clematis cuttings before, these would be the ideal ones to begin with. The best time to take cuttings from clematis grown in the garden is between late spring and mid-summer when the growth is fresh and has not yet ripened into a woody state. Nurseries usually grow their stock plants under cover, which ensures that cutting material is ready earlier in the season. Once the first cuttings have been taken the plants will grow on quickly and probably produce enough material for a second batch of cuttings to be taken. In England, nurseries are usually taking cuttings between April and August, a much longer season than would be possible from garden cutting material.

Preparation

Prepare the compost in pots or seed trays before removing the cutting material from the plant. Once the stem has been cut it is essential to prepare the cuttings and get them into moist compost without delay. If there has to be a delay, the vines should be placed in a large damp polythene bag which should then be sealed, avoiding damage to the stems! Alternatively, they can be laid in a tray and covered over with a damp cloth or newspaper. However this is only a temporary measure and the cutting material will deteriorate quickly.

Ready-mixed cutting compost usually consists of equal proportions of peat or peat substitute and grit or sharp sand. If you are mixing your own compost you can change this ratio to whatever suits your needs best, but it is always better to have more grit and less peat, thus keeping the structure of the compost open.

The pots or seed trays should be filled level with compost and then firmed down and watered. It is then a good idea to put a thin layer of grit or sharp sand on top of the compost, bringing it level with the top of the pot or tray. This will prevent the risk of the leaf on the cutting touching the damp compost. The grit dries out more quickly than the compost underneath and thus prevents leaf rotting.

Having prepared the pots or trays in advance, you can now take the cuttings.

Soft Wood Cuttings

These are the most common type taken. The clematis stem should be in a strong state of growth and semi-ripe. It is better to avoid using the new soft growing tip, or the vine which is changing colour from green to brown as this will be too ripe. This strong growth will feel firm to the touch, not soft nor woody. You must avoid using damaged stems, as they will simply rot off very quickly and be wasted. Avoid, too, using leaf joints which have sent out flowering stems, because they will have no viable buds in the leaf-joints from which the new plant can grow.

Having selected a good vine, cut it from the plant and take it to a bench (which is out of the strong sunlight) to prepare the cuttings. It is best to use a very sharp penknife, Stanley knife or razor blade to prepare the cuttings. Scissors should be avoided, as they will not make a clean enough cut.

The majority of clematis cuttings are taken inter-nodal. This involves cutting through the stem immediately above a leaf joint (node), being careful not to damage the joint itself. The second cut is made approximately 1½in (3cm) below the leaf joint. One set of leaves should be removed from the leaf joint, and the other set reduced to one or two good leaflets. This will prevent the leaf losing too much moisture through transpiration (*see diagram below*). Only healthy leaves should be left on the cutting, as a damaged leaf could be the source of infection by Botrytis fungus, which will cause rotting.

The bottom ½in (1cm) of the cutting can then be dipped into hormone rooting powder, which will improve the chances of the cutting striking.

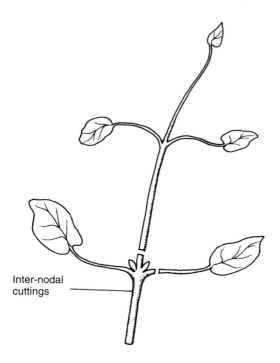

Inter-nodal cuttings

Inter-nodal cutting (most commonly used).

There are many hormone rooting powders available; we use one which is recommended for hard wood cuttings, which suits clematis cuttings very well. Gently shake off any excess powder and then place the cuttings in the compost. Do not push the stem directly into the compost; it is better to make a hole first with a narrow piece of cane or the like. If many cuttings are to be placed in a seed tray, put the stem of the cutting into the compost at an angle so that the leaf is held erect in the air (*see diagram page 105*) This will avoid having the leaves lying on top of one another, and air will be able to circulate. This in turn will help to avoid disease and the risk of the cuttings rotting. You will find it helpful to spray the cuttings weekly with fungicide to prevent rot. If you notice a leaf rotting, remove it immediately, again to avoid the spread of infection. When only a few cuttings are taken, they can be arranged around the edge of a flower pot, thus allowing each leaf to hang over the edge of the pot.

Once all cuttings are in the compost, the pot or tray should be carefully labelled, watered and placed on a bench or window sill out of full sun. The ideal condition for striking clematis is a warm, moist atmosphere. A small plant propagator is therefore useful, or a glass-house bench with heating cables underneath. On an open glass-house bench conditions will probably not be humid enough, so try making a small polythene tunnel over the bench with stiff wire hoops and a sheet of polythene or bubble-wrap. Our propagating bench is designed like this: the bench itself has a layer of sand which is kept at about 20°C by heating cables. Every few hours during the day, the polythene cover is removed and the leaves of the cuttings are lightly sprayed with water. This, along with the bottom heat, keeps the cuttings warm and moist, while the polythene cover keeps the atmosphere humid. During very hot, sunny weather the cuttings may need dampening several times a day. They should not be drenched in water from a watering can, but sprayed with a fine mist from a hand-held garden sprayer. On sunny days, when there is the risk of scorching, make sure the cuttings are provided with some shade.

After about three weeks test to see whether the

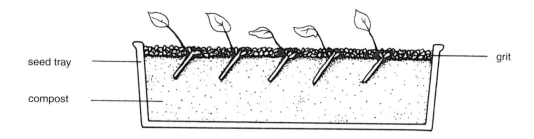

Placing cuttings in a seed tray.

cuttings have struck. Gently pull the cutting: if it moves easily it has not rooted, but if there is resistance the roots have begun forming. Leave for another week or two, after which if you hold up the pot or tray you may find roots beginning to grow through the drainage holes. The tray of cuttings should then be removed from the propagator and placed in the open, but shaded glass-house, to sit for about one month before potting. This period allows the roots to increase and become stronger to withstand the disturbance of potting-up.

Hard Wood Cuttings

Hard wood cuttings are taken during the winter while the parent plant is in a dormant state. Not all clematis propagate successfully from hardwood cuttings, and certainly the majority are better taken from soft wood.

Those which have proved successful are the Armandii, Heracleifolia and Montana Groups. Because the *C. armandii* cultivars are evergreen they have no real dormant period, and their cuttings, like the deciduous Montana Group, can be taken almost year round. *C. armandii* and its cultivars can however be quite difficult to root. They will form a callus at the base of the cutting but not send out any roots. With this particular clematis it is worth trying both hard and soft wood cuttings at different times of the year.

Hard wood cuttings will need to be taken internodal, as described for soft woods, but, to encourage rooting, a small sliver of the bark about ½ in

(1cm) long should be cut off the stem at the base of the cutting. The compost, rooting powder and method of placing the cuttings into a pot or tray remains the same as for soft woods, although if they have no leaves the cuttings can be put vertically into the compost, rather than at an angle.

Heating a propagator bench in a glass-house during the winter can be expensive and it is not essential to provide heat for hard wood cuttings, but they may take all winter to strike without any artificial heat. The cuttings should be kept damp

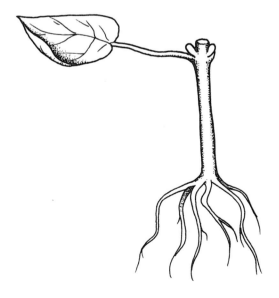

Rooted cutting.

rather than very wet, and there is no need to keep them misted as with the softwood cuttings which were in full leaf.

Double Noded Cuttings

These are used for a few cultivars of clematis with hollow stems which, because of their structure, will not strike from the more normal inter-nodal cutting. You will find, when cutting through the stems of clematis such as Flammula and Heracleifolia Group cultivars, the stems are hollow. Select a stem and cut through immediately above a leaf-joint (node), then, moving down the stem, cut immediately below the next joint. The cutting will then consist of a piece of stem perhaps 4–6in (10–15cm) long, with a node at the top and the bottom. Remove the leaves from the bottom node

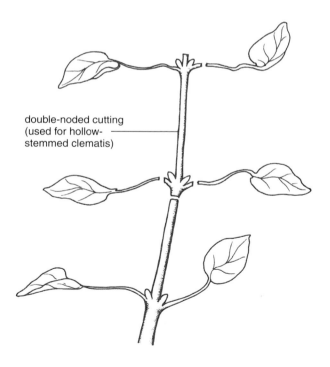

double-noded cutting
(used for hollow-
stemmed clematis)

Double-noded cuttings.

and dip into hormone rooting powder and place in a deep pot of compost as before.

Potting Up Cuttings

Potting up cuttings is a task which needs care. Loosen the compost in the cuttings tray so the roots can be eased out gently without having to pull them. The plants at this stage are quite fragile and all parts of the cutting and roots can be easily damaged. They can be potted directly into 2-litre pots, but we find it best to pot into small 3in (7cm) pots to grow on, as a first step. Either way, use a good potting compost with slow-release fertilizer and bury each cutting so that the leaf joint (node) is about ¼in (0.5cm) below the surface of the compost. This will encourage the young plant to shoot from the leaf-joint and grow on strongly.

As they grow the young plants will need pruning down at least twice, to encourage a strong root system to form. When the plant has made about 12in (30cm) of growth, prune it down to just above the first set of leaves above the compost. This should make the leaf-joints break into growth and send out more fresh stems. Allow the plant to make another 12–18in (30–45cm) of growth, then prune again, this time to just above the second set of leaves. At this stage, if you originally potted into a 3in (7cm) pot, the young plant should be re-potted into a 2-litre pot. When re-potting, place the young plant into its new pot so that the first

---

QUICK CUTTINGS GUIDE

1. Cuttings compost equal proportions of peat or peat substitute and grit.
2. Level off compost in pot or tray, firm down and water.
3. Layer of grit on top of compost.
4. Inter-nodal cuttings, remove one leaf (for hard woods, chip the bark)
5. Hormone powder.
6. Place cuttings in compost at an angle.
7. Water.
8. Bottom heat (68°F./20°C.)
9. Shade and keep humid (mist spray).

leaf joint is covered with compost. This will encourage the buried joint to shoot out yet again whenever the plant is pruned. It can also encourage the production of more roots.

DIVISION

Division is a most successful way of propagating herbaceous clump-forming clematis where only a few new plants are required. The cultivars of the Integrifolia Group, for example, can all be divided, the best time being from late winter to mid-spring when the ground is frost-free. After growing for several years these herbaceous clematis will have made quite large clumps of growth and, if split up, each division will form another plant.

To prepare the plant for division prune the clematis in the normal way, and lift the plant out of the ground with a fork. The clump can then be divided either with a sharp spade or old carving knife cutting the plant into three or four pieces, or using two garden forks placed back to back, pushing down into the centre of the clump and prizing apart. The two resulting clumps can then each be divided once again (*see* diagram below).

Each divided piece will make a new plant, providing it has some roots and either new shoots or some old stems with viable buds from which to grow.

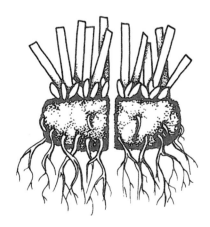

Division.

These new plants can then be re-planted straight into the garden or potted up if required. Whichever you do, the young plants must be kept watered until re-established.

HYBRIDIZING

Clematis hybridizing has proved to be a fascinating challenge for professional nurserymen and amateur gardeners alike for the last 150 years.

George Jackman was among the first Englishmen to achieve success in hybridizing clematis, and it was largely due to him that hybridizing clematis became so popular in the late nineteenth century. His book *The Clematis as a Garden Flower*, written jointly with Thomas Moore and published in 1872, spread the word about the genus, tempting others to grow and propagate these versatile plants.

Today's hybridizers have to meet the challenge not only of producing more and better flowers but also of producing stronger, healthier, and more compact plants for modern, smaller gardens. This task has been undertaken by many nurserymen, and we are seeing some exceptional new clematis hybrids commercially available.

If you are a gardener who enjoys a horticultural challenge and who has plenty of space together with abundant patience, then hybridizing can be rewarding. Remember, however, that you may have to produce hundreds of clematis plants before finding one worthy of naming and marketing! And these plants, as previously stated, demand much time and space to nurture effectively. This is no undertaking for the faint-hearted, since you must be prepared to abandon ruthlessly hundreds of your infant plants.

If you decide to go ahead with the challenge, have a specific target in mind. For instance, a good, double red clematis may be your aim, and with this intent you will need to select appropriate parents, perhaps 'Sylvia Denny', a good strong, healthy, double white, crossed with a compact, floriferous red, such as 'Westerplatte'. Or perhaps a double light blue is to be sought, by crossing ARCTIC QUEEN with 'Fujimusume'. Always select as parents clematis that have the assets of strong, healthy growth, and which produce numerous, well-shaped flowers. These characteristics should then be passed on to the offspring.

Be prepared for disappointments, for few hybridizers actually achieve what they set out to do, and the excitement of seeing your seedling flower can take what seems like an eternity; in fact it is usually around three to four years.

Technique to Apply

Wait until the buds of your chosen clematis are almost ready to open into flower and catch them before they do; otherwise nature may take over and pollination could be initiated by bees or insects. Having selected nice, fat flower buds, decide which cultivar is to be the 'seed' parent and which the 'pollen' parent.

To prepare the 'seed' parent carefully remove the tepals and then the anthers which contain the pollen. By removing the anthers you will prevent the seed parent from pollinating itself. To do this use either a very sharp knife or fine-tipped sharp scissors. The central stigma of the pistil must be left to receive the pollen (*see* diagram below). A polythene bag should then be put over the prepared head and tied in place to prevent pollination from an un-wanted source.

The 'pollen' parent must also be prepared in advance, to prevent insects from depositing un-wanted pollen from another cultivar onto the anthers. For this it is only necessary to remove the tepals, then cover with a polythene bag tied below the flower head.

After a few days the stigma of the seed parent will be ready to pollinate, having become shiny and covered with a sticky fluid. When the seed parent is ready the polythene bags can be removed and the pollen parent flower cut from its plant. Gently brush the two heads together so that the pollen is transferred from the anthers of the one to the stigma of the other. Having completed this process, replace the polythene bag to prevent additional unwanted pollination. Tie it below the seed head, not too tightly but so as to allow a small breathing space between the stem and the poly-thene to prevent a build-up of condensation.

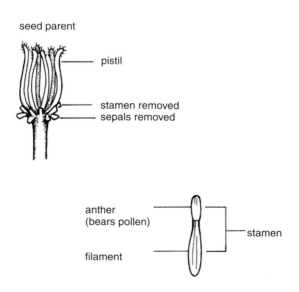

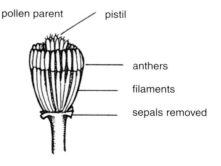

Hybridizing – preparing the blooms.

Attach a label to the head with the names of the clematis parents and the date pollinated. Once the pollen is placed on the stigma, it moves down the style to the ovary where fertilization takes place and the seed is produced.

In order to be certain that the pollen and stigma are both at the right stage of development and ready for pollination it is wise to repeat the procedure. The same pollen parent flower can be used if it has been saved, or another flower from the same plant that has also been covered earlier as described above. The second pollination should be a few days after the first, with the seed parent flower being covered between times.

Leave the bag in place for two to three weeks until the flower has 'died' naturally and it can then be removed without any concern that stray pollen from another clematis would cause further cross-pollination. Make sure the stem of the developing seed head is labelled.

The seed head can then be left to develop and ripen. This can take three to four months, or longer, before the seed can be collected. The seed is ripe when it turns brown and when the individual seeds easily break away from the head if touched.

Late-flowering clematis will not set seed late in the year in the garden. Therefore, if you wish to hybridize any of these clematis it would be more successful to grow them in pots in a glass-house to encourage them to flower earlier. The seed will then have a chance to ripen before the onset of winter.

When crossing clematis with two different flowering periods (one may be an early flowerer and one a late flowerer, for example), the pollen from the early flowerer can be kept in an airtight container in the refrigerator until required.

If you decide to make several crosses it is useful not only to label the 'seed' parent at the time of pollination but also to keep a log of crossings, recording dates and other details. When the time comes to pot up the resulting seedlings, each one can be given a number so that a complete record of their history can be kept for future reference.

Whatever the modern hybridizers manage to achieve is often outclassed by nature, which by itself can produce masterpieces. This most natural event can take us by surprise and has produced some stunning new clematis hybrids over the years. Certainly, many new cultivars nowadays have come not just from the hybridizers but as chance seedlings.

GROWING CLEMATIS FROM SEED

This method of propagating clematis can be an interesting and rewarding pastime. It is more of a hobby than a profitable means of producing clematis. Usually the only time a nurseryman raises clematis from seed is when a specific hybridizing programme is underway.

Seed from species clematis will germinate quickly and easily when given ideal conditions, the offspring produced being similar but not necessarily identical to the parent plant. In the wild, literally thousands of seeds will fall to the ground from one clematis, but only a few will develop into plants. This natural method of reproduction will also happen in our gardens. It is worthwhile keeping a close watch when weeding around the base of your clematis, for seedlings may well be growing there. The seedlings that a clematis will produce in the garden could have been produced by self-pollination, or pollen could have been transferred by bees from another clematis growing nearby. When this happens the identity of the 'pollen' parent will not be known, unlike controlled hybridization where both 'seed' and 'pollen' parents have been selected for their best attributes.

Seed from clematis is more often sown in the hope of discovering a unique new cultivar worthy of naming and marketing. Many hundreds of seedlings can be produced (each one will be unique), but unfortunately the chances of producing one of commercial interest is minimal. When the hybrid seedlings begin to flower, the producer who has lovingly tended these plants for three or four years must reluctantly discard the majority. Success comes from the one special plant found lurking among the seedlings.

Clematis seeds must be allowed to ripen on the plant. This ripening will take place during the summer and autumn, and the seed heads must be watched closely so that collection can take place before they drop naturally. As the seeds ripen the seed head changes colour from green through to brown, and in the case of the species, from silver to brown. The styles, or tails, of each seed of the species clematis will become feathery, while the hybrid seeds will have a slightly hairy appearance. Not all the seeds on each seed head will be viable; only those that have swollen achenes have been pollinated and will germinate (*see* diagram below).

The seeds are best collected on a warm sunny day when they have dried off naturally. They can then be sown immediately or stored in paper bags in a cool, dry place. If it is necessary to collect seeds on a damp day and they are not to be sown immediately, spread them out on a sheet of newspaper in a warm place, away from direct heat, to allow them to dry before storage. Avoid storing damp seed as they will quickly go mouldy. Seeds should also be dried slowly to retain a certain amount of internal moisture to allow them to germinate.

When storing seeds, label the bag or container, for it is only too easy to forget which plant they were from and seeds look very similar. If seeds need to be stored long term they can be kept sealed in a polythene bag in a refrigerator for up to one year. Do not store seed longer than this, or freeze them, as they are unlikely to germinate.

Before sowing or storage, the styles (tails) can be removed, although this is not absolutely necessary and can be fiddly. If you do wish to remove the style from a seed, cut it off making sure not to cut into the achene (seed).

When sowing the seed, depending on the quantity to be sown, you could use either a flower pot or a half- or full-size seed tray. This should be filled with seed compost which can either be purchased ready-mixed or you could mix your own. We use a compost containing 50 per cent peat and 50 per cent grit or sharp sand. The compost should be lightly firmed down and watered. Once it has drained the seeds can be sprinkled over it. They should then be covered with a fine layer of compost, grit or sharp sand, which will prevent moss growing on the top of the compost.

For successful germination ensure the compost never dries out; on the other hand it should not be regularly saturated. Place the tray or pot in a situation where it will be free-draining – the open nature of the gritty compost will then prevent water-logging. Keeping the compost slightly moist is ideal.

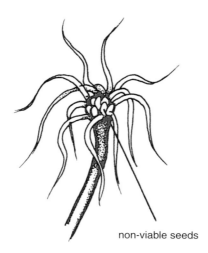

non-viable seeds

viable seeds

Clematis seed heads.

Germination will take place more quickly if some form of heat is available; a propagator kept between 15 and 20°C is useful, although not essential. Seeds will germinate well if kept in a cold glass-house or cold-frame but they will simply take a little longer. The seeds will also germinate on a window sill in the house, but a shaded or north-facing window is best to avoid extreme heat on a sunny day.

Do not cover the pot or tray with a sheet of glass or cling-film, often mistakenly considered necessary, but allow air to circulate, which stops mould growing and the seeds rotting. There is no need either to use any feed until the seedlings are growing on as the seed itself contains all the feed necessary for germination.

Once the seed has germinated keep direct sunlight off the seedlings, otherwise their tender growth will scorch. On the other hand, do not keep them completely shaded as this could cause the young plants to grow up weak and spindly. Ensure there is adequate ventilation.

You will find that many of the species clematis germinate in a few weeks. Seeds which germinate quickly have a very thin shell protecting the inner seed. The thicker and larger this casing is, the longer the seed will take to germinate, as is the case with many hybrid clematis. *C. campaniflora*, although a species, has relatively large seeds and takes about a year to germinate.

Seeds can germinate quicker if they are collected and stored in a refrigerator over winter, and sown the following spring. These seeds will often germinate before those which were sown fresh the previous autumn.

Generally, seed from the large-flowered clematis will take longer to germinate than the species. They can however sprout very erratically, perhaps only one or two in the first year but, if left alone, more seeds will germinate during the next year, or even the next two years. Never be too eager to throw away a tray of seed assuming it has failed; keep it for at least two years before giving up.

Transplant the seedlings when they are large enough to handle but not before they have made at least one proper pair of leaves. They should ideally go into 3in (7cm) pots in a standard potting compost, and be kept shaded from direct sunlight for three or four days.

You will find that having been transplanted the seedlings will grow very quickly. They will need pruning down at least twice before allowing them to go on to flower. This encourages the young plant to produce a strong root system. At this stage fertilizer can be used, either a slow release one mixed into the compost, or a half strength liquid feed applied once a week.

Allow each seedling to make 12in (30cm) of growth, and then prune it just above the first set of leaves. This pruning should encourage the node to 'break' so that two stems will be produced. Allow the plant to grow another 12–18in (30–45cm), then prune it again above the second set of leaves. As the plant begins to make fresh growth, this time it can be potted up into a 2-litre pot where it can stay until it has flowered.

Overall, this is a long process, from hybridizing and collecting seed in the first year, sowing and germinating in the second, transplanting and growing on in the third year and, finally, flowering in the fourth year. Do not be too disappointed with the quality of the plants' first flowers, as they can sometimes take until their second or third flowering before producing their 'true' blooms.

When labelling your seedlings, particularly if they are to be passed on to others, it is important to label them correctly. For example, take the label 'Seedling from 'Nelly Moser'': it would be wrong to label it as 'Nelly Moser' because it has been created by pollination and is therefore a mixture of two parents. The only clematis entitled to be called by a specific hybrid name would be one that has been vegetatively propagated.

The excitement and anticipation this all creates, despite the work involved, is reward enough. But if you do produce a masterpiece, 'clematis fame' can be yours with the naming of the new cultivar!

Many gardeners find that they are able to propagate plants from their own gardens. Clematis are among the slightly more difficult category, but are by no means impossible to do this with. You may discover you have 'the knack' to produce more of your favourite cultivars to pass on to your gardening friends.

CHAPTER 11

Diseases and Pests

Clematis are generally fairly trouble-free plants, compared to many we struggle to grow. However, as with all plants there is the occasional problem, and once identified, we can usually hope to find a solution that keeps the plant alive in the process.

DISEASES AND OTHER PROBLEMS

Clematis Wilt

Wilt is probably the most well-known disease to affect clematis. While it is alarming, it is not all that common. To put it into perspective, for many years we have had around 300 clematis in our garden, and the number which have wilted is only one or two in a year. With the help of modern fungicides and specialist nurseries offering advice on planting and after-care, clematis are once again a popular garden plant, with today's gardeners not needing to worry so much about 'the dreaded wilt'.

The problem began back in the late 1800s when hybridizers were using three large-flowered species in their hybridization programmes. These were *C. florida*, introduced from Japan by Thunberg during the late 1700s; *C. patens*, introduced from Japan by

Von Siebold in the early 1830s; and *C. lanuginosa*, introduced from China by Robert Fortune in 1851. *C. lanuginosa* was considered by the early hybridizers as being probably the best large-flowered species and was therefore widely used in their hybridization programmes. It is now thought, however, that *C. lanuginosa* was the 'rogue' of the three, being susceptible to attack by the wilt fungus. By the early 1900s, clematis wilt had become such a problem that hybridizing had virtually stopped. Wilt had so affected the stock of clematis around the world that research was carried out to try and find the cause and, it was hoped, a cure for the condition.

There were various theories as to the cause of clematis wilt, such as: bursting of the cells through excessive moisture or injury from frost; too much water, nourishment or heat; or over-propagation. During the early part of the last century, the majority of clematis were produced by grafting, and this was considered as a possible cause of the infection entering the plant. However, despite the fact that most nurserymen rarely graft clematis as a method of propagation, today we still sometimes experience cases of clematis wilt. Indeed those that are propagated by grafting are no more prone to clematis wilt than those produced from cuttings.

In America in 1915 the fungus *Ascochyta clematidina* was first recorded as being the cause of stem rot and leaf-spot in clematis. These findings were not confirmed for fifty years, but in 1965 British researchers agreed that this same fungus was the one responsible for causing clematis wilt.

The small-flowered species clematis and the late-flowering hybrids we now grow are almost

OPPOSITE: Snails – showing typical leaf damage.

immune to clematis wilt and seem better able to defend themselves against attack by fungi. It is thought likely though, that the same fungi can infect them, only without such devastating results. The cultivars which seem rather more prone to wilt are the early large-flowered hybrids which took their characteristics from *C. lanuginosa*, some cultivars appearing more susceptible to attack than others.

Modern research has identified a second fungus which can cause clematis wilt, *Coniothyrium clematidis-rectae*. Both this and the previously mentioned fungus *Ascochyta clematidina* are thought to be activated by particular conditions of temperature and humidity. This is possibly why some years there seems to be hardly any clematis wilt, whilst in others the problem can be more of a nuisance. The rise in temperature and humidity in the British Isles is usually at its greatest during May, and this is when we are most likely to witness a case of clematis wilt. Of course, this is also a time when the plant is bursting forth in the full surge of growth, preparing itself for flowering following its winter dormancy. This rush of sap puts the clematis in a very vulnerable position at a time when the weather conditions are especially favourable to the fungi.

How to Identify Wilt

As we have said, the most likely time of year for an attack of wilt will probably be during mid to late spring. Unfortunately, this is the time of year when our early large-flowered hybrid clematis are budding up in preparation for their spectacular display of flowers. All will appear well until one day when quite suddenly one or more of the clematis stems will droop, or you may notice the flower buds drooping their heads or that the new growing tips are sadly hanging limp instead of being in their normal erect state. The whole plant will look as though it has been starved of water.

Before immediately blaming the problem on clematis wilt, do check to see whether the problem could be caused by something else – perhaps severing of the stems by a quietly guilty 'strimmer driver', or an attack by snails or mice, who often

enjoy a clematis stem to chew through, may be the cause.

Taking Action

However, if these possibilities have been eliminated you can take appropriate action. It may be possible to detect a lesion, caused by the fungus, around the affected stems; this could be at a leaf joint or on the stem somewhere between two leaf joints. Each affected stem must be pruned out, below the lesion. If the whole plant is affected, or you cannot trace the point of infection, then the whole plant will need to be pruned down. It would then be advisable, if possible, to burn the resulting waste material, as this will help to reduce the spread of infection.

Having done this pruning, we would strongly advise the use of a systemic fungicide to kill off the fungi. Mix the solution, as recommended by the manufacturer, in a hand sprayer or watering can and drench any remaining foliage and stems to a height of 18in (45cm) above the soil, plus the surrounding earth to a diameter of approximately 18in. The spores of these fungi lurk in the soil, so drenching the soil is essential. We would suggest then that, having bought the fungicide, it is a good idea to repeat this procedure at weekly intervals for at least two more drenchings. As it is a systemic fungicide the roots will take it up to the remaining stems and foliage.

With the pruning and the use of fungicide as described, we can be quite confident that your plant will be well on the road to recovery. This is where our deep planting comes in useful. When planting was discussed in an earlier chapter we strongly advised that some of the leaf joints should be buried below soil level when planting. An attack of wilt is one of those situations where, following the loss of all top growth, the clematis will almost always re-shoot from these buried nodes. After drenching the clematis, do wait for several weeks before assuming it has died completely, as the buried nodes can take weeks, sometimes even months, before showing their new shoots above ground.

If, having patiently waited for perhaps a year, the worst has happened and your clematis does not recover, and you decide to replant a clematis in that same position, then firstly, try to choose a clematis less susceptible to wilt, perhaps a Viticella Group cultivar, or one of the species clematis.

Secondly, it would be advisable to change the soil. If possible, a cube 18in (45cm) square and deep needs to be removed and replaced, either with topsoil from elsewhere in the garden, or with manure, garden compost and so on (as described in Chapter 4), or a sack of loam-based compost, such as John Innes No.3.

Thirdly, having planted your new clematis, we would recommend watering it in with a solution of systemic fungicide. This is a real 'belt and braces' job, but one which is well worth trying. Clematis wilt usually only affects quite young plants; it seems that when a clematis has been in the ground for some years the stems become quite woody and less susceptible to attack. Clematis plants in nursery production very rarely suffer from wilt, possibly due to the necessary occasional use of fungicides.

With a little forethought it may be possible to protect your clematis against wilt. For example, it is a good idea when purchasing a plant to check the stems, making sure there are no damaged areas above the soil where the fungi could enter. Another point to bear in mind is that if you leave a lot of heavy top growth on your clematis over the winter this will catch the wind, and in rocking back and forth, will cause damage to the stems lower down, thus providing another possible site of entry for the fungus. It would therefore be advisable to check your clematis before the onset of any autumnal gales and carry out a quick, light pruning to tidy the growth back to its support. Further pruning, however, should wait until early spring.

Mildew

Mildew tends only to be a problem in the garden from mid to late summer onwards. It is quite noticeable, and appears to be a fine, white powder covering the leaves, stems, buds and flowers. The flowers, on opening, are misshapen, and the whole plant looks very poorly. Some clematis seem more

prone to mildew than others, the Texensis Group being one.

It is thought by some that if the garden is open to the wind and weather, mildew may not be a problem, but where a garden is very sheltered the risk of mildew is much greater. Our garden is both open and windy, yet we still have the odd plants getting mildew. This can be controlled successfully using the occasional spray with fungicide from midsummer onwards, but this may not be necessary at all in some years, unless your garden is particularly prone to mildew. One factor that does seem to make clematis more susceptible is dry soil. If the roots do not have enough moisture then the plant is stressed and this leaves it more easily attacked by the mildew fungus. A south facing spot is therefore often more likely to be home to a mildew stricken clematis.

Slime Flux

Ruth first came across this problem several years ago at our local agricultural show where we were displaying our clematis, along with other trade exhibitors, in the floral marquee. During the show a lady came up to us and asked if we could identify the problem she had with her montana. She explained how the growth had suddenly all gone limp a few weeks before and, upon examining it, she had discovered this 'smelly stuff' oozing out of the stem. When Ruth opened the bag to see what she had brought, the most foul smell emerged. (You do not expect smells like that at a flower show amongst the roses and sweet peas!) The cause was slime flux.

This problem very rarely happens, but late one spring a 'Marjorie' (Montana Group) and a *C. flammula* in our garden were both struck down by slime flux. There had been some unusually late hard frosts, coinciding with a spell of rather mild days. At this time of year the sap is rising very quickly through the clematis stems, allowing them to become vulnerable to damage by these hard frosts. The frost damage opens the stems, and out leaks the sap. On this will grow fungi, yeast and bacteria, which cause the awful smell.

As soon as the problem is discovered, the affected stems should be pruned out below the diseased area. The clematis will sometimes re-shoot, grow on and may never have the problem again. However, in many cases slime flux is fatal to the clematis.

We have not known this problem to occur on the finer-stemmed clematis; slime flux seems to confine itself to types of clematis which, over the years, make very thick, woody trunks.

Brown Leaves

Sometimes the leaves of clematis will turn brown and crisp, and with the evergreen cultivars such as those in the Armandii and Cirrhosa Groups this can be due to severe heat or cold winds, or lack of moisture for the roots. Damaged leaves will not recover, but often the stem will be unharmed and new leaves will be produced and the plant will continue to thrive.

In mid-summer the Cirrhosa Group cultivars can go into a summer dormancy if there is a long hot spell. Again, it is only the leaves that will die off. Do not be tempted to cut back the stems, and do not over-water during this dormant spell. Once some cool rains come it will re-shoot and usually flower well over the coming winter.

Summer flowering clematis will sometimes lose their leaves, particularly after their early summer flowering. This is also not usually fatal, but in these types the whole stem will often be affected and needs to be removed, often quite low down. Fresh shoots should appear within a few weeks, especially if the clematis was planted deep initially.

Brown leaf tips or margins, especially on young growth, is usually due to lack of moisture, espe-cially on a young plant where the roots have not become established. Lower leaves turn brown naturally and in some cultivars this can be surpris-ingly early in the summer; moisture stress will hasten this process.

Also remember that slugs and snails can kill a stem, as noted below, so take precautions against them if this effect is seen.

Green Flower Tips

In cold dull summers it is more common to see the green tips on some clematis flowers. This is due to insufficient temperature and sunlight to turn the tepal from a photosynthesizing leaf-type of growth into the coloured 'petal-like' structure we expect to see. This is only a temporary effect, and with warmer weather the flowers will form correctly. One cultivar that exhibits this most frequently is 'Alba Luxurians'; some people, flower arrangers amongst them, like this effect and grow the plant in a cool shady position to encourage this to happen. Others dislike it, and to avoid the problem you should choose a warm sunny aspect for this cultivar.

PESTS

Snails and Slugs

Snails and slugs can also cause damage to your plants' stems. These pests can cause tremendous problems if their numbers are not kept under control.

Following a wet winter and spring there is often a population explosion of snails, not just the little ones but the really enormous snails which wreak havoc in the garden. In the eastern counties of Britain, which are quite dry, we are normally fortunate not to suffer too badly from snails. However, when we do have a wet winter our clematis suffer from attack by snails during the following spring. After their winter hibernation they emerge hungry and go onto the attack. We have a sunken garden laid out with clipped box hedging. In the centre of each 'knot' is an obelisk planted with a clematis. Unfortunately, snails seem to adore living in box hedging, and when they come out at night they do their best to annihilate our clematis.

We first noticed the problem in late spring when, at a quick glance the symptoms were identi-cal to clematis wilt. The plants, which were full in bud and had been growing vigorously, were hang-ing their heads down and all the foliage was limp.

RIGHT: Bark stripped off clematis stems by slugs or snails.

BELOW: Clematis are generally fairly problem-free plants, but it is as well to keep an eye out for any signs of trouble.

Not every stem was affected, just the odd one or two on each plant; this led me to think the problem might be caused by wilt. When we came to prune down the affected stems, as part of our wilt treatment, we noticed the tell-tale signs that snails had been the cause of our problem. The bark on each of the affected stems had been stripped off, up to a height of about 18in (45cm) above soil level. Instead of the stems being their normal dark brown, you could see the paler, beige inner wood of the stems. This stripping of the bark was enough to cause the stem to collapse. Snails are also partial to the odd new green shoot bursting through the soil, as well as the leaves; in fact they will enjoy any part of a clematis!

Slugs in a clematis garden can be as big a menace as snails. They are as partial to a diet of clematis as the snails, but seem to much prefer the tender young shoots of the hard prune cultivars as they begin to sprout forth during the spring.

Taking Action

If you have problems with either snails or slugs in your garden there are one or two different courses of action you can take. First of all, prune out the damaged stems; the damage will usually go right down to soil level.

Next you will have to take measures to control the pests. We usually squash these pests – good stout gardening boots are ideal! Alternatively slug pellets could be used as these will kill both slugs and snails. A few sprinkled and lightly worked into the soil around the base of your clematis should provide sufficient control. Nowadays most pellets available are 'animal and bird friendly' so should not harm any frogs, toads, hedgehogs or birds that may live in your garden. The suggested use of concrete slabs or roof tiles to shade the root systems of our clematis will provide a perfect refuge for slugs and snails, so these should be checked regularly and the offending beasts removed and slug pellets sprinkled beneath them.

Biological control has been a fairly recent introduction regarding the destruction of slugs; it involves introducing a microscopic nematode by mixing it in water and watering it onto the soil. At first sight, the price for this method of control may appear rather high, although a single application is meant to last for six weeks.

There are one or two cheaper methods of controlling slugs and snails, without the use of chemicals, which have been developed over the years by some people. (They often involve a night raid, armed with torch and bucket!)

We do feel strongly that we should all make an effort to use fewer chemicals where possible, and we should be looking more to encouraging natural predators into our gardens, which will help to alleviate the worst of our problems. Birds adore slugs and snails; thrushes particularly enjoy cracking open snail shells on large stones. Hedgehogs are also another 'garden friendly' animal to have around, as they too, enjoy feasting on slugs and snails. Despite being absolutely terrified of frogs and toads, Ruth cannot help but admit that these are some of the most useful pest controllers around. Many people have a pond in their garden, and to introduce some frog or toad spawn from a friend's pond could be one of the best moves ever made. It will be only a short while before your slug population has decreased noticeably.

Another slug or snail deterrent which we have heard is successful, but have not tried ourselves, is the use of very sharp sand, grit or egg shells placed around the base of each clematis. Apparently these pests do not enjoy sliding over something sharp and will move off elsewhere. This means, however, the other plants in your garden may be more vulnerable as a result.

Earwigs

These are creatures of the night; they prefer to sleep hidden in cracks and crevices by day, to emerge with a voracious appetite as dusk falls. The damage they cause is similar to that of slugs and snails, in that they will attack the leaves and new shoots of the clematis. They also enjoy eating the centre parts of flowers and flower buds.

Earwigs tend not to be a big problem early in the year but, as summer progresses, especially if we have a very dry summer, their numbers seem to increase tenfold. Dahlia growers will sympathize with clematarians (clematis growers) as earwigs are equally fond of these wonderful border plants. So, later in the summer, if you discover holes in the leaves and flowers of your clematis, but can find no pest munching happily, we would be almost certain the culprits are earwigs. You may also find that the fat flower buds have had their tips and centres completely eaten away, even down to their stamens, which the earwigs find delicious.

Again you have two choices of pest control: the use of chemicals, or a 'green', environmentally friendly method. If you decide to try the 'green' method, one which has been favoured by dahlia growers for many a year is the 'up-turned flower pot'. This will require a bamboo cane or stick, a flower pot and some straw, hay or dried grass. The idea is to stuff the straw, hay or dried grass into the flower pot. (If you have none of these, newspaper will do just as well.) Up-turn the filled pot on top of the cane and place strategically, close to your clematis. This needs to be checked every morning by carefully removing the 'stuffing' which should contain some earwigs. Then all you need to do is dispose of the earwigs and the stuffing material. Of course this procedure will need to be repeated each day. We must add that although it seems a bit of an effort it really does work.

Another environmentally friendly method to try is one which involves soaking mint in just enough boiling water to cover it, in a large container. Allow this to ferment for a few days and then add two gallons of cold water, strain off the liquid and spray this concoction over your plants. Try this during mid-summer; one dose is meant to be enough.

If you decide that all this is too much trouble and you resort to using insecticides, to be really effective they need applying during the evening. Your local garden centre should be able to suggest a suitable insecticide to kill earwigs; most of these come ready to use, thus avoiding the need to handle chemicals.

Spider Mite

Some semi-hardy clematis cultivars are grown in conservatories and these, like greenhouses, provide a near perfect environment for pests to establish themselves. While greenfly and whitefly are easily detected, spider mite (often called red spider) is not. A check must be kept on the condition of the leaves of your plant and any changes investigated. When infested with spider mite, the leaves have a mottled, rather rusty appearance. If the leaf is then turned over so that the underside can be seen, a very fine cobweb may be visible. The minute mites, which are sometimes only visible through a magnifying glass, can be seen crawling all over the under-side of the leaf. They are not red as their popular name suggests, being more a rusty beige colour. They are also not spiders, but very tiny mites.

There are insecticidal sprays available to tackle this pest, but the biological controls are equally as effective. These mites thrive when conditions are dry and warm, so if adequate humidity is maintained the problem is less likely to occur. A daily spray with clean water to keep up the humidity must be the cheapest and most environmentally friendly pest control available.

Greenfly and Whitefly

These again are not so much of a problem in our gardens as they can be in conservatories and greenhouses. Usually greenfly cluster along the new growing tips of the clematis, whilst whitefly more often confine themselves to the undersides of the leaves.

There are both insecticides and biological controls for use under glass against these pests. In the garden, however, if you are unfortunate enough to have a sudden infestation by one of these, a quick spray with insecticide is a simple solution to the problem.

These pests can also be controlled to a certain extent by the use of foliar feed. This will keep the plants in a healthy state, seemingly making them better able to fight off infestation. We were never sure of any scientific explanation as to why this works, but recent trials have shown how effective a 'sticky spray' can be in controlling many foliage pests. It seems that its main effect is to prevent the pests from moving, meeting and breeding. Suffice it to say that for many years Ruth's father used a seaweed foliar feed with excellent results. This helps to keep down the numbers of insect pests, thus reducing the need for regular spraying with insecticides.

Rabbits and Mice

We will deal with these two pests together as they are similar in many ways. If you live in a built-up area, you may never suffer from the effects that rabbits can create in a garden, but both rabbits and mice are very fond of clematis, especially in spring, when new clematis shoots are particularly tempting. During the winter, mice will chew through clematis stems and take these away with a few dead leaves to make a nest.

The mouse problem can be controlled in two ways, with the aid of traps or bait. Both methods need shielding from unwary birds, cats and dogs. The traps can be baited with one of a number of tasty morsels: mice like not only cheese but they also eat chocolate, unsalted peanuts and runner bean seeds. The prepared trap can then be placed near the base of the clematis and shielded with a roof tile.

Rabbits are more of a menace to those of us living in the country. If rabbits are a real problem to you, the only real deterrent is to 'rabbit-proof' your whole garden using fine mesh netting. The galvanized netting can be obtained from an agricultural supplier. We would suggest buying a fine mesh because baby rabbits are extremely agile and can squeeze themselves through small holes. The netting needs to be at least 3ft (1m) tall, so that about 9–12in (20–30cm) can be buried below soil level to prevent rabbits from burrowing underneath it. This is an expensive exercise, but if it is done well, using galvanized netting which will not rust, then it should last for many years. It should relieve you of much anxiety and all the expense of replacing costly plants. A cheaper course to take would be to net each individual clematis, a course that we are now taking!

We have been told that crushed mothballs placed around the base of clematis can deter

rabbits, but we have not tried this. One theory we are currently testing is the use of garlic flakes as a deterrent. These can be obtained from animal feed suppliers.

Moles

These deceptively delightful little creatures are, again, usually only a pest to those living in the country. Unfortunately, moles usually seem to root around right underneath our favourite plants, causing enormous damage to the root systems. Again, trapping is one course of action to take, although it may be worth employing a professional 'mole trapper', as moles are quite devious creatures and difficult to catch. A deterrent is worth a try; you will find various mole scarers in garden centres nowadays.

USING CHEMICALS

There are a few important points to consider when using chemicals in gardens and greenhouses and, as responsible gardeners, we must all bear these in mind.

Firstly, it is wise to wear rubber gloves when handling and using any chemicals. But even so, your hands should always be washed thoroughly afterwards. The gloves can then be stored along with the chemicals to avoid them being used for other purposes.

Secondly, make absolutely sure that your garden chemicals are stored safely between use. A small, lockable cabinet in your garden shed or garage could be a sensible precaution to take against possible disaster, especially if you have children or grandchildren around.

Thirdly, *always*, with no exceptions, follow the manufacturer's instructions.

Nurserymen as well as gardeners are becoming increasingly aware of the need to reduce the amount of chemicals used. One way of achieving this is through biological control which can be very satisfactory in a greenhouse environment, where serious infestations can build up if not controlled in some way. There are now effective biological controls for spider mite, whitefly and greenfly, all of which can be a real problem to the amateur and professional alike.

Not only have the gardening public become much more aware of the need to reduce the use of chemicals to safeguard the environment, but nurserymen too are becoming conscious of the need to help. The less we use sprays, the more we will give our beneficial insects and animals, such as ladybirds, frogs and toads, a better chance to reproduce and therefore continue the battle against pests on our behalf.

CHAPTER 12

Clematis Profiles

INTRODUCTION

This section contains detailed descriptions of around 400 clematis cultivars and species, their flowering seasons, approximate heights and flower sizes, preferred aspects and so on. The cultivars are listed in alphabetical order under either their species name or hybrid name. The descriptions are intended as a guide, to give a helpful indication of what you can reasonably expect from these clematis, how they can be grown and any particular points of interest.

Much of this information has been gleaned from years of experience growing them in our garden. Ours, like all gardens, has changed and developed over the years. Structures and shrubs have come and gone, with new ones planted in their place – gardens are living things, they don't stand still – but the changes that we have made have given us huge opportunities to try many different clematis in many different situations in our difficult and dry East Anglian garden, and some of these we will share with you in the descriptions that follow.

To simplify and clarify the information, all descriptions in the Profiles assume that flowers are single, unless otherwise stated.

Seasons

Flowering periods vary greatly up, down and across the country, so instead of using flowering months we have preferred to work with the seasons, thus leaving the reader to interpret these within their own garden – for instance spring in the far north of Scotland arrives later than on the south coast of England, so please bear this in mind.

Size of Plant

Heights and flower sizes are approximate as these also vary greatly between gardens and gardeners; the richer the soil, plus thoughtful attention to feeding and watering will obviously have an increased effect on height and flower size as well as the depth and richness of flower colour. Poor growing conditions will inevitably reduce the overall height and flower size one can reasonably

An informal arrangement of late summer blooms.

OPPOSITE: An autumnal arrangement.

expect. For example, in our dry East Anglian garden, where 'Perle d'Azur' is rather neglected, it grows about 8ft (2.6m) tall each year, whereas in more favourable growing conditions it could make 10–12ft (3.3–4m) by flowering time.

Clematis which have two periods of bloom in a year will usually produce large flowers from the old wood early in summer, with slightly smaller blooms later in the season from the growth made in the current year. It is often found that clematis flowering twice in the year will produce flowers of a different shade in the second flush (this is particularly noticeable in 'Dr Ruppel' for example).

Aspect

The aspect suggested for each cultivar should again be used purely as a flexible guide; some gardens are open and exposed to the elements, while others are sheltered and several degrees warmer. A few clematis will fade, losing their colour quite badly, if grown in full sun, and therefore we have indicated that these should be grown in a shady or semi-shady position, which will preserve their colour. Other clematis will actually benefit from being grown in a sunny position, which can help to improve their colour and will encourage the very late flowering cultivars to bloom a little earlier. Also scented clematis will have their fragrance enhanced if grown in full sun.

Colour Perception

We have described the flower colours as we see them, which *could* be slightly different from how you and others see them. To quote the International Clematis Register and Checklist 2002, 'There are some cultivars whose flowers have a surprisingly wide colour range. This may be because the plants produce flowers that have different colours or tints when grown in sun or shade. To add to the problem, the light conditions under which a colour is viewed, often have an influence on how a colour is perceived. Colour perception also varies between individuals: different people may see the same colour in different

ways, resulting in apparent colour variation. Even those who apparently see a colour in the same way may describe it in different terms.'

Photographs can also vary greatly in the accuracy of their colour. Some clematis are notorious for the difficulty in producing a photograph of the correct shade, and printing of photographs, whether in a book, magazine, plant label or website adds yet another opportunity for slight inaccuracies.

White flowered clematis are much simpler to describe, and it should be noted here that generally, unlike other white flowered plants, white clematis flowers are less susceptible to weather damage, that is, frost, wind and wet.

Use in Flower Arrangements

Clematis and their seed heads make very interesting additions to flower arrangements, and we have noted this in the details of those that we have tried, with success, lasting at least four or more days when cut and kept in water.

Suitability for Growing in Pots

We have indicated those cultivars that we recommend as being suitable for growing in pots; these tend to be the more compact growing, lower and more free-flowering cultivars. There are various reasons that we have not recommended some as being suitable; perhaps they are too tall and 'leggy', and others may be too vigorous and therefore far more suited to ground planting. However, any clematis could be grown in a container if that is the only option available and providing an appropriately sized container is used, such as a half oak barrel for the more vigorous growers.

Awards

We have listed awards made to clematis by the Royal Horticultural Society with their Award of Garden Merit (AGM) and First Class Certificate (FCC) and also those awards made following trials by the British Clematis Society (for example, BCS Certificate of Merit).

Plant Breeders' Rights

Those clematis listed here with PBR in their details are protected by Plant Breeders' Rights, and therefore unlicensed propagation is prohibited in certain territories. No attempt has been made to declare trademarks or registered trademarks, as the legal implications of these vary from country to country. Therefore as noted on the title page no legal rights can be extracted from this book. Where appropriate we have included trade designations that are known to us.

Trade Designations

Many plants nowadays have a name that is used for commercial purposes which differs from the botanically defined name. The International Code for the Nomenclature of Cultivated Plants (ICNCP) governs the botanical name, but a trade designation name can be used instead and often is, especially when a 'code name' has been used for the plant during its assessment for Plant Breeders' Rights, for example. We have used the trade designation for clematis that are commonly sold under

NOMENCLATURE

For many years we have used 'Groups' in our nursery catalogue and website to aid the gardener in plant selection. At the time of Ruth's first book in 1996 our main reference for nomenclature was Wim Snoeijer's *Clematis Index*. Since then there have been many discussions and other works published. In 2002 the Royal Horticultural Society published the *International Clematis Register and Checklist*, which we have used as a standard reference work in recent years.

In 2008 Wim Snoeijer published another invaluable book, *Clematis Cultivar Group Classification*. The main change to earlier systems is the application of Cultivar Groups defined by the actual appearance of the plant rather than its history. We have adopted a number of these Cultivar Groups where his conclusions match ours. In other cases we have retained the use of Pruning Groups (Early Large Flowered and Late Large Flowered) as these are well known and we feel they reflect the more relevant aspect of allocating groups.

Our aim is to try to avoid confusion and to simplify and clarify the naming of clematis whenever possible. But as more and more breeding produces more complex hybrids, boundaries become increasingly blurred. No one method is perfect, there is often no clear 'right or wrong', and we have therefore made some decisions based on a pragmatic approach whilst trying to be consistent. In a few cases we have not applied a group name if we felt this would not aid the gardener.

One example of compromise is the cultivar *C. florida* 'Alba Plena'. This has had many alternative names, some of which were very involved. As Wim Snoeijer states on page 15 of his book, 'The name 'Alba Plena' was published by Boucher & Mottet (1898) and is the only publication of such a combination of Latin words which makes it impossible to mix the name up for other plants and can therefore be used safely.' We agree that this is much better than *C. florida* var. *flore-pleno*, however we have retained the use of *florida* in our profile listing as this also helps to avoid confusion with 'Albina Plena' (Atragene Group). So we may offend some rules whichever way we go, but we feel that the final guide for us has to be clarity for the gardener.

It often proves difficult though to find a certain clematis which may have been listed under one name but is also commonly found under another. Let us take Texensis Group cultivar 'Duchess of Albany' as an example: in many situations this clematis may have been found listed alphabetically under the Ts as *texensis* 'Duchess of Albany'; it can however, often be found listed under the Ds as purely 'Duchess of Albany'. The latter is botanically correct due to the origin of this clematis being a cross between *C. texensis* and 'Star of India'.

We have decided to list the clematis in the Profiles under their commonly known name but have added, after the name, the Cultivar Group, or Pruning Group, associated with that plant as this will offer cultural guidance. For example, the clematis cultivar known as 'Black Prince' will be found under B with the note 'Viticella Group' after the name.

these names (for example GOLDEN TIARA which is the trade designation for 'Kugotia'). Occasionally a clematis is given a trade designation to help make it more marketable; for example, 'Fairy Blue' is better known as CRYSTAL FOUNTAIN and similarly 'Kakio' is better known as PINK CHAMPAGNE.

CULTIVAR GROUPS

We have chosen to use Cultivar Groups for many of the clematis listed. In each Clematis Profile the group is shown after the cultivar name, for example 'Columbine', Atragene Group, which gives you the opportunity to check on its cultural requirements.

Armandii Group

These spring flowering clematis produce clusters of sweetly scented flowers from their old ripened wood, and we recommend growing these in a sunny position to enhance their fragrance. Whilst hardy, they prefer free-draining conditions and a situation that is sheltered from the worst of the cold winds, as this can damage their foliage.

Their long narrow glossy leaves are evergreen, leathery in texture and are similar, in many ways, to those of the common laurel.

If space allows, pruning is unnecessary, but when required, should be carried out in late spring or early summer, immediately flowering has finished, enough to simply tidy the plant.

Atragene Group

This group includes the alpinas, koreanas, macropetalas and their various hybrids. All these clematis are spring flowering and have either single, semi-double or double nodding bell-shaped flowers that are borne from their old ripened wood. A few will continue to produce some blooms throughout the summer months from their current season's growth, and these are indicated by a + sign in the details of their flowering months.

As their flowers fade, pretty silky seed heads are left in their place. Both their flowers and seed heads are lovely to use in flower arrangements and

posies; the cut flowers will last about four to five days in water.

The Atragenes are all extremely hardy and easy to grow, but require free-draining conditions and will not tolerate water-logged soil. They do not need the 'rich' growing conditions nor deep planting that the large flowered cultivars prefer.

They can be left unpruned, but if pruning is required it should be carried out in late spring or early summer, immediately after the main flowering period has finished. It is probably better to remove a little growth each year to keep the plant tidy.

Cirrhosa Group

These winter and early spring flowering clematis are derived from the species *C. cirrhosa* that was introduced to Britain from the Mediterranean and southern Europe around 1590. They all produce masses of dainty nodding bell-shaped flowers from their old ripened wood.

Their attractive evergreen foliage looks at its best in autumn, winter and spring. Whilst classed as evergreen, they do have a natural dormant period in summer when the leaves can look 'tired' and sometimes go brown during very long, hot periods. If this happens, reduce watering to a minimum and leave well alone; the plant is not dead, it is simply resting and will re-shoot into fresh growth as soon as nature permits.

The Cirrhosa Group cultivars flower better in a sunny position, which is also free draining and sheltered from the worst of the cold winds that could damage their foliage.

If space allows, pruning is unnecessary, but when required, should be carried out in late spring or immediately flowering has finished.

Diversifolia Group

Long flowering periods and a wide range of flower shapes are the key features of this most 'diverse' group.

All members of this group are derived directly or indirectly from *C. integrifolia* for at least one parent. The variation that is seen in this group is

A posy of clematis from the Atragene Group.

due to the use of other, often large flowered clematis, in their cross-breeding. This gives a range of stem lengths from 3ft (90cm) to 8ft (2.6m) depending on the cultivar. Their stems do not cling, and therefore they can be allowed to scramble or trail amongst host plants in a border. Alternatively they are excellent at adding height to a border, but they need to be tied into a support or trained up through an obelisk to achieve this.

This is one of the newer Group classifications and contains many that have previously been listed as members of the Integrifolia Group. However, the Diversifolia Group cultivars form viable buds low down on their old stems, whereas the integrifolias normally die down completely.

They should be hard pruned in winter or early spring.

All the clematis in this group are excellent to use as cut flowers, and many of them have lovely seedheads that can also be used in arrangements.

A selection of clematis from the Diversifolia Group.

Elegant whorls of seedheads from the Early Large Flowered Group.

The dramatic centre of CRYSTAL FOUNTAIN, one of the Early Large Flowered Group.

C. mandschurica seedheads.

Early Large Flowered Group

This large group contains many of the most popular clematis that generally have two quite distinct flowering periods in the year (such as 'Nelly Moser'). Many have their origins in the species *C. patens*, but their pedigree is often complex and also often unknown.

Light pruning in late winter or early spring is normally recommended, followed by deadheading after the first flush of flowers has finished. This will encourage a second, spectacular display of flowers in late summer and early autumn. They enjoy a rich moist soil with plenty of nutrients.

Some of the taller growing cultivars in this group can be hard pruned to reduce their overall height and this is indicated in their details as 'Prune Light or Hard'. This will also affect whether they flower earlier or later in the year. For further guidance see 'Optional Pruning' in Chapter 6.

Many of the more recent introductions that are designed to be good 'patio clematis' for growing in pots are recommended to be hard pruned to keep them compact. Therefore, even if they are really Group 2 Light Prune types in nature, they respond very well to hard pruning both in early spring and again after their first flush of flowers. This way you keep the plant compact and tidy and you get more

C. mandschurica (Flammula Group) scrambling in a border.

than one period of flowering. These cultivars *could* be lightly pruned, but they would then grow much taller.

Flammula Group

These hardy, summer flowering, herbaceous perennial, clump-forming clematis can make useful additions to our gardens. A few such as *C. terni-flora* will naturally climb, but others are shorter growing and ideal for the border. *C. recta* and its crosses produce literally hundreds of star-like flowers which have a delicate, hawthorn-like perfume that helps to attract bees and butterflies to the garden.

The young purply-bronze foliage of *C. recta* 'Purpurea' and 'Velvet Night' makes a wonderful backdrop to other shorter growing herbaceous plants during late spring and early summer, which is an added bonus before their flowers open.

Whilst these can be grown in any aspect, they prefer a free-draining situation and will flower better, and their perfume will be stronger if grown in a sunny position.

The shorter growing members can be allowed to scramble freely in a border, or perhaps for some of them to look their best, their non-climbing stems could be given some support to hold them erect.

Their stems naturally die down over the winter, when they should be hard pruned, but protect the newly emerging shoots in the spring from slugs and snails.

Florida Group

These exotic looking clematis are all very free flowering and make excellent specimen plants when grown in containers for the patio or conservatory. They will flower continually throughout the summer and autumn, and often into the winter given ideal conditions.

Because they are not considered to be fully hardy they tend to be more reliable when grown in pots that can be stood in the garden during the summer months and then moved into cold glasshouse conditions to over-winter. There they will remain semi-evergreen and may continue to flower

until their hard pruning becomes necessary in late winter – they are well worth the extra care.

However, if you have a very sheltered or courtyard garden, they can be planted out and require free draining conditions and possibly some winter protection. You may also find that they will flower more profusely if given a warm, sunny location.

Forsteri Group

The clematis in this group are species, or are derived from species, native to New Zealand. They all have attractive evergreen foliage and flower in the spring from their old ripened wood.

Because they are not fully hardy they are well suited to being grown in pots using very free-draining gritty compost and may prefer the winter protection of a cold glasshouse or conservatory. However, given ideal conditions of a fairly sunny, sheltered site and exceptionally free-draining soil, they can survive winters outdoors in some areas.

These clematis are dioecious – in other words, they produce male *or* female flowers on separate plants. 'Lunar Lass' and 'Early Sensation' have female flowers and produce amazing seed heads when grown alongside 'Joe', for instance, whose flowers are male.

Whilst these do not have to be pruned and can simply be left, we prefer to hard prune those that we grow in pots immediately they have finished flowering each year. They then make fresh growth through the summer and early autumn, which ripens over the winter to flower again the following spring. Whilst evergreen, they do have a natural dormant period in summer when their foliage can look tired.

They require extremely gritty compost and very few nutrients, so beware not to overfeed these types.

Heracleifolia Group

These summer flowering clematis are classed as herbaceous sub-shrubs; they have woody stems that die back, more or less, to a woody base during the winter.

Most have erect stems and produce large clusters of hyacinth-shaped flowers. Others produce more star-shaped flowers whose tepal tips recurve, and their woody stems have a scrambling or semi-climbing habit.

These hardy clematis can be grown in any aspect; however, they generally flower and perform better in sunny, free draining conditions. Indeed, a sunny border is ideal to enhance the fragrance of the scented cultivars in this group.

We find, in our exposed garden, that it is better to prune the erect growing members of this group in two stages. Over the winter, their old flowering stems can be reduced by half in order to tidy the garden. Then wait until mid-spring, when the weather has improved, to prune them back to just above the fresh young shoots at the base of the plant. The scrambling or semi-climbing members can be hard pruned over the winter or early spring, back to viable, dormant buds about 12in (30cm) from their woody base.

Integrifolia Group

These hardy herbaceous perennial, summer flowering clematis are derived from the wild *C. integrifolia* species that originated in Europe.

They are all very free flowering, clump-forming 'scramblers' that die back more or less to soil level each winter.

Their non-clinging stems can be held erect with supports, or allowed to scramble at will through herbaceous borders. They also make excellent companions in beds of bush roses. Their stems vary in length from approximately 12in (30cm) to 36in (1m) depending on the cultivar.

Because they die back in winter, they should be hard pruned to within an inch or so of their base during that time. Their new shoots will quickly emerge from the base in spring, but beware, these make tasty treats for slugs and snails as they also emerge from their winter quarters!

All the clematis in this group are excellent to use as cut flowers.

Late Large Flowered Group

This group contains many popular larger flowered

A collection of clematis from the Heracleifolia Group.

clematis that generally only flower on their new growth each year (such as 'Jackmanii'), and therefore hard pruning in late winter or early spring is required. There are a few exceptions, and these can be either hard or light pruned, which will affect whether they flower later or earlier in the year. Where applicable this is noted in the individual profiles.

These are all hardy and reliable clematis that enjoy a rich moist soil with plenty of nutrients.

Many have similar origins to 'Jackmanii' but their pedigree is often complex and also often unknown.

Montana Group

The spring flowering *C. montana* originated in the Himalaya where their natural habit is to clamber up into large trees, making them ideal in our garden settings for softening the outline of buildings, covering fences or growing up large mature trees. But beware, they can be very vigorous. 'Freda' is probably the only 'lady-like' montana!

Whilst the majority of the Montana Group cultivars bear single flowers, some such as 'Jenny Keay' have semi-double blooms. The semi-double cultivars tend to begin their flowering period around two to three weeks later than singles and continue to bloom for several weeks after the singles have finished, and are therefore ideal to use to extend the flowering season of the Montana Group.

Flowering profusely in the spring from their old ripened wood, the Montana Group cultivars do not have to be pruned unless they have filled their allotted space. If required, pruning should be carried out immediately flowering has finished, a simple 'hair-cut' with garden shears will normally suffice to remove the unwanted growth. But if you wish to grow a montana and space is very limited, try hard pruning it each year after it has finished flowering. The plant then needs to make its new growth in time to ripen through the autumn and winter, in order to bloom the following spring.

As the Montana Group cultivars have a relatively short flowering period, good interesting foliage is of utmost importance. Generally, we find that the montanas bearing pale to very deep pink blooms tend to have purply-bronze leaves, whereas those that have white or salmon-pink blooms have brighter green leaves.

The shorter growing members of this group could be grown in huge pots if there is no way of planting directly into the ground. However, this is not ideal, so ground planting is always the preferred method of cultivation for these vigorous clematis.

Tangutica Group

The clematis in this group are derived from the species *C. tangutica* or *C. orientalis*, and all, except 'Anita', have nodding bell-shaped flowers in vari-

An arrangement of clematis from the Tangutica Group.

ous shades of yellow. They are all hardy, extremely free flowering and useful in the garden as they flower for long periods throughout the summer and autumn, with most producing excellent seedheads for added interest during the winter months. Both their flowers and seed heads are excellent to use in flower arrangements.

They enjoy free draining soil, cope happily with poorer growing conditions and are drought resistant. However, they will not tolerate very heavy clay soil that waterlogs, nor over-watering, and do not appreciate too much feeding either.

Flowering from growth made in the current season, they require hard pruning in late winter or early spring to roughly 12–18in (30–45cm) above the soil. Because they do not generally form viable buds in their leaf joints as other clematis do, it is unnecessary to cut each individual stem above a leaf joint. Simply cut straight through all stems. For weeks the stems may appear dead, and then all of a sudden it will sprout into growth and be in bloom again in a matter of weeks. We have never known one to die due to incorrect pruning!

The glorious silky seedheads of 'Lambton Park'.

Texensis Group

The cultivars in this group are very much sought-after garden plants, especially those derived from the species *C. texensis*, whose 'trumpet' shaped blooms are exquisite. They are all hardy, summer flowering and are excellent plants which deserve space in anyone's garden.

Used as climbers, they all perform best in a situation that is sunny yet not too windy. Alternatively they can be allowed to scramble at will, down out of the wind, growing over and through other plants in beds and borders.

Clematis in the Texensis Group are herbaceous in habit; in other words their stems die down, very often to ground level, every winter, and this old growth should be removed during late winter or early spring. New shoots quickly appear from below soil level in spring, and these should be protected from damage by slugs and snails.

Consistent watering in summer, whilst ensuring free drainage, will reduce the risk of attack by

powdery mildew to which some can occasionally be prone. If this does occur, at the first signs of mildew infection quickly take appropriate action, such as applying a fungicide spray after sundown, and the problem should be easily contained.

Viorna Group

The members of this group have smaller nodding bell or urn-shaped flowers and many produce attractive seedheads. They are summer flowering and their stems die down completely in winter so hard pruning is required.

They prefer well-drained conditions, although they need moist roots in their growing season. Their requirements are very similar to the Texensis Group noted above.

Vitalba Group

These clematis are small flowered, vigorous growing plants. *C. vitalba*, our native British clematis, is not very garden worthy and only suitable for natural planting schemes; however it does produce many wonderful seed heads. 'Paul Farges' is a valuable addition to the larger garden, flowering for many weeks, but it has no seedheads of any significance.

Flowering only on new wood each year they need to be hard pruned in garden situations to keep them under control. These are very tolerant of drier soil conditions.

Viticella Group

Included here are those clematis commonly thought of as Viticellas and hybrids derived from the species *C. viticella*. Some of these clematis have been crossed and re-crossed so many times over the years that their 'blood' is somewhat question-able. In addition we have included some cultivars in this group because their growth, habit and general appearance is so similar to that of *C. viticella* and, for ease of selection by gardeners, we feel justified in placing them within this 'very loose' group.

These summer flowering clematis are extremely hardy; they can be grown in any aspect, some are suitable to grow in pots, they are all very free flowering, their pruning is simple and they cannot be recommended highly enough. They are especially useful for people new to growing clematis as they are extremely tolerant of whatever the gardener does to them!

These all need to be hard pruned in late winter or early spring.

Clematis Profiles A–Z

'Abundance'

Viticella Group
AGM 2002

Flowering Period Mid summer to early autumn
Aspect Any
Pruning Hard
Height or Spread 8–10ft (2.6–3.3m)
Flower Size 3in (7.5cm)

Deciduous climber. Raised by Morel in France around 1900, it was introduced to Britain by Jackman's of Woking in 1939. The pretty semi-nodding to outward facing flowers are pinky-red and it is very aptly named as its flowers are indeed produced in abundance. Their four to six broad tepals have dark pinkish-red running through veins across their deeply textured surface and the serrated margins recurve as they taper to blunt, strongly recurved tips. The anthers are a greenish yellow. This used to flaunt itself over a huge wooden arch in our garden where it made a wonderfully eye-catching display every year. Best suited for planting in the garden.

'Ai-Nor'

Early Large Flowered Group

Flowering Period Early summer to early autumn
Aspect Any
Pruning Light
Height or Spread 6–8ft (2–2.6m)
Flower Size 4–6in (10–15cm)

Deciduous climber. Raised by M.A. Beskaravainaya, Russia, 1968. These beautiful flowers open the most fabulous shade of rich peachy-pink that gradually matures to pale peachy-pink yet retains the slightly deeper shade towards the broad rounded tips. There is a hint of deep reddy-purple shading at the base of each tepal. The stamens have white filaments that merge to primrose yellow anthers. We are particularly fond of this charming clematis which our son Peter fell in love with when he was on 'clematis' work experience in New Zealand several years ago. Suitable for growing in containers or planting in the garden.

'Akaishi'

Early Large Flowered Group

Flowering Period Late spring to early summer and early autumn
Aspect Any
Pruning Light
Height or Spread 8–10ft (2.6–3.3m)
Flower Size 5–6in (12.5–15cm)

Deciduous climber. Introduced from Japan. The rich violet-purple blooms have broad, bright crimson bars, which really bring the flowers to life. The seven or eight broad, over-lapping tepals taper via wavy margins to pointed tips that gently recurve with age. The stamens have pinkish-white filaments and deep red anthers. A glorious sight when in full bloom. Suitable for growing in containers or planting in the garden.

ALABAST 'Poulala'   Early Large Flowered Group
                                                                              AGM 2002

Flowering Period Late spring to early summer and late summer to early autumn
Aspect Shaded, to preserve colour
Pruning Light
Height or Spread 8–10ft (2.6–3.3m)
Flower Size 5–6in (12.5–15cm)

Deciduous climber. Raised by D.T. Poulson, Denmark and introduced in 1970. The pale primrose yellow flowers have a deeper bar and a lovely satin sheen. They mature to creamy-white. The early blooms sometimes have a pale green bar. The filaments are cream with butter yellow anthers. When gown in shade this will hold the primrose yellow colouring for longer. Suitable for growing in containers or planting in the garden. PBR: Unlicensed propagation prohibited.

'Alba Luxurians'   Viticella Group
                                                                              AGM 1993

Flowering Period Mid summer to mid autumn
Aspect Any
Pruning Hard
Height or Spread 8–10ft (2.6–3.3m)
Flower Size 2in (5cm)

Deciduous climber. W.J. Bean suggested that this was probably raised at Veitch's Coombe Wood Nursery (around 1900). The semi-nodding, somewhat irregular shaped white flowers have green 'leaf-like' tips to its early flowers. The margins of the four to six tepals recurve as they taper to blunt recurved tips and the reverse bears a hint of mauve and a pale green bar along the mid-ribs. The short stamens have contrasting purply-black anthers. This grows over a double-flowering gorse bush in our garden where its later blooms extend the period of interest against the spring flowering shrub. These unusual white and green flowers are much sought-after by flower arrangers, and their cut blooms keep well in water. Best suited for planting in the garden.

'Albina Plena'   Atragene Group

Flowering Period Mid to late spring
Aspect Any, with free drainage
Pruning Tidy after flowering
Height or Spread 8–12ft (2.6–4m)
Flower Size 1½–2in (4–5cm)

Deciduous climber. Raised by Magnus Johnson, Sweden in 1982. The pure white semi-double nodding bell-shaped flowers are creamy-white when first open. It has a distinctive reddy-purple ring at the base of the tepals where they join the flower stalk. Extremely hardy, one of the best double whites in the Atragene Group. Best suited for planting in the garden.

'Alice Fisk'   Early Large Flowered Group

Flowering Period Late spring to early summer and late summer to early autumn
Aspect Any
Pruning Light
Height or Spread 6–8ft (2–2.6m)
Flower Size 5–7in (12.5–18cm)

Deciduous climber. Introduced by Fisk's Clematis Nursery, Suffolk, in 1967 and named after Jim Fisk's mother. The star-shaped blooms first open a mid violet-blue which matures to light mauve-blue. Normally bearing six broad textured tepals which taper via lightly crimped margins to pointed tips. The contrasting stamens have white filaments and deep wine-red anthers. The cut blooms keep well in water. Suitable for growing in containers or planting in the garden.

'Alionushka'   Diversifolia Group
Synonym: 'Aljonushka'   BCS Certificate of Merit 1998 and AGM 2002

Flowering Period Early summer to early autumn
Aspect Any
Pruning Hard
Height or Spread 5–7ft (1.6–2.3m)
Flower Size 2½in (6cm)

Semi-herbaceous, deciduous, non-clinging, semi-climber or scrambler. Raised in 1961 by A.N.
Volosenko-Valenis, Nikitsky State Botanic Garden, Ukraine. This beautiful clematis has
deep, mauve-pink nodding bell-shaped flowers. The four 'twisted' tepals have deep, rich-
pink along their prominent mid-ribs with a lighter mauve-pink radiating out towards the crimped margins that recurve
as they taper to pointed recurved tips. As the tips flare out and twist the inner deeply textured surface is revealed. The
tips of the yellow anthers can be seen deep in the throat of the flowers. We grow this in two completely different situations: one grows up through an obelisk on a bank of mixed shrubs, and the other was through a white shrub rose called
'Swany' which looked lovely. Recently the rose had to be removed and has been replaced by a tree peony, which should
work equally well. The cut flowers keep well in water. Suitable for growing in containers or planting in the garden.

'Allanah'   Early Large Flowered Group

Flowering Period Early summer to early autumn *or* late summer to late autumn
Aspect Sunny, to encourage flowering
Pruning Light *or* Hard
Height or Spread 10–12ft (3.3–4m) *or* 6–8ft (2–2.6m)
Flower Size 5–6in (12.5–15cm)

Deciduous climber. Raised by Alister Keay in New Zealand. Rich velvety red on first opening, then fading slightly towards the margins; the six to eight tepals taper at both ends
making the flowers appear rather gappy (but not to their detriment). The tepals have
blunt tips which give the flower a very round appearance. The stamens have white filaments with very dark, almost black, anthers. Adapt your pruning technique to suit your
growing conditions and to encourage a better display of flowers – in a mild climate or a
sheltered garden, hard pruning will be necessary, but in colder districts, light pruning and
a sunny position will improve performance. Hard pruning will keep the plant more
compact but will delay the flowering period by a few weeks. Suitable for growing in
containers if hard pruned, or for planting in the garden.

alternata
Synonym: *Archiclematis alternata*

Flowering Period Early summer to mid autumn
Aspect Sunny, sheltered and free draining.
Pruning Light
Height or Spread 6–10ft (2–3.3m)
Flower Size 1in (2.5cm)

Deciduous climber. A species originating from Nepal and Tibet, discovered by the Japan
Himalayan Expedition, 1955. This has delightful little red, nodding flowers dangling on
long stems from the leaf axils. The four deeply textured tepals form a tubular shaped
bloom whose pointed tips recurve to reveal the boss of greeny-cream anthers. The name
alternata reflects its leaf format – normally clematis leaves are borne in pairs opposite one
another along the vine, whereas *C. alternata* produces its leaves singly and alternately
along the vine. The attractive mid-green leaves often take on a bronze tint in autumn, are
heart shaped, have serrated margins and they are covered in fine hairs. This is a novel, yet very attractive addition to the
east facing wall of our terrace. Its long flowering period means we can admire it all summer and most of the autumn.
Suitable for growing in containers or planting in the garden.

'Ameshisuto'   Early Large Flowered Group

Flowering Period Late spring to early summer and late summer to early autumn
Aspect Any
Pruning Light
Height or Spread 6–8ft (2–2.6m)
Flower Size 5–6in (12.5–15cm)

Deciduous climber. Raised in Japan by Kozo Sugimoto before 1998. The gorgeous rich lilac-blue flowers have the merest hint of rose-pink when first open. It normally bears eight broad, overlapping tepals that taper via slightly incurved margins, to blunt tips. The beautiful contrasting stamens have white filaments and butter yellow anthers. It is possible that this is the same plant as 'Amethyst', also of Sugimoto, Japan. Suitable for growing in containers or planting in the garden.

AMETHYST BEAUTY **'Evipo043'**   Late Large Flowered Group

Flowering Period Early summer to early autumn
Aspect Not north
Pruning Hard
Height or Spread 4–6ft (1.3–2m)
Flower Size 5–6in (12.5–15cm)

Deciduous climber. Raised, and introduced in 2010, by Raymond Evison, Guernsey. The velvety deep reddy-purple flowers mature to bluey-purple with a slightly paler bar. They have six broad overlapping tepals that taper to pointed tips via lightly crimped and wavy margins; the anthers are deep wine-red. Suitable for growing in containers or planting in the garden. PBR: Unlicensed propagation prohibited.

'Andromeda'   Early Large Flowered Group

Flowering Period Late spring to early summer and early autumn
Aspect Partial shade, to preserve colour
Pruning Light
Height or Spread 6–8ft (2–2.6m)
Flower Size 5–6in (12.5–15cm)

Deciduous climber. Raised by Ken Pyne, Chingford, in 1987. The early blooms are semi-double and are a very pretty creamy-white with raspberry red bars along the centre of each tepal. The margins recurve slightly and taper to pointed tips. The stamens have white filaments and cream anthers. The later flowers are single. Suitable for growing in containers or planting in the garden.

ANGÉLIQUE **'Evipo017'**   Early Large Flowered Group

Flowering Period Early to mid summer and early to mid autumn
Aspect Any
Pruning Hard
Height or Spread 3–4ft (1–1.3m)
Flower Size 4½–5½in (11–13cm)

Deciduous climber. Raised, and introduced in 2002, by Raymond Evison, Guernsey. The exceptionally pretty pale lilac-blue star-shaped flowers have six to eight broad, overlapping tepals whose crimped and wavy margins taper to pointed tips. The stamens have white filaments and light brown anthers. Hard pruning will keep this very compact. Suitable for growing in containers or planting in the garden. PBR: Unlicensed propagation prohibited.

'Anita'   Tangutica Group
                                          BCS Certificate of Merit 2000

Flowering Period Early summer to early autumn *or* mid summer to mid autumn
Aspect Any, and free draining
Pruning Light *or* Hard
Height or Spread 15–20ft (5–6m) *or* 10–12ft (3.3–4m)
Flower Size 1–1½in (2.5–4cm)

Deciduous climber. Raised in 1988 by R. Zwijnenburg, The Netherlands. The pretty
creamy-yellow buds open to white, outward-facing flowers which have four, occasionally
five, broad tepals whose margins incurve slightly as they taper towards the pointed tips.
The stamens have greeny-yellow filaments and primrose yellow anthers. Hard pruning will keep the plant more
compact but will delay the flowering period by a few weeks. Best suited for planting in the garden.

ANNA-LOUISE 'Evithree'   Early Large Flowered Group
                                                             AGM 2002

Flowering Period Late spring to early summer and late summer to early autumn
Aspect Any
Pruning Light
Height or Spread 6–8ft (2–2.6m)
Flower Size 6–7in (15–17cm)

Deciduous climber. Raised, and introduced in 1993, by Raymond Evison, Guernsey, and named after his second daughter. The bluey-purple flowers have a bright cerise bar and a lovely velvety sheen. The tepals have an undulating surface
and slightly frilly margins. They are offset perfectly by a crown of contrasting stamens which have white filaments and
coffee coloured anthers. Suitable for growing in containers or planting in the garden. PBR: Unlicensed propagation
prohibited.

'Aotearoa'   Late Large Flowered Group

Flowering Period Mid summer to early autumn
Aspect Any
Pruning Hard
Height or Spread 8–10ft (2.6–3.3m)
Flower Size 3–4in (7.5–10cm)

Deciduous climber. Raised in New Zealand by Alister Keay in 1992. Its name translates as
'Land of the long white cloud' and is the Maori name for New Zealand. Normally bearing six broad overlapping tepals that are a lovely deep purply-blue, with a lightly textured
surface. The undulating margins taper to pointed, slightly recurved tips. The greenish-
yellow stamens make a good contrast against their dark background. Best suited for planting in the garden.

'Apple Blossom'   Armandii Group
                                                        AGM 2002

Flowering Period Early to late spring
Aspect Sunny, to enhance perfume, sheltered and free draining
Pruning Tidy after flowering
Height or Spread 15–20ft (5–6m)
Flower Size 2in (5cm)

Evergreen climber. The clusters of deep pink flower buds open to reveal pinky-white flowers the exact colour of apple blossom. Like the species *C. armandii* they have a gorgeous
vanilla-like perfume. The evergreen leaves are a glossy dark green, they are long, oval and
are borne in threes. Best suited for planting in the garden.

'Arabella'

Diversifolia Group
AGM 2002

Flowering Period Late spring to early autumn
Aspect Any
Pruning Hard
Height or Spread 4–5ft (1.3–1.6m)
Flower Size 2–3in (5–7.5cm)

Semi-herbaceous, deciduous, non-clinging scrambler. Raised, and introduced in 1990, by Barry Fretwell, Devon. The mid mauvy-blue flowers have a hint of a rose pink bar when first open. The four to six tepals have slightly incurved margins. The stamens have bluey-mauve filaments and pale yellow anthers. We have two 'Arabella' in our garden, one growing in full sun, the other in partial shade, and both are fantastic, when they come into bloom they just carry on flowering all summer. Suitable for growing in containers or planting in the garden.

Arctic Queen 'Evitwo'

Early Large Flowered Group
AGM 2002

Flowering Period Early summer to early autumn
Aspect Any
Pruning Light
Height or Spread 6–8ft (2–2.6m)
Flower Size 4–6in (10–15cm)

Deciduous climber. Raised, and introduced in 1994, by Raymond Evison, Guernsey. Arctic Queen is a very free flowering clematis producing gorgeous double and semi-double white blooms over a very long period. The cascading layers of tepals appear slightly creamy-white due to the large array of yellow anthers enhancing their centre. Suitable for growing in containers or planting in the garden. PBR: Unlicensed propagation prohibited.

armandii

Armandii Group

Flowering Period Early to late spring
Aspect Sunny, to enhance perfume, sheltered and free draining
Pruning Tidy after flowering
Height or Spread 15–20ft (5–6m)
Flower Size 1½–2in (4–5cm)

Evergreen climber. Introduced from China by E.H. Wilson in 1900, *C. armandii* bears clusters of white flowers from the leaf axils which have a gorgeous vanilla-like perfume. The evergreen leaves are a glossy dark green, they are long, oval and are borne in threes, each leaflet is about 6in (15cm) long and 2in (5cm) wide. The young leaves and stems have a bronze tinge. Best suited for planting in the garden.

'Aromatica'

Flammula Group

Flowering Period Mid summer to early autumn
Aspect Sunny, to enhance perfume
Pruning Hard
Height or Spread 3–5ft (1–1.6m)
Flower Size 2in (5cm)

Herbaceous, deciduous, clump-forming, semi-erect stems. Thought to be a cross between *C. integrifolia* and *C. recta* (or *C. flammula*) that originated in France around the mid 1800s. When first open the pretty star-shaped flowers are reddy-purple but as they mature the colour changes to violet-blue, their four narrow tepals taper via incurved margins to pointed tips. The prominent stamens have white filaments and butter yellow anthers. Because of its lax habit it is best grown with some support to hold the stems erect; a sunny border is ideal as the warmth from the sun will help to enhance its spicy fragrance. Suitable for growing in containers or planting in the garden.

'Asagasumi'
Trade designation: OPALINE

Early Large Flowered Group

Flowering Period Late spring to early summer and late summer to early autumn
Aspect Any
Pruning Light
Height or Spread 8–10ft (2.6–3.3m)
Flower Size 5–7in (12.5–17cm)

Deciduous climber. Raised in Japan by Yoshio Kubota pre-1939. The elegant bluey-white star-shaped flowers have a satin sheen and a mauve-blue 'wash' along the central bar, the ribs of which are mid mauve-blue. The eight broad, overlapping tepals taper via slightly recurved margins to pointed tips. The stamens have white filaments and butter yellow anthers. Best suited for planting in the garden.

'Asao' (pronounced Asow)

Early Large Flowered Group

Flowering Period Late spring to early summer and late summer to early autumn
Aspect Any
Pruning Light
Height or Spread 6–8ft (2–2.6m)
Flower Size 5–7in (12.5–18cm)

Deciduous climber. Raised by Kazushige Ozawa, Japan, in 1971. The single star-shaped flowers have broad, rich, deep pink margins with the same deep pink running through veins across a white bar. The bright golden anthers make this flower a stunning sight early in the summer. Suitable for growing in containers or planting in the garden.

'Ascotiensis'

Late Large Flowered Group

Flowering Period Mid summer to early autumn
Aspect Any
Pruning Hard
Height or Spread 8–10ft (2.6–3.3m)
Flower Size 5–6in (12.5–15cm)

Deciduous climber. Raised by J. Standish, Ascot, in 1871. 'Ascotiensis' is one of the best and easiest blue clematis for the garden. The broad, rich mid mauvy-blue tepals taper to pointed tips, do not lie flat and are inclined to both incurve and recurve giving the whole bloom a wavy appearance. The stamens have white filaments and coffee coloured anthers. Best suited for planting in the garden.

'Ashva'

Early Large Flowered Group

Flowering Period Late spring to early summer and early autumn *or* early summer to early autumn
Aspect Any
Pruning Light *or* Hard
Height or Spread 6–8ft (2–2.6m) *or* 4–5ft (1.3–1.6m)
Flower Size 3–3½in (5–6cm)

Deciduous climber. Originating from Lithuania. The six or seven very broad tepals overlap and taper via ruffled margins to rounded tips. Bluey-violet on opening, the colour matures to violet-blue with a crimson 'half' bar. The stamens have white filaments and dark chocolate anthers. Hard pruning will keep the plant more compact but will delay the flowering period by a few weeks. Suitable for growing in containers or planting in the garden.

'Avalanche'   Forsteri Group
Synonyms: *C. × cartmanii* 'Avalanche' (1999) and 'Blaaval'   AGM 2002

Flowering Period Mid to late spring
Aspect Sheltered, free draining and winter protection
Pruning Tidy after flowering
Height or Spread 10–12ft (3.3–4m)
Flower Size 3in (7.5cm)

Evergreen climber. Bred by Robin White of Blackthorn Nursery, Hampshire in 1990 from two New Zealand species *C. paniculata* and *C. marmoraria.* The clusters of greeny-cream buds open to glorious pure white male flowers whose stamens have greenish filaments and yellow anthers. The evergreen foliage is very dark green, a perfect background for its floral display. For many years we grew 'Avalanche' in a half oak barrel on our terrace where it clambered up through our wisteria, the two were a wonderful sight as they bloomed together. Best grown in containers (*see* Forsteri Group notes on page 130). PBR: Unlicensed propagation prohibited.

AVANT-GARDE 'Evipo033'   Viticella Group

Flowering Period Early summer to early autumn
Aspect Any
Pruning Hard
Height or Spread 6–8ft (2–2.6m)
Flower Size 2in (5cm)

Deciduous climber. A sport from 'Kermesina' introduced in 2004 by Raymond Evison, Guernsey. The four broad tepals are a deep pinky-red, they have a textured surface and serrated margins that taper to blunt, recurving tips. The centre is like a pink pom-pom of staminodes. An unusual yet very pretty flower. Suitable for growing in containers or planting in the garden. PBR: Unlicensed propagation prohibited.

'Barbara'   Early Large Flowered Group

Flowering Period Late spring to early summer and late summer to early autumn *or* early summer to early autumn
Aspect Any and free draining
Pruning Light *or* Hard
Height or Spread 8–10ft (2.6–3.3m) *or* 6–8ft (2–2.6m)
Flower Size 5–6in (12.5–15cm)

Deciduous climber. Raised in 1993 by Szczepan Marczyński in Poland and named after his wife. The six tepals are a vivid deep, slightly purplish, pink with a textured surface. A stunning colour, quite unusual in clematis. The tepals are broad and overlap at the base tapering along lightly crimped margins to pointed tips. In autumn the colouring is more purplish red. The stamens have pinky-white filaments and deep purply-red anthers. Hard pruning will keep the plant more compact but will delay the flowering period by a few weeks. Suitable for growing in containers if hard pruned, or planting in the garden.

'Barbara Jackman'   Early Large Flowered Group

Flowering Period Late spring to early summer and late summer to early autumn
Aspect Any
Pruning Light
Height or Spread 6–8ft (2–2.6m)
Flower Size 4–5in (10–12.5cm)

Deciduous climber. Raised in 1947 by George Jackman and Son, Woking. The seven or eight overlapping, round edged tepals have pointed tips and are light mauve-blue with a central bar of very deep, rich purply-pink. The stamens have white filaments with primrose yellow anthers. The cut flowers keep well in water. Suitable for growing in containers or planting in the garden.

'Beauty of Worcester'   Early Large Flowered Group

Flowering Period Late spring to early summer and late summer to early autumn
Aspect Not north
Pruning Light
Height or Spread 6–8ft (2–2.6m)
Flower Size 5–6in (12.5–15cm)

Deciduous climber. Raised, and introduced in 1890, by Messrs. Richard Smith and Co., of Worcester. The early blooms from the old ripened wood are double or semi-double, their outer ring of six reddish-purple tepals have rounded edges and pointed tips. The further layers of overlapping tepals are slightly smaller than the previous. These inner layers are deep mid-blue with a hint of pink. Single flowers are produced later in the season from the new growth. The stamens have white filaments and yellow anthers. Suitable for growing in containers or planting in the garden.

'Bees' Jubilee'   Early Large Flowered Group

Flowering Period Late spring to early summer and late summer to early autumn
Aspect Any
Pruning Light
Height or Spread 8–10ft (2.6–3.3m)
Flower Size 6–7in (15–17cm)

Deciduous climber. Raised, and introduced in 1958, by Bees Nursery, Chester, to commemorate their 25th anniversary. The seven or eight broad, overlapping tepals each taper to a blunt tip and have a deep carmine bar radiating out towards the pale mauve-pink margins. The stamens have white filaments and beige anthers. A lovely old free-flowering cultivar. Suitable for growing in containers or planting in the garden.

'Belle of Woking'   Early Large Flowered Group

Flowering Period Early to mid summer and early to mid autumn
Aspect Any
Pruning Light
Height or Spread 6–8ft (2–2.6m)
Flower Size 4–5in (10–12.5cm)

Deciduous climber. Raised, and introduced in 1881, by George Jackman and Son, Woking.
One of the first double clematis to be introduced in the UK and is still available today. The rosette-like double blooms have many layers of broad tepals each tapering to a point. They open a silvery-mauve but quickly lose the mauve tint, turning instead to a beautiful silvery-grey. The stamens have white filaments and cream anthers. For years we grew this with a flamboyant cerise rose 'Sophie's Perpetual', the two looked wonderful together and the rose gave support to a clematis that is not a particularly strong grower. Suitable for growing in containers or planting in the garden.

'Bells of Émei Shan'
Synonym: *C. repens*

Flowering Period Early summer to early autumn
Aspect Sheltered and free-draining
Pruning Hard
Height or Spread 6–8ft (2–2.6m)
Flower Size 1–1¼in (2.5–3cm)

Semi-evergreen, semi-climber or scrambler. Originally introduced in 1996 by Dan Hinckley of Heronswood Nursery, USA, from seed collected in Sichuan, China, and thought to possibly be a selection of *C. repens*. It has subsequently been given a cultivar name, that of the area where the seed was collected. The pretty yellow nodding urn-shaped flowers dangle by flimsy stalks from the leaf axils. With winter protection it can remain semi-evergreen. We grew this in a hanging basket for 'fun' one year, it 'flowered its socks off', but did require a lot of water! Suitable for growing in containers or planting in the garden.

'Best Wishes'   Florida Group

Flowering Period Early summer to early autumn +
Aspect Sheltered, free-draining and winter protection
Pruning Hard
Height or Spread 6–8ft (2–2.6m)
Flower Size 4–5in (10–12.5cm)

Deciduous climber. Raised in 1996 by Geoffrey Tolver, Reymerston and introduced in 2009 by Thorncroft Clematis Nursery. The mauvy-white tepals have a deep pinky-mauve bar and are heavily overlaid with purple freckles. The depth of colour can change considerably during the course of the flowering period, adding to its unique charm. The six to eight broad, overlapping tepals have a lovely satin sheen, their margins incurve slightly and gently undulate towards pointed tips. At the centre is a most attractive crown of stamens which have white filaments merging through deepest purply-red to almost black anthers. Best grown in containers (*see* Florida Group notes on page 130). PBR applied for.

'Betty Corning'   Viticella Group
                                                                              AGM 2002

Flowering Period Mid summer to early autumn
Aspect Any
Pruning Hard
Height or Spread 6–8ft (2–2.6m)
Flower Size 2in (5cm)

Deciduous climber. Betty Corning, a former President of the Garden Club of America, discovered this clematis in 1933 growing on a side street in Albany, New York. These gorgeous pale bluey-mauve nodding bell-shaped flowers are slightly deeper bluey-mauve on their textured inside. The four tepals have crimped margins that taper to pointed, recurved and somewhat twisted tips. This has a delicate scent that is difficult to describe, but grow her in a nice sunny position and the lovely perfume will be very noticeable. She looks lovely clambering up into our small dark green leaved holly tree. The cut flowers keep well in water. Suitable for growing in containers or planting in the garden.

'Betty Risdon'   Early Large Flowered Group

Flowering Period Late spring to early summer and early autumn
Aspect Sheltered
Pruning Light
Height or Spread 8–10ft (2.6–3.3m)
Flower Size 6–8in (15–20cm)

Deciduous climber. Raised in 1983 by Vince and Sylvia Denny, Preston, and named after a founding member of the British Clematis Society. The huge blooms have eight broad tepals which overlap and taper to blunt tips, the margins are slightly wavy. The background colour is pale mauvy-pink which is heavily overlaid with very deep mauvy-pink and has a wonderful satin sheen. The deeper colouring is particularly pronounced along the margins and the reverse. Cream mottling is apparent along the bar and at the tips of the tepals on some blooms. The filaments are pinky-white with golden anthers. Best suited for planting in the garden.

Bɪᴊᴏᴜ 'Evipo030'   Early Large Flowered Group

Flowering Period Late spring to late summer
Aspect Any
Pruning Hard
Height or Spread 1–3ft (30cm–1m)
Flower Size 3–4in (7.5–10cm)

Deciduous climber. Raised, and introduced in 2003, by Raymond Evison, Guernsey. The pointed and ruffled tepals are light violet-mauve with a slight pink bar and pinkish-beige anthers. With hard pruning it keeps extremely compact and is perfect as a 'front of border' plant, in a pot or even in a hanging basket! Suitable for growing in containers or planting in the garden. PBR: Unlicensed propagation prohibited.

'Bill MacKenzie'   Tangutica Group
                                                                 AGM 1993

Flowering Period Late summer to late autumn
Aspect Any, and free-draining
Pruning Hard
Height or Spread 10–15ft (3.3–5m)
Flower Size 2½–3in (6–7.5cm)

Deciduous climber. A seedling discovered by Bill MacKenzie (a past Curator of the Chelsea Physic Garden in London) in 1968 on a visit to Waterperry Gardens in Oxfordshire. Its bright yellow nodding, lantern-shaped flowers have distinctive dark reddish-brown stamens that become visible as the flowers open. The four broad tepals have a wax-like textured surface and taper to pointed, gently recurved tips. The flowers are followed by an excellent display of silky seed heads that remain on the plant right through the winter. When buying 'Bill MacKenzie', check to make sure the young plants were produced from cuttings, not from seed, as those from seed will not come true to type. This is a vigorous grower that requires plenty of space in the garden. The cut flowers and seedheads keep well in water. Best suited for planting in the garden.

'Black Prince'   Viticella Group

Flowering Period Mid summer to early autumn
Aspect Any
Pruning Hard
Height or Spread 8–10ft (2.6–3.3m)
Flower Size 2in (5cm)

Deciduous climber. Raised by Alister Keay, New Zealand, in 1990. The deep reddish-purple flowers are such a dark purple when first open that they appear almost black and their semi-nodding or outward facing habit reveals their silvery reverse. The four tepals have undulating margins which taper to pointed slightly recurved tips. The stamens have creamy-white filaments and dark red anthers. Best suited for planting in the garden.

'Błękitny Anioł'   Viticella Group
Trade designation: BLUE ANGEL   AGM 2002

Flowering Period Early summer to early autumn
Aspect Any
Pruning Hard
Height or Spread 8–10ft (2.6–3.3m)
Flower Size 3–4in (7.5–10cm)

Deciduous climber. Raised, and introduced in 1988, by Brother Stefan Franczak, Poland. The pale, slightly mauvy, blue flowers have a very deeply textured surface and a pretty satin sheen, their four tepals have crimped, undulating margins that taper to pointed tips. The stamens have white filaments and creamy-beige anthers. We have grown this with a pale pink rose, 'Eden Rose '88' on an obelisk in our sunken garden where at dusk the blooms had an ethereal beauty, it was stunning! We now grow it in a different situation together with another Viticella Group cultivar, 'Mary Rose'. Best suited for planting in the garden.

'Blue Boy'   Diversifolia Group
Synonym: *C.* × *diversifolia* 'Blue Boy'

Flowering Period Early summer to early autumn
Aspect Any
Pruning Hard
Height or Spread 6–8ft (2–2.6m)
Flower Size 2–3in (5–7.5cm)

Semi-herbaceous, deciduous, non-clinging, semi-climber or scrambler. Raised by Dr Frank Skinner, Canada, in 1947. The outside of the open nodding bell-shaped flowers is light mauvy-blue with three prominent dark blue 'ribs' running down the centre of the tepals towards the pointed, recurved tips. The inside is light to mid blue with a deeply textured surface and crimped margins. The stamens have cream filaments and yellow anthers. This grows up through an obelisk in our garden, along with 'Alionushka', and the blue and pink are charming together. The cut flowers keep well in water. Suitable for growing in containers or planting in the garden.

'Blue Dancer'   Atragene Group

Flowering Period Mid to late spring
Aspect Any, with free drainage
Pruning Tidy after flowering
Height or Spread 6–8ft (2–2.6m)
Flower Size 2–3in (5–7.5cm)

Deciduous climber. Introduced in 1995 by Valley Clematis Nursery. The four long, narrow light to mid-blue tepals form nodding bell-shaped flowers. The staminodes are white with primrose yellow tips. Suitable for growing in containers or planting in the garden.

'Blue Dwarf'   Heracleifolia Group
Synonym: *C. heracleifolia* 'Dwarf Blue'

Flowering Period Mid summer to mid autumn
Aspect Sunny and free-draining
Pruning Hard
Height or Spread 1–1½ft (30–45cm)
Flower Size ¾–1in (2–2.5cm)

Herbaceous, deciduous, clump-forming, erect woody stems. Selected by Kozo Sugimoto, Japan, introduced to the UK by Thorncroft Clematis Nursery in 2002. This unusual *C. heracleifolia* cultivar has, as its name implies, a very dwarf habit. The large clusters of silvery-blue hyacinth shaped flowers look good with the glaucous foliage. Very free flowering, some clusters have as many as thirty to forty individual flowers! The short woody stems are self-supporting making it a perfect front of border plant. Suitable for growing in containers or planting in the garden.

'Blue Eclipse'   Atragene Group
                                                                                   BCS Certificate of Merit 2007

Flowering Period Mid spring to late summer
Aspect Any, with free drainage
Pruning Tidy after flowering
Height or Spread 6–8ft (2–2.6m)
Flower Size 2–2¼in (5–6cm)

Deciduous climber. Raised by Vince and Sylvia Denny, Preston, in 1987. The four tepals of the nodding bell-shaped flowers are a rich, deep, somewhat mottled purply-blue and are outlined by cream margins. The inside of the bells is cream. The cut flowers keep well in water. Suitable for growing in containers or planting in the garden.

'Blue Eyes'   Early Large Flowered Group

Flowering Period Late spring to early summer and late summer to early autumn *or* early summer to early autumn
Aspect Any
Pruning Light *or* Hard
Height or Spread 6–8ft (2–2.6m) *or* 4–5ft (1.3–1.6m)
Flower Size 3–4in (7.5–10cm)

Deciduous climber. Raised by Ken Pyne, Chingford, in 1987. The pretty sky blue flowers are offset by contrasting stamens that have white filaments and yellow anthers. When first open they are a more lavender-blue but quickly lose the pinkish tinge as the bloom matures. The five or six broad overlapping tepals taper to blunt tips via slightly undulating margins. Hard pruning will keep the plant more compact but will delay the flowering period by a few weeks. Suitable for growing in containers or planting in the garden.

'Blue Light'   Early Large Flowered Group

Flowering Period Early summer to early autumn
Aspect Any
Pruning Light
Height or Spread 5–6ft (1.6–2m)
Flower Size 3½–5in (9–12.5cm)

Deciduous climber. Introduced by Frans van Haastert in the Netherlands in 1998, as a sport from 'Mrs Cholmondeley'. Pale to light mauvy-blue very double rosette-like blooms are produced from the old ripened wood, then later in the season very spiky double blooms come from the current season's growth. Suitable for growing in containers or planting in the garden. PBR: Unlicensed propagation prohibited.

BLUE PIROUETTE 'Zobluepi'   Diversifolia Group
         BCS Commended Certificate 2008

Flowering Period Early summer to early autumn
Aspect Any
Pruning Hard
Height or Spread 4–6ft (1.3–2m)
Flower Size 3–4in (7.5–10cm)

Semi-herbaceous, deciduous, non-clinging, semi-climber or scrambler. Raised in 1992 by Wim Snoeijer, The Netherlands. The very pretty violet-blue flowers have four 'twisted' tepals. When first open the blooms nod slightly, turning more upright as they mature. The tepals have a textured surface with crimped margins tapering to pointed recurved tips. The edges of the tepals both incurve and recurve giving the twisted appearance – BLUE PIROUETTE is aptly named! The stamens have violet filaments and butter yellow anthers. The cut flowers keep well in water. Suitable for growing in containers or planting in the garden. PBR: Unlicensed propagation prohibited.

'Blue Ravine'   Early Large Flowered Group

Flowering Period Late spring to early summer and early autumn
Aspect Any
Pruning Light
Height or Spread 6–8ft (2–2.6m)
Flower Size 5–7in (12.5–17cm)

Deciduous climber. Raised by Conrad Erlandson, Canada in the 1970s. The light bluey-violet flowers open with deep mauvy-pink bars which pale as the bloom matures. The six to eight tepals have slightly incurving margins that taper to pointed tips. The glorious crown of contrasting stamens have deep pink filaments and wine red anthers. Suitable for growing in containers or planting in the garden.

BLUE RIVER 'Zoblueriver'   Diversifolia Group

Flowering Period Early summer to early autumn
Aspect Any
Pruning Hard
Height or Spread 4–5ft (1.3–1.6m)
Flower Size 2½–3in (6–7.5cm)

Semi-herbaceous, deciduous, non-clinging, semi-climber or scrambler. Raised in 2000 by Wim Snoeijer, the Netherlands. Following their trials in 2009, BLUE RIVER received high praise from *Gardening Which?* (May 2010): 'This was our favourite clematis of all the ones we grew last year'. The bluish-lilac star-shaped flowers are produced in abundance over a long period. Their six narrow tepals have a deeper lilac bar and taper via somewhat incurved margins to pointed tips. The stamens have white filaments and cream anthers. It is certainly a good plant in our garden. The cut flowers keep well in water. Suitable for growing in containers or planting in the garden. PBR: Unlicensed propagation prohibited.

BONANZA 'Evipo031'   Viticella Group

Flowering Period Mid summer to early autumn
Aspect Any
Pruning Hard
Height or Spread 5–6ft (1.6–2m)
Flower Size 2–3in (5–7.5cm)

Deciduous climber. Raised, and introduced in 2006, by Raymond Evison, Guernsey. This lovely mid mauvy-blue clematis has five or six broad, overlapping tepals that have a textured surface, their undulating margins taper to blunt, gently recurved tips. The contrasting stamens have white filaments and butter yellow anthers. Suitable for growing in containers or planting in the garden. PBR: Unlicensed propagation prohibited.

BOURBON 'Evipo018'   Early Large Flowered Group

Flowering Period Early to late summer
Aspect Any
Pruning Light
Height or Spread 6–8ft (2–2.6m)
Flower Size 5–6in (12.5–15cm)

Deciduous climber. Raised, and introduced in 2002, by Raymond Evison, Guernsey. The broad tepals which overlap and taper towards blunt tips are a glorious vibrant red which is deeper at the margins; they are made even more eye-catching by a wonderful crown of bright yellow anthers. In our opinion, it's one of the nicest reds and always looks wonderful in our Chelsea Flower Show exhibit. Suitable for growing in containers or planting in the garden. PBR: Unlicensed propagation prohibited.

'Broughton Bride'   Atragene Group
                                                                      BCS Gold Medal Certificate 2003

Flowering Period Mid spring to late summer
Aspect Any, with free drainage
Pruning Tidy after flowering
Height or Spread 8–10ft (2.6–3.3m)
Flower Size 2½–3in (6–7.5cm)

Deciduous climber. Raised by Vince and Sylvia Denny, Preston, in 1990. This lovely clematis bears both single and double nodding bell-shaped flowers that are white, speckled with lilac, having opened from cream buds. The four tepals of the single blooms are longer than those of the double blooms and taper to very pointed tips. There is a splash of deep rose-pink at the base of each flower where the tepals join the stalk. The staminodes are pale yellow. The cut flowers keep well in water. Best suited for planting in the garden.

'Broughton Star'   Montana Group

BCS Certificate of Merit 1998 and AGM 2002

Flowering Period Late spring to early summer
Aspect Any
Pruning Tidy after flowering
Height or Spread 20–30ft (6–10m)
Flower Size 2in (5cm)

Deciduous climber. Raised in 1986 by Vince and Sylvia Denny, Preston. The gorgeous semi-double flowers are *very* deep plumy-pink, almost red, and the foliage is a good purply-bronze. Grow it in a fairly sunny position to enhance the colour of both the flowers and foliage. This is one of the best *C. montana* cultivars, a real eye-catching gem, it is both Ruth and Jon's favourite in this group. The cut flowers keep well in water. Best suited for planting in the garden.

'Brunette'   Atragene Group
Synonym: 'Catullus'

Flowering Period Mid to late spring +
Aspect Any, with free drainage
Pruning Tidy after main flowering
Height or Spread 8–10ft (2.6–3.3m)
Flower Size 1½–2in (4–5cm)

Deciduous climber. Raised by Magnus Johnson, Sweden, in 1979. The very deep glossy purply-red bell-shaped flowers have four broad tepals tapering to pointed tips. The staminodes are creamy-white. A most beautiful colour seen against the light green foliage. The cut flowers keep well in water. Best suited for planting in the garden.

'Burma Star'   Early Large Flowered Group

Flowering Period Late spring to early summer and late summer to early autumn *or* early summer to early autumn
Aspect Any
Pruning Light *or* Hard
Height or Spread 6–8ft (2–2.6m) *or* 4–5ft (1.3–1.6m)
Flower Size 4½–5in (11–12.5cm)

Deciduous climber. Raised and introduced by Barry Fretwell, Devon, about 1990. The gorgeous deep velvety purple flowers have a purply-red bar when first open which fades as the bloom matures. The six broad tepals overlap and taper via undulating margins towards pointed tips. The stamens have pinky filaments and wine red anthers. Hard pruning will keep the plant more compact but will delay the flowering period by a few weeks. Compact and very free-flowering, excellent! Suitable for growing in containers or planting in the garden.

campaniflora   Viticella Group
Synonym: *C. viticella* subsp. *campaniflora*

Flowering Period Mid summer to early autumn
Aspect Any
Pruning Hard
Height or Spread 12–15ft (4–5m)
Flower Size ¾–1in (2–2.5cm)

Deciduous climber. A native of Portugal and Western Spain and introduced to Britain in 1820. The plant has dainty little bluey-white nodding bell-shaped flowers. The four slightly twisted tepals have a textured surface and crimped, recurved margins that taper to pointed and strongly recurved tips. The inner surface is pure white and glistens like sugar-icing, feeling waxy to the touch. It is so pretty that this 'wild' clematis is worthy of space in our gardens. Best suited for planting in the garden.

'Carmencita'   Viticella Group

Flowering Period Mid summer to early autumn
Aspect Any
Pruning Hard
Height or Spread 8–10ft (2.6–3.3m)
Flower Size 2½–2¾in (6–7cm)

Deciduous climber. Raised in 1952 by Magnus Johnson, Sweden. The semi-nodding blooms are rich carmine-red, slightly paler at the base and have a very pretty textured surface and ruffled margins. It normally bears four, occasionally five, broad tepals which taper to rounded tips. The stamens have lime green filaments merging to dark red at the tips of the anthers. Best suited for planting in the garden.

'Carnaby'   Early Large Flowered Group

Flowering Period Late spring to early summer *or* mid to late summer
Aspect Partial shade, to preserve colour
Pruning Light *or* Hard
Height or Spread 6–8ft (2–2.6m) *or* 4–5ft (1.3–1.6m)
Flower Size 4–6in (10–15cm)

Deciduous climber. Introduced from America in 1983 by Treasures of Tenbury, Worcestershire. The bright reddy-pink blooms have almost frilly paler pink margins. The six to eight tepals are broad, overlap and taper via crimped margins to pointed tips. The stamens have white filaments and wine red anthers. The depth of colour varies considerably from garden to garden, the aspect and light levels also have a marked effect, but not to its detriment. Hard pruning will keep the plant more compact but will delay the flowering period by a few weeks. Suitable for growing in containers or planting in the garden.

'Caroline'   Late Large Flowered Group

Flowering Period Mid summer to early autumn
Aspect Any
Pruning Hard
Height or Spread 6–8ft (2–2.6m)
Flower Size 4–5in (10–12.5cm)

Deciduous climber. Raised by Barry Fretwell, Devon, around 1990 and named after Lady Caroline Todhunter. 'Caroline' has the most delightful satin sheen across the pinky-white blooms with a hint of raspberry pink shading along the central bar and margins. The six broad tepals overlap and taper to pointed tips. The stamens have white filaments and butter yellow anthers. Gorgeous delicate colouring, and very free-flowering. The cut flowers keep well in water. Suitable for growing in containers or planting in the garden.

'Cassandra'   Heracleifolia Group

Flowering Period Mid summer to early autumn
Aspect Sunny to enhance perfume, and free draining
Pruning Hard
Height or Spread 2–3ft (60cm–1m)
Flower Size 1½in (4cm)

Herbaceous, deciduous, clump-forming, erect woody stems. A selection originating from Germany in the 1990s. The clusters of hyacinth-shaped flowers are a rich deep blue and each small bloom has strongly reflexed tips. The inside of the flowers is smooth along the bar whilst the textured margins have crimped edges. The reverse is silvery-blue near the flower stalk deepening to mid blue towards the tips. The stamens have white filaments and bright yellow anthers. The woody stems are self-supporting. It is very strongly scented, a delicious, 'heady' fragrance which, combined with the rich colouring, makes this our personal favourite of all the heracleifolias. Suitable for growing in containers or planting in the garden.

CASSIS 'Evipo020'   Florida Group

Flowering Period Early summer to early autumn +
Aspect Sheltered, free draining and winter protection
Pruning Hard
Height or Spread 6–8ft (2–2.6m)
Flower Size 3–4in (7.5–10cm)

Deciduous climber. Raised, and introduced in 2003, by Raymond Evison, Guernsey. These gorgeous blooms have a cream base which is heavily overlaid by blackcurrant-purple and have a stunning rosette-like centre of staminodes that are also mottled purple and cream. The six broad, outer tepals taper via slightly incurved margins to pointed tips. These are exceptionally pretty, yet quite unusual blooms. Best grown in containers (*see* Florida Group notes on page 130). PBR: Unlicensed propagation prohibited.

'Celebration'   Early Large Flowered Group

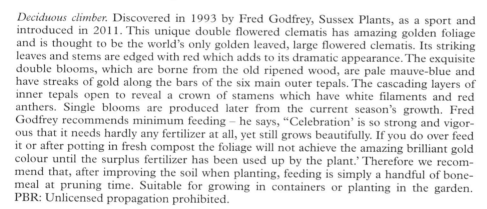

Flowering Period Late spring to early summer and late summer to mid autumn
Aspect Sunny, to enhance colour
Pruning Light
Height or Spread 6–8ft (2–2.6m)
Flower Size 5–6in (12.5–15cm)

Deciduous climber. Discovered in 1993 by Fred Godfrey, Sussex Plants, as a sport and introduced in 2011. This unique double flowered clematis has amazing golden foliage and is thought to be the world's only golden leaved, large flowered clematis. Its striking leaves and stems are edged with red which adds to its dramatic appearance. The exquisite double blooms, which are borne from the old ripened wood, are pale mauve-blue and have streaks of gold along the bars of the six main outer tepals. The cascading layers of inner tepals open to reveal a crown of stamens which have white filaments and red anthers. Single blooms are produced later from the current season's growth. Fred Godfrey recommends minimum feeding – he says, "Celebration' is so strong and vigorous that it needs hardly any fertilizer at all, yet still grows beautifully. If you do over feed it or after potting in fresh compost the foliage will not achieve the amazing brilliant gold colour until the surplus fertilizer has been used up by the plant.' Therefore we recommend that, after improving the soil when planting, feeding is simply a handful of bonemeal at pruning time. Suitable for growing in containers or planting in the garden. PBR: Unlicensed propagation prohibited.

CEZANNE 'Evipo023'   Early Large Flowered Group

Flowering Period Early summer to early autumn
Aspect Any
Pruning Hard
Height or Spread 3–4ft (1–1.3m)
Flower Size 4–5in (10–12.5cm)

Deciduous climber. Raised, and introduced in 2002, by Raymond Evison, Guernsey. The pretty light sky blue flowers have seven broad tepals that taper via undulating margins to pointed tips. The contrasting stamens have creamy-white filaments and pale yellow anthers. A really lovely colour combined with a compact and exceptionally free-flowering plant. Hard pruning will keep this very compact. Suitable for growing in containers or planting in the garden. PBR: Unlicensed propagation prohibited.

'Chalcedony' Early Large Flowered Group

Flowering Period Late spring to early summer and late summer to early autumn
Aspect Any
Pruning Light
Height or Spread 6–8ft (2–2.6m)
Flower Size 5–6in (12.5–15cm)

Deciduous climber. Raised by Strachan, 1984. This glorious clematis has very pale silvery-mauve-grey blooms which are fully double when borne from the old ripened wood and have many layers of broad tepals that taper to pointed tips via slightly wavy margins. The later blooms tend to be less full. The anthers are pale yellow. Suitable for growing in containers or planting in the garden.

CHANTILLY 'Evipo021' Early Large Flowered Group

Flowering Period Early to mid summer and early to mid autumn
Aspect Any
Pruning Hard
Height or Spread 3–4ft (1–1.3m)
Flower Size 4–6in (10–15cm)

Deciduous climber. Raised, and introduced in 2003, by Raymond Evison, Guernsey. CHANTILLY is the palest pink with a lovely deeper pink bar which becomes more pronounced as the bloom fades to white. The broad tepals overlap and taper to rounded tips making a very pretty bloom. Hard pruning will keep this very compact. Suitable for growing in containers or planting in the garden. PBR: Unlicensed propagation prohibited.

'Charissima' Early Large Flowered Group

Flowering Period Late spring to early summer and late summer to early autumn
Aspect Any
Pruning Light
Height or Spread 6–8ft (2–2.6m)
Flower Size 5–7in (12.5–18cm)

Deciduous climber. Raised by Walter Pennell, Lincoln, 1961. The pale satin pink blooms are heavily overlaid with deep cherry pink which is even darker along the bars, extreme margins and tips. The six to eight broad tepals have a delicately textured surface and taper via lightly crimped margins to pointed tips. The stamens are a good contrast with white filaments and dark purply-red anthers. Suitable for growing in containers or planting in the garden.

CHEVALIER 'Evipo040' Early Large Flowered Group

Flowering Period Late spring to early summer and late summer to early autumn
Aspect Any
Pruning Hard
Height or Spread 4–5ft (1.3–1.6m)
Flower Size 4–5in (10–12.5cm)

Deciduous climber. Raised, and introduced in 2009, by Raymond Evison, Guernsey. The velvety purple flowers mature to a mid blue and have a contrasting crown of pale yellow anthers. The broad tepals overlap and taper via undulating margins to pointed tips. Hard pruning will keep this very compact. Suitable for growing in containers or planting in the garden. PBR: Unlicensed propagation prohibited.

'Cicciolina'

Viticella Group

Flowering Period Mid summer to early autumn
Aspect Any
Pruning Hard
Height or Spread 8–10ft (2.6–3.3m)
Flower Size 1½–2in (4–5cm)

Deciduous climber. Raised, and introduced in 1995, by Hans Vermeulen, the Netherlands. These lovely deep carmine-red semi-nodding flowers have a greeny-white bar with carmine-red veins running through them. As the blooms mature the bars lose their green tinge and clear to creamy white. The four tepals have a deeply textured surface and very crimped margins that taper to blunt, gently recurved tips. The stamens have greenish-cream filaments and pale yellow anthers. Best suited for planting in the garden.

cirrhosa var. *balearica*

Cirrhosa Group

Flowering Period Mid winter to early spring
Aspect Sunny, to encourage flowering, sheltered and free draining
Pruning Tidy after flowering
Height or Spread 10–12ft (3.3–4m)
Flower Size 1½in (4cm)

Evergreen climber. Introduced from the Balearic Islands in 1783. The nodding bell-shaped flowers open yellowy-cream and mature to creamy-white, with a peppering of rusty-maroon freckles inside. The attractive foliage is finely cut, similar to a coarse parsley leaf, the young leaves are light bronze which mature to dark green. Best suited for planting in the garden.

Clair de Lune 'Evirin'

Early Large Flowered Group

Flowering Period Late spring to early summer and late summer to early autumn
Aspect Any
Pruning Light
Height or Spread 8–10ft (2.6–3.3m)
Flower Size 6–7in (15–17cm)

Deciduous climber. Raised, and introduced in 1997, by Raymond Evison, Guernsey, when it was called Blue Moon. The gorgeous white, star-shaped blooms have broad, ruffled margins of the palest lilac-blue. It normally bears eight tepals that overlap, have textured surfaces and a pretty satin sheen. The crown of stamens make an elegant contrast with white filaments and dark chocolate-red anthers. The cut blooms keep well in water. Suitable for growing in containers or planting in the garden. PBR: Unlicensed propagation prohibited.

'Columbine'

Atragene Group

Synonym: *C. alpina* 'Columbine'

Flowering Period Mid to late spring
Aspect Any, with free drainage
Pruning Tidy after flowering
Height or Spread 6–8ft (2–2.6m)
Flower Size 1½–2in (4–5cm)

Deciduous climber. Raised by Ernest Markham, East Grinstead, and exhibited by him in 1937. The light to mid-blue bell-shaped flowers change to powder blue as the blooms mature. The staminodes are white with pale yellow tips. The cut flowers keep well in water. Suitable for growing in containers or planting in the garden.

'Columella'
Atragene Group

Flowering Period Mid to late spring
Aspect Any, with free drainage
Pruning Tidy after flowering
Height or Spread 6–8ft (2–2.6m)
Flower Size 1½–2in (4–5cm)

Deciduous climber. Raised by Magnus Johnson, Sweden, in 1979. The outside of the nodding bell-shaped flowers is a deep rich pink, when first open it is so deep as to be almost red and each is outlined by a pale pink margin. The inside of the bells is pale pink. The cut flowers keep well in water. Suitable for growing in containers or planting in the garden.

'Comtesse de Bouchaud'
Late Large Flowered Group
AGM 1993

Flowering Period Early to late summer
Aspect Any
Pruning Hard
Height or Spread 6–8ft (2–2.6m)
Flower Size 4–5in (10–12.5cm)

Deciduous climber. Raised, and introduced in 1900, by Morel, France. The blooms are a lovely mid, slightly mauvy, pink and have a pretty satin sheen across their textured surface. The six tepals are broad and taper via undulating margins to blunt recurved tips. The stamens have white filaments and cream anthers. A lovely old cultivar that for years grew up our holly tree, until the rabbits ate la Comtesse! The cut flowers keep well in water. Suitable for growing in containers or planting in the garden.

CONFETTI 'Evipo036'
Viticella Group

Flowering Period Mid summer to mid autumn
Aspect Any
Pruning Hard
Height or Spread 6–8ft (2–2.6m)
Flower Size 1½–2½in (4–6cm)

Deciduous climber. Raised, and introduced in 2006, by Raymond Evison, Guernsey. The pretty little nodding bell-shaped flowers are a gorgeous mid-pink, upturn them to see the inside of their four deeply textured tepals that is a really rich pink. The crimped and recurved margins taper to pointed, reflexed tips. This looks fantastic on an arch where its charming flowers can be fully appreciated. The cut flowers keep well in water. Suitable for growing in containers or planting in the garden. PBR: Unlicensed propagation prohibited.

'Constance'
Atragene Group
AGM 2002

Flowering Period Mid to late spring
Aspect Any, with free drainage
Pruning Tidy after flowering
Height or Spread 6–8ft (2–2.6m)
Flower Size 1½–2in (4–5cm)

Deciduous climber. Raised by Mrs K. Goodman in 1986. The semi-double nodding, bell-shaped flowers are a wonderful deep reddish-pink and have a white inner skirt. The cut flowers keep well in water. Suitable for growing in containers or planting in the garden.

'Continuity'
Synonym: *C. chrysocoma* 'Continuity'

Montana Group

Flowering Period Late spring to autumn
Aspect Sheltered and free-draining
Pruning Tidy after main flowering
Height or Spread 15–20ft (5–6m)
Flower Size 2–3in (5–7.5cm)

Deciduous climber. Understood to have originally been from Jackman's of Woking. The four mid-pink tepals have a satin sheen across their textured surface and taper via crimped margins to rounded, gently recurved tips. The huge crown of stamens have white filaments with very long yellow anthers. The blooms have an unusually long flower stalk and produce their flowers over many weeks through the summer. The mid-green leaves have a bronze tint and are covered in fine hairs. The cut flowers keep well in water. Best suited for planting in the garden.

'Corona'

Early Large Flowered Group

Flowering Period Late spring to early summer and late summer to early autumn
Aspect Partial shade, to preserve colour
Pruning Light
Height or Spread 6–8ft (2–2.6m)
Flower Size 5–6in (12.5–15cm)

Deciduous climber. Raised in Sweden by John Gudmundsson, 1955. The eight broad, overlapping tepals are rich purply-cerise and have paler mauvy-cerise margins that taper to pointed, lightly reflexed tips. The stamens have white filaments and dark red anthers. Suitable for growing in containers or planting in the garden.

'Countess of Lovelace'

Early Large Flowered Group

Flowering Period Late spring to early summer and early autumn
Aspect Any
Pruning Light
Height or Spread 6–8ft (2–2.6m)
Flower Size 6–7in (15–17cm)

Deciduous climber. Raised, and introduced in 1872, by Jackman's of Woking. This lovely old mid bluey-mauve clematis is still much sought-after today. Its early blooms, produced from the old ripened wood, are double with six to eight broad, pointed outer tepals over which are several layers of shorter, narrower, pointed tepals. Later blooms from the current season's growth, are single; they have six open, gappy tepals of the same mid bluey-mauve. The stamens have white filaments and yellow anthers. We used to grow this with a flamboyant orangey-apricot climbing rose called WESTERLAND, they looked fabulous together. Suitable for growing in containers or planting in the garden.

'Cragside'

Atragene Group

Flowering Period Mid to late spring +
Aspect Any, with free drainage
Pruning Tidy after main flowering
Height or Spread 6–8ft (2–2.6m)
Flower Size 1½–2in (4–5cm)

Deciduous climber. Raised in 1995 by Ed Phillips and named after the National Trust property in Northumberland, his home county. The semi-double nodding, bell-shaped flowers are a gorgeous deep purply-rose, with slightly paler margins. The insides of the four main tepals are paler, with the narrower inner staminodes being white with purply-rose margins. A really lovely addition to this group of clematis. The cut flowers keep well in water. Suitable for growing in containers or planting in the garden.

'Crimson King'   Early Large Flowered Group
Trade designations: CRIMSON STAR in USA and RED COOLER in Japan

Flowering Period Late spring to early summer and early autumn
Aspect Any
Pruning Light
Height or Spread 8–10ft (2.6–3.3m)
Flower Size 5–7in (12.5–17cm)

Deciduous climber. Raised by Jackman's of Woking about 1915. The beautiful blooms are deep cerise pink with a slightly paler bar, they have a lightly textured surface and pretty satin sheen. The six or seven broad overlapping tepals taper via undulating margins to pointed tips. The stamens have creamy-white filaments and dark coffee coloured anthers. Occasionally the early blooms are semi-double. The cut blooms keep well in water. Best suited for planting in the garden.

crispa   Viorna Group

Flowering Period Early summer to early autumn
Aspect Any, with free drainage
Pruning Hard
Height or Spread 4–6ft (1.3–2m)
Flower Size 1in (2.5cm)

Herbaceous, deciduous climber. A native of south-eastern USA, first documented in 1726, whose common name is The Marsh Clematis. The colour of the nodding urn-shaped flowers varies from the palest mauvy-white to mid purplish-blue and deep rosy-mauve. The four 'ribbed' tepals taper via crimped margins to strongly recurved, pointed tips revealing the pale yellow anthers and the inner colouring, which is usually similar to the outer. The inside has a white bar and a deeply textured surface. The colour variation is due to this normally being propagated from seed. The stems of this herbaceous clematis will die down to ground level each winter with new shoots appearing in the spring from beneath the soil. Suitable for growing in containers or planting in the garden.

CRYSTAL FOUNTAIN 'Fairy Blue' 'Evipo038'   Early Large Flowered Group

Flowering Period Late spring to early summer and late summer to early autumn
Aspect Any
Pruning Light
Height or Spread 4–6ft (1.3–2m)
Flower Size 5–6in (12.5–15cm)

Deciduous climber. Originally named 'Fairy Blue' in Japan, it is understood to be a sport from 'H.F. Young' and was found by Hiroshi Hayakawa in 1994. The unusual lilac-blue flowers have dozens of paler, long narrow petaloid stamens which make a fountain-like centre that has, in turn, a pale green 'eye'. The eight broad outer tepals taper to pointed tips and those on the early flowers are often flushed with pink and have a greenish bar that clears as the bloom matures. Suitable for growing in containers or planting in the garden. PBR: Unlicensed propagation prohibited.

DANCING QUEEN 'Zodaque'   Early Large Flowered Group

Flowering Period Late spring to early summer and late summer to early autumn
Aspect Any
Pruning Light
Height or Spread 4–5ft (1.3–1.6m)
Flower Size 3–4in (7.5–10cm)

Deciduous climber. Raised in 1999 by Wim Snoeijer, The Netherlands. The double and semi-double blooms first open a pretty candy pink that gradually matures to pinky-white. The layers of broad tepals taper to blunt tips. The stamens have white filaments and cream anthers. Suitable for growing in containers or planting in the garden. PBR: Unlicensed propagation prohibited.

'Daniel Deronda'   Early Large Flowered Group
                                                                 AGM 1993

Flowering Period Late spring to early summer and late summer to early autumn
Aspect Any
Pruning Light
Height or Spread 8–10ft (2.6–3.3m)
Flower Size 6–8in (15–20cm)

Deciduous climber. Raised around 1880 by Charles Noble, Bagshot, and named after the last book written by George Eliot (1819–80). The large rich bluey-purple flowers have paler almost white bars overlaid with bluey-purple. The broad tepals overlap and taper to pointed tips. Occasionally the early flowers are semi-double. The crown of stamens have white filaments and pale yellow anthers. Best suited for planting in the garden.

'Dark Eyes'   Viticella Group

Flowering Period Mid summer to early autumn
Aspect Any
Pruning Hard
Height or Spread 6–8ft (2–2.6m)
Flower Size 2–3½in (5–9cm)

Deciduous climber. Raised in 2001 by Willem Straver, Germany. The four, sometimes five broad tepals are the deepest velvety purple, almost black on opening, their margins and blunt tips recurve. The dusting of creamy-white pollen on the reddy-purple anthers makes a lovely contrast against the dark tepals. The cut flowers keep well in water. Suitable for growing in containers or planting in the garden.

'Dawn'   Early Large Flowered Group

Flowering Period Late spring to early summer and late summer
Aspect Any
Pruning Light
Height or Spread 6–8ft (2–2.6m)
Flower Size 5–6in (12.5–15cm)

Deciduous climber. Raised in Sweden by Tage Lundell around 1960. One of the earliest large flowered clematis to bloom in the spring, it is very pale pearly-pink, the colour deepening through the veins and towards the deeper pearly-pink margins. Because of its early flowering nature the blooms occasionally have a green bar which disappears as they mature. The eight tepals are broad, overlapping and taper to rounded tips. The stamens have white filaments and dark wine-red anthers. Suitable for growing in containers or planting in the garden.

'Débutante'   Early Large Flowered Group

Flowering Period Early to mid summer and early autumn
Aspect Sheltered
Pruning Light
Height or Spread 6–8ft (2–2.6m)
Flower Size 4–6in (10–15cm)

Deciduous climber. Raised, and introduced in 1990, by Frank Watkinson, Doncaster. On first opening one can only describe the colour of the blooms as 'Shocking' pink. As the flowers age the colour softens to a deep mauvy-pink but retains a darker bar. The eight tepals are narrow where they join the stamens, which makes the bloom look rather gappy. The slightly wavy margins taper to pointed recurved tips. The stamens have white filaments and dark purply-red anthers. Suitable for growing in containers or planting in the garden.

'Denny's Double'   Early Large Flowered Group

Flowering Period Late spring to early summer and late summer to early autumn
Aspect Not north
Pruning Light
Height or Spread 6–8ft (2–2.6m)
Flower Size 4–5in (10–12.5cm)

Deciduous climber. Raised in 1977 by Vince and Sylvia Denny, Preston. The double flowers that are produced on both the old and new wood are a mid bluey-mauve and have the merest hint of pink when first open; they mature to a very pretty pale silvery-mauve. The eight outer tepals are broad and they, along with the further layers of narrower tepals, taper via slightly incurved margins to pointed tips. The stamens have white filaments and cream anthers. Suitable for growing in containers or planting in the garden.

Diamantina 'Evipo039'   Early Large Flowered Group

Flowering Period Early summer to early autumn
Aspect Not north
Pruning Light
Height or Spread 6–8ft (2–2.6m)
Flower Size 4–6in (10–15cm)

Deciduous climber. Raised, and introduced in 2010, by Raymond Evison, Guernsey. The many layers of tepals taper to pointed tips via lightly crimped and wavy margins and form a 'pom-pom'-like double flower. They are a mid bluish-purple with a hint of deep rose-pink in the centre. Suitable for growing in containers or planting in the garden. PBR: Unlicensed propagation prohibited.

'Diana' (Estonian pronunciation Deearna)   Late Large Flowered Group

Flowering Period Mid summer to early autumn
Aspect Any
Pruning Hard
Height or Spread 6–8ft (2–2.6m)
Flower Size 5–7in (12.5–18cm)

Deciduous climber. Raised by Uno and Aili Kivistik, Estonia, in 1985. The blooms have a white centre and broad margins of increasingly deeper shades of violet-blue, the outer edges are mid violet-blue. Their six broad overlapping tepals have a lightly textured surface and a pretty satin sheen. The huge crown of stamens have creamy-white filaments and pale yellow anthers. The stems and new leaves on the young growth are a very distinctive shiny bronze. An excellent plant for those gardeners who like large flowers but prefer to hard prune! Suitable for growing in containers or planting in the garden.

DIANA'S DELIGHT 'Evipo026' Early Large Flowered Group

Flowering Period Late spring to early summer and late summer to early autumn
Aspect Any
Pruning Hard
Height or Spread 4–6ft (1.3–2m)
Flower Size 6–7in (15–17cm)

Deciduous climber. Raised, and introduced in 2009, by Raymond Evison, Guernsey. The attractive blooms are pale mauvy-blue in the centre merging to deeper bars and margins. The six to eight broad tepals overlap and taper to rounded tips. They have a crown of contrasting stamens with white filaments and pale yellow anthers. Hard pruning will keep this very compact. Suitable for growing in containers or planting in the garden. PBR: Unlicensed propagation prohibited.

'Dominika' Late Large Flowered Group

Flowering Period Mid summer to early autumn
Aspect Any
Pruning Hard
Height or Spread 6–8ft (2–2.6m)
Flower Size 4–5in (10–12.5cm)

Deciduous climber. Raised in 1972 by Brother Stefan Franczak, Poland. The pretty light mauve-blue flowers have a paler mauvy-white bar. Depending upon the climatic conditions some years the colour seems more intense and the flowers can open with a rosy hue. The surface of the four to six broad tepals is deeply textured and their crimped margins incurve slightly and taper to pointed, gently recurved tips. The stamens have white filaments and pale yellow anthers. The cut blooms keep well in water. Suitable for growing in containers or planting in the garden.

'Dorothy Barbara' Montana Group

Flowering Period Late spring to early summer
Aspect Any
Pruning Tidy after flowering
Height or Spread 20–30ft (6–10m)
Flower Size 2–3in (5–7.5cm)

Deciduous climber. Selected by Mrs Val Le May Neville-Parry, Collection Holder of the Montana Group of Clematis in Hampshire and named in 2007 after the late Dorothy Brown, wife of Mike Brown a past chairman of the British Clematis Society. A lovely new montana whose pretty white flowers have four to six broad tepals with a textured surface, crimped margins and rounded tips that gently recurve. The stamens have greenish-cream filaments and primrose yellow anthers. If grown in a warm, sunny position you will find it has a slight fragrance. Best suited for planting in the garden.

'Dorothy Tolver' Early Large Flowered Group

Flowering Period Late spring to early summer and early to mid autumn
Aspect Any
Pruning Light
Height or Spread 8–10ft (2.6–3.3m)
Flower Size 5–6in (12.5–15cm)

Deciduous climber. Raised in 1987 by Jonathan Gooch and introduced by Thorncroft Clematis Nursery in 1993, it is named after Ruth's mother. The vibrant deep mauve-pink blooms have a satin sheen and lightly textured surface. Their six to eight broad, overlapping tepals have gently crimped margins tapering to pointed tips. The stamens have white filaments and bright yellow anthers. The early flowers are occasionally semi-double. In 2010 it began flowering at the end of April in its sheltered position in a south-east facing corner of our terrace where its rich colouring stands out well against the cream house walls. Suitable for growing in containers or planting in the garden.

'Dr Ruppel' (pronounce the U short, as in umbrella)   Early Large Flowered Group
Synonym: 'Doctor Ruppel'

Flowering Period Late spring to mid summer and early autumn
Aspect Any
Pruning Light
Height or Spread 8–10ft (2.6–3.3m)
Flower Size 5–7in (12.5–18cm)

Deciduous climber. Originally from Argentina, it was introduced in Britain in 1975 by Jim Fisk, Westleton. The early flowers have deep pinky-mauve tepals with pale mauve margins and a glorious rich cerise-pink bar, whereas the slightly smaller later flowers have a more intense colouring and lack the paler margins. The six to eight broad tepals taper to pointed tips via wavy, lightly crimped margins. The stamens have white filaments and coffee-coloured anthers. A flamboyant clematis that could stir any heart! The cut flowers keep well in water. Suitable for growing in containers or planting in the garden.

'Duchess of Albany'   Texensis Group
                                            Award of Merit 1897

Flowering Period Mid summer to mid autumn
Aspect Sunny, to encourage flowering
Pruning Hard
Height or Spread 8–10ft (2.6–3.3m)
Flower Size 2–2½in (5–6cm)

Semi-herbaceous, deciduous climber. Raised in 1890 by Arthur Jackman, Woking. The trumpet or tulip shaped flowers, which are upward or outward facing, are mid pink with paler candy-pink margins. The four (occasionally five or six) tepals taper to pointed, gently recurved tips that reveal the textured candy-pink inner surface which has a bright deep pink bar. A lovely old cultivar that blooms more freely if planted in a sunny position. The cut flowers keep well in water. Best suited for planting in the garden.

'Duchess of Edinburgh'   Early Large Flowered Group

Flowering Period Early to late summer
Aspect Any
Pruning Light
Height or Spread 6–8ft (2–2.6m)
Flower Size 4–4½in (10–11cm)

Deciduous climber. Raised, and introduced in 1874, by Jackman's of Woking. The double, almost dahlia-like blooms are made up of layer upon layer of white tepals, in the centre of which is a boss of cream stamens. A few inches below the bloom is a ring of leaflets on long stalks and above this, just underneath the bloom is a ring of what appear to be half leaf and half tepals, being a mixture of green and white. The growth tends to be on the weak side and is therefore best grown through another plant, perhaps a climbing rose such as 'Zéphirine Drouhin', to give the clematis some support. Best suited for planting in the garden.

'Durandii'
Synonym: *C.* × *durandii*

Diversifolia Group
AGM 1993

Flowering Period Early summer to early autumn
Aspect Any
Pruning Hard
Height or Spread 5–6ft (1.6–2m)
Flower Size 3–4in (7.5–10cm)

Semi-herbaceous, deciduous, non-clinging, semi-climber or scrambler. Raised, and introduced in 1870, by Durand Frères, Lyon, France, a cross between *C. integrifolia* and *C. lanuginosa.* Ruth's favourite herbaceous 'scrambler' has gorgeous rich indigo blue flowers that are semi-nodding bell-shaped when first opening, losing their bell-shape as they mature to 'open' outward or upward facing blooms. The four, five or occasionally six, broad tepals are narrow at base, their reverse has deeper colouring along the three prominent mid-ribs with rather paler violet-purple margins, the richly coloured surface is textured. As the flowers mature, the margins recurve slightly and twist as they taper to pointed, gently recurving tips. The stamens have creamy-white filaments, sometimes with a violet-blue 'wash' and pale yellow anthers. The cut flowers keep well in water. Suitable for growing in containers or planting in the garden.

'Dutch Sky'

Viticella Group

Flowering Period Mid summer to early autumn
Aspect Any
Pruning Hard
Height or Spread 6–8ft (2–2.6m)
Flower Size 3–4in (7.5–10cm)

Deciduous climber. Unfortunately the origin is unknown at present. The pretty outward facing flowers have bluey-white bars that merge to wide light blue margins. The five or six broad tepals overlap and taper via gently undulating margins to pointed slightly recurved tips. The stamens have greenish-cream filaments and butter yellow anthers. It is exceptionally free flowering. The cut flowers keep well in water. Suitable for growing in containers or planting in the garden.

'Early Sensation'

Forsteri Group

Flowering Period Mid to late spring
Aspect Sheltered, free-draining and winter protection
Pruning Tidy after flowering
Height or Spread 6ft (2m)
Flower Size 2in (5cm)

Evergreen climber. Raised by Graham Hutchins, Essex and introduced in 1995. The female flowers are greeny-cream when first open but quickly clear to pure white that has a pretty satin sheen. Usually bearing seven broad tepals that taper via lightly crimped margins to blunt tips. The evergreen foliage is a rich dark green. Best grown in containers (*see* Forsteri Group notes on page 130).

'Edith'   Early Large Flowered Group
                                                                                 AGM 1993

Flowering Period Late spring to early summer and late summer
Aspect Any
Pruning Light
Height or Spread 8–10ft (2.6–3.3m)
Flower Size 5–6in (12.5–15cm)

Deciduous climber. Raised by Raymond Evison and named after his mother. The cultivar was introduced in 1974 by Treasures of Tenbury. The white blooms have a lightly textured surface with a pretty satin sheen. The six to eight broad, overlapping tepals are rather gappy at their base and taper via gently recurved margins to blunt tips. The huge crown of contrasting stamens have white filaments and deep wine-red anthers. Best suited for planting in the garden.

'Edward Prichard'   Heracleifolia Group

Flowering Period Mid summer to early autumn
Aspect Sunny, to enhance perfume and free draining
Pruning Hard
Height or Spread 3–5ft (1–1.6m)
Flower Size 1½–2½in (4–6cm)

Herbaceous, deciduous, semi-erect woody stems. Raised before 1950 by Russell Prichard, Australia. The pretty scented, star-like flowers are borne in clusters, each flower has four narrow tepals that are white with mauve-pink tips. As the flowers mature the margins recurve. The stamens are cream and it has a delicious almond-like perfume. The woody stems relax and 'arch' as they grow over the course of the summer. This is one of those clematis that can prove to be a bit of a challenge; however, it is so lovely that we believe the challenge to be worthwhile. Suitable for growing in containers or planting in the garden.

'Eetika'   Viticella Group

Flowering Period Mid summer to mid autumn
Aspect Any
Pruning Hard
Height or Spread 6–8ft (2–2.6m)
Flower Size 3–4in (7.5–10cm)

Deciduous climber. Raised in 1984 by Uno and Aili Kivistik, Estonia. The glorious deep rose-pink flowers have a satin sheen and a deeply textured surface. The four to six tepals are narrow at the base, broad across the centre and taper via crimped margins to blunt tips. The contrasting stamens have white filaments and deep dusky red anthers. The cut flowers keep well in water. Suitable for growing in containers or planting in the garden.

'Ekstra'   Late Large Flowered Group

Flowering Period Mid summer to early autumn
Aspect Any
Pruning Hard
Height or Spread 4–6ft (1.3–2m)
Flower Size 4–5in (10–12.5cm)

Deciduous climber. Raised, and introduced in 1982, by Uno and Aili Kivistik, Estonia. The pale, almost luminous blue bar gradually deepens in colour towards the very ruffled margins which taper to pointed tips. The six or seven deeply textured tepals also bear a hint of rose-pink along the bar when first open. The contrasting stamens have white filaments and dark wine red anthers. The cut flowers keep well in water. Suitable for growing in containers or planting in the garden.

'Elizabeth'   Montana Group
                                                               AGM 1993

Flowering Period Late spring to early summer
Aspect Sunny, to enhance perfume
Pruning Tidy after flowering
Height or Spread 20–30ft (6–10m)
Flower Size 2½in (6cm)

Deciduous climber. Raised, and introduced in 1953, by Jackman's of Woking. The very pale
pink, powerfully vanilla-scented flowers have a pretty satin sheen. The four broad tepals
have textured surfaces and taper to blunt, slightly recurved tips. The stamens have white
filaments and pale yellow anthers. Best suited for planting in the garden.

'Elsa Späth'   Early Large Flowered Group

Flowering Period Early to mid summer and early autumn
Aspect Any
Pruning Light
Height or Spread 6–8ft (2–2.6m)
Flower Size 6–7in (15–17cm)

Deciduous climber. Raised in Germany by L. Späth in 1891. The deep violet-blue flowers mature to mid-blue and have
a very slightly paler bar. The six to eight broad, overlapping tepals have slightly undulating margins tapering to pointed
tips that occasionally have a hint of deep pink. The stamens have white filaments and wine red anthers. Suitable for
growing in containers or planting in the garden.

'Emilia Plater'   Viticella Group
                                                               BCS Certificate of Merit 2002

Flowering Period Mid summer to mid autumn
Aspect Any
Pruning Hard
Height or Spread 8–10ft (2.6–3.3m)
Flower Size 3–4in (7.5–10cm)

Deciduous climber. Raised in Poland by Brother Stefan Franczak in 1967 and named after
a young female officer killed during the 1830 Polish uprising against the Russian occupation, who became the symbol of women fighting for Poland's independence. The light
mauvy-blue tepals have a deeply textured surface which makes them appear almost
mottled; they also have bluey-violet shading along the central bar. The four (occasionally
five) broad tepals taper via crimped, undulating margins to lightly recurved tips. The
stamens have cream filaments and pale yellow anthers. Best suited for planting in the
garden.

EMPRESS 'Evipo011'   Early Large Flowered Group

Flowering Period Early summer to early autumn
Aspect Sunny, to enhance colour
Pruning Light
Height or Spread 5–6ft (1.6–2m)
Flower Size 4–5in (10–12.5cm)

Deciduous climber. Introduced in 2004 by Raymond Evison, Guernsey, as a sport from the hugely popular double pink
clematis JOSEPHINE, so EMPRESS therefore is very similar in colour, a light mauvy-pink with a deep pink bar. It has a
huge crown of spiky mauvy-pink petaloid stamens which makes a fountain-like centre to the bloom. Suitable for growing in containers or planting in the garden. PBR: Unlicensed propagation prohibited.

'Entel'   Viticella Group

Flowering Period Mid summer to early autumn
Aspect Any
Pruning Hard
Height or Spread 6–8ft (2–2.6m)
Flower Size 2–3½in (5–9cm)

Deciduous climber. Raised in 1984 by Uno and Aili Kivistik, Estonia. The semi-nodding flowers are the prettiest pale 'icing sugar' pink and have a satin sheen and a somewhat deeper pink bar along the centre of their deeply textured surface. Their four or five tepals have crimped margins that taper to pointed tips and the reverse has rose-pink bars. The stamens are cream. The cut flowers keep well in water. Suitable for growing in containers or planting in the garden.

'Ernest Markham'   Early Large Flowered Group
                                                                                    AGM 1993

Flowering Period Early to late summer *or* late summer to mid autumn
Aspect Sunny, to encourage flowering
Pruning Light *or* Hard
Height or Spread 10–12ft (3.3–4m) *or* 6–8ft (2–2.6m)
Flower Size 4–5in (10–12.5cm)

Deciduous climber. Named after William Robinson's head gardener at Gravetye Manor in East Sussex. The original plant was one of a batch of seedlings given to Jackman's of Woking who, following Ernest Markham's death in 1937, named the red seedling after him in recognition of his work with clematis. The six broad, light magenta-red tepals have a deeply textured surface, they overlap and taper to a recurved, pointed tip via crimped and somewhat reflexed margins that make the bloom appear round. The stamens are a rather dull beige and quite insignificant. Adapt your pruning technique to suit your growing conditions and to encourage a better display of flowers – in a mild climate or a sheltered garden, hard pruning will be necessary, but in colder districts, light pruning and a sunny position will improve performance. Suitable for growing in containers if hard pruned, or planting in the garden.

'Étoile Rose'   Viticella Group
Synonym: *C. texensis* 'Étoile Rose'

Flowering Period Early summer to early autumn
Aspect Any
Pruning Hard
Height or Spread 6–8ft (2–2.6m)
Flower Size 2–2½in (5–6cm)

Deciduous climber. Raised, and introduced in 1903, by Lemoine et fils, France, 'Étoile Rose' has, for the last century, been classed by most growers as a Texensis hybrid. However, in 1999 Wim Snoeijer classified this in the Viticella Group, with The International Clematis Register and Checklist 2002 confirming his opinion. The open semi-nodding bell-shaped flowers are pale dusky pink on the outside, but upturn them to appreciate the inside which is a rich deep pink, merging to light mauve-pink margins with a lovely satin sheen over their textured surface. The margins and tips recurve to reveal the wonderful colour beneath. The stamens have creamy-white filaments and pale yellow anthers. We grow two of these in our garden, one over an arch and the other clambering into a weeping cherry tree, where we can look up to fully appreciate their beauty. Unfortunately it can sometimes be prone to mildew; if this should happen, and you prefer not to use spray, try moving it to another position in the garden. Some years, one of ours gets an attack of mildew, the other never does! The cut flowers keep well in water. Suitable for growing in containers or planting in the garden.

'Étoile Violette'

Viticella Group
AGM 1993

Flowering Period Mid summer to early autumn
Aspect Any
Pruning Hard
Height or Spread 8–10ft (2.6–3.3m)
Flower Size 3–3½in (7.5–9cm)

Deciduous climber. Raised, and introduced in 1885, by Morel, France. The dark bluey-purple flowers have a textured surface, and a deep reddy-purple bar when first open. The blooms produce between four and six broad tepals which taper via undulating margins to pointed and strongly recurving tips. The stamens have white filaments and pale yellow anthers. We have grown 'Étoile Violette' through the bright yellow climbing rose CASINO which makes a glorious combination. Best suited for planting in the garden.

'Fascination'

Diversifolia Group

Flowering Period Early to late summer
Aspect Any
Pruning Hard
Height or Spread 4–5ft (1.3–1.6m)
Flower Size 1–1½in (2.5–4cm)

Semi-herbaceous, deciduous, non-clinging, semi-climber or scrambler. Raised in 1992 in The Netherlands by Wim Snoeijer. The gorgeous dark glossy violet-blue nodding bell-shaped flowers have four deeply ribbed tepals with pale violet margins which taper to pointed strongly recurved tips. The stamens have violet-white filaments and pale beige anthers. A super plant that should be more widely grown. The cut flowers keep well in water. Suitable for growing in containers or planting in the garden. PBR: Unlicensed propagation prohibited.

FILIGREE 'Evipo029'

Early Large Flowered Group

Flowering Period Late spring to late summer
Aspect Any
Pruning Hard
Height or Spread 1–3ft (30cm–1m)
Flower Size 3–4in (7.5–10cm)

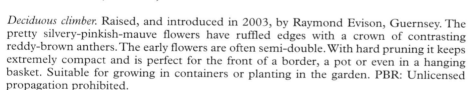

Deciduous climber. Raised, and introduced in 2003, by Raymond Evison, Guernsey. The pretty silvery-pinkish-mauve flowers have ruffled edges with a crown of contrasting reddy-brown anthers. The early flowers are often semi-double. With hard pruning it keeps extremely compact and is perfect for the front of a border, a pot or even in a hanging basket. Suitable for growing in containers or planting in the garden. PBR: Unlicensed propagation prohibited.

'Fireworks'　　　　　　　　　　　　　　Early Large Flowered Group

Flowering Period Late spring to early summer and early autumn
Aspect Any
Pruning Light
Height or Spread 8–10ft (2.6–3.3m)
Flower Size 6–8in (15–20cm)

Deciduous climber. Raised in 1980 by John Treasure, Tenbury Wells. This eye-catching clematis has bright cerise-pink bars merging to pinkish-mauve undulating margins. The six to eight tepals overlap at their base, then narrow towards pointed tips. The stamens have white filaments and wine-red anthers. The rather twisted shape and vibrant colouring of this lovely clematis make it very aptly named. Suitable for growing in containers or planting in the garden.

flammula　　　　　　　　　　　　　　　　Flammula Group

Flowering Period Late summer to mid autumn
Aspect Sunny, to enhance perfume and free draining
Pruning Hard
Height or Spread 8–10ft (2.6–3.3m)
Flower Size ¾–1in (2–2.5cm)

Deciduous, or semi-evergreen climber. When introduced to Britain from southern Europe in 1590 *C. flammula* was known as 'The Fragrant Virgin's Bower', a very appropriate name because of its clouds of small white star-like flowers that have a sweet hawthorn scent, reminiscent of country hedgerows in the spring. Each tiny flower bears four narrow, blunt-tipped tepals that recurve as the flowers mature. The stamens have white filaments and primrose yellow anthers which can give the satin-white tepals a creamy hue. Certainly one of the most strongly perfumed clematis, which fills its corner of the garden with scent on a late summer's evening. Gertrude Jekyll described *C. flammula* as one of the chief beauties of September and we would agree with her. Because *C. flammula* is difficult to propagate it is sometimes grown from seed, therefore the plants being sold can be somewhat variable. It is not always the easiest of clematis to establish in the garden, but it is so lovely that every effort should be made to try this one! Best suited for planting in the garden.

Fleuri 'Evipo042'　　　　　　　　　　　Early Large Flowered Group

Flowering Period Early summer to early autumn
Aspect Not north
Pruning Hard
Height or Spread 3–4ft (1–1.3m)
Flower Size 3–4in (7.5–10cm)

Deciduous climber. Raised, and introduced in 2008, by Raymond Evison, Guernsey. The pretty star-shaped blooms are a rich, velvety, bluey-purple with a bright purply-red bar and it has a beautiful satin sheen. The six tepals taper to pointed tips via slightly incurved and wavy margins. It has an elegant crown of stamens with deep mauve filaments and dark red anthers whose cream pollen adds to the starry effect. Hard pruning will keep this very compact. Suitable for growing in containers or planting in the garden. PBR: Unlicensed propagation prohibited.

florida   Florida Group

Flowering Period Early summer to early autumn
Aspect Sheltered, free draining and winter protection
Pruning Hard
Height or Spread 6–8ft (2–2.6m)
Flower Size 3–4in (7.5–10cm)

Deciduous climber. There is some confusion over the introduction of C. *florida* to Europe. It was almost certainly a native of Western and Southern China, being found by Augustine Henry (1857–1930) in about 1885 near Ichang in the province of Hupeh, and later by E.H. Wilson in the same area. There is also reference to Thunberg finding it growing in Japan and introducing it to Europe in 1776. The six (occasionally four) broad, overlapping, lightly textured creamy-white tepals have a distinctive pale green bar on their reverse. The purply-black stamens are fertile and will readily set seed. Best grown in containers (*see* Florida Group notes on page 130).

florida 'Alba Plena'   Florida Group
Synonyms: C. *florida* 'Plena' and C. *florida* var. *flore-pleno*

Flowering Period Early summer to early autumn +
Aspect Sheltered, free draining and winter protection
Pruning Hard
Height or Spread 6–8ft (2–2.6m)
Flower Size 3–4in (7.5–10cm)

Deciduous climber. Introduced from Japan around 1835, this extraordinarily pretty double flowered clematis has greeny-cream rosette-like blooms. The six broad, overlapping outer tepals taper to a point and have a green bar on their reverse; there are then many layers of staminodes forming the 'rosette'. Each flower can take two to three weeks to open fully, as each layer gradually unfurls; it takes equally long to die, losing the outer layer of tepals first, the flower gradually diminishing in size. Because of this slow process, each of these sterile flowers is displayed for several weeks. Best grown in containers (*see* Florida Group notes on page 130).

florida 'Sieboldiana'   Florida Group
Synonyms: C. *florida* 'Sieboldii', C. *florida* 'Bicolor' and C. *florida* var. *sieboldiana*

Flowering Period Early summer to early autumn +
Aspect Sheltered, free draining and winter protection
Pruning Hard
Height or Spread 6–8ft (2–2.6m)
Flower Size 3–4in (7.5–10cm)

Deciduous climber. Introduced to Europe from Japan in 1829 by Philipp F. von Siebold (1796–1866). The stunning blooms have an outer layer of five or six broad, overlapping creamy-white tepals that taper to pointed tips. In the centre is an enormous crown, about 2–2½in (5–6cm) across, made of many layers of rich purple staminodes. As the flowers die, they lose their outer tepals first, leaving their purple crowns on the stems for several more days. These unusual blooms are normally sterile but very occasionally a fertile flower will be produced and the blooms will sometimes revert, or partially revert to *florida* 'Alba Plena'. Best grown in containers (*see* Florida Group notes on page 130).

florida 'Thorncroft'   Florida Group

Flowering Period Early summer to early autumn
Aspect Sheltered, free draining and winter protection
Pruning Hard
Height or Spread 6–8ft (2–2.6m)
Flower Size 3–4in (7.5–10cm)

Deciduous climber. We (Thorncroft Clematis Nursery) first introduced this in 1994 as the then very rare *C. florida* which, at the time, was on the NCCPG (or Plant Heritage as it is now) 'Pink Sheet', meaning it was a very rare or endangered plant. But over the years others reproduced this from seeds with very variable results and often inferior blooms. We therefore decided to give a specific name to our selected form of this beautiful species in order to identify it from other poorer forms. The elegant satin-white flowers have a lightly textured surface with six broad, overlapping tepals tapering to pointed tips via undulating margins. The boss of contrasting purply-black stamens gradually deposits a fine powdering of purply-black pollen onto the white tepals which is most attractive and, being fertile, it produces interesting spiky seedheads. The reverse of the tepals is white with distinctive green bars. Best grown in containers (*see* Florida Group notes on page 130).

'Fond Memories'   Late Large Flowered Group

Flowering Period Early summer to early autumn +
Aspect Not north
Pruning Hard
Height or Spread 6–8ft (2–2.6m)
Flower Size 5–7in (12.5–17cm)

Deciduous climber. Raised by Geoffrey Tolver, Reymerston and introduced in 2004 by Thorncroft Clematis Nursery. The exceptionally pretty blooms are the palest pinky-white with an elegant satin sheen and its margins are outlined with deep rosy-lavender. Each tepal is beautifully marked with feathering radiating out from the central bar towards the margins. The six broad tepals overlap and taper to pointed, gently recurved, deep rosy-lavender coloured tips. The reverse is very deep rosy-lavender with slightly paler bars across which are three prominent deep rose coloured ribs. The stamens make an attractive contrast to the tepals having white filaments and dark purple anthers. Very free-flowering and extremely hardy – it can make a wonderful gift. Suitable for growing in containers or planting in the garden. PBR: Unlicensed propagation prohibited.

FOREVER FRIENDS 'Zofori'   Late Large Flowered Group
Plantarium, Boskoop Silver Medal 2009

Flowering Period Early summer to early autumn
Aspect Any
Pruning Hard
Height or Spread 6–8ft (2–2.6m)
Flower Size 3½–4in (9–10cm)

Deciduous climber. Raised, and introduced in 2009, by Wim Snoeijer, the Netherlands, and named in memory of his father. The four to six broad tepals have a textured surface and lightly crimped margins that taper to blunt tips. The very pretty satin-white flowers have contrasting stamens with creamy-white filaments and dusky red anthers. An exceptional new introduction that received much attention when exhibited at the Chelsea Flower Show for the first time in 2010. Suitable for growing in containers or planting in the garden. PBR: Unlicensed propagation prohibited.

forsteri Forsteri Group

Flowering Period Mid to late spring
Aspect Sheltered, free-draining and winter protection
Pruning Tidy after flowering
Height or Spread 8–10ft (2.6–3.3m)
Flower Size 1in (2.5cm)

Evergreen climber. A native of New Zealand whose semi-nodding, citrus scented flowers have six to eight tepals with pointed tips. They open a rather attractive greenish-cream and as they mature the green clears to leave a very pretty cream flower. Male and female flowers are borne on separate plants; however, it is the male form which is perhaps more commonly seen. The crown of stamens are primrose yellow and the foliage is evergreen. Best grown in containers (*see* Forsteri Group notes on page 130).

'Frances Rivis' Atragene Group
Synonym: *C. alpina* 'Frances Rivis', 'Francis Rives' AGM 1993

Flowering Period Mid to late spring
Aspect Any, with free drainage
Pruning Tidy after flowering
Height or Spread 6–8ft (2–2.6m)
Flower Size 2–2½in (5–6cm)

Deciduous climber. Raised from seed obtained by Mrs F.E. Rivis, Suffolk, around the mid 1900s. The deep, rich blue nodding bell-shaped flowers open to reveal a white inner skirt of petaloid stamens. The flowers can be an irregular shape with the tepals sometimes twisting and blunt in appearance, which adds to their charm. There are currently two completely different clematis being sold under the name of 'Frances Rivis', the one described here is most widely considered to be the original and therefore correct cultivar. The other 'Frances Rivis' is paler blue with very long, narrow tepals which we (and others) believe to be 'Blue Dancer'. The cut flowers keep well in water. Suitable for growing in containers or planting in the garden.

'Frankie' Atragene Group
AGM 2002

Flowering Period Mid to late spring +
Aspect Any, with free drainage
Pruning Tidy after main flowering
Height or Spread 6–8ft (2–2.6m)
Flower Size 1½–2in (4–5cm)

Deciduous climber. Raised by Frank Meechan and introduced in 1991. The deep mauve-blue nodding bell-shaped flowers pale slightly as they mature and open to reveal a creamy-white inner skirt that has blue shadings on the outer ring. As the blooms mature the edges of the four tepals recurve, but it remains a well-shaped, balanced flower produced in abundance in the spring, and which the plant continues to produce in lesser numbers throughout the summer. The cut flowers keep well in water. Suitable for growing in containers or planting in the garden.

FRANZISKA MARIA 'Evipo008'   Early Large Flowered Group

Flowering Period Late spring to early summer and late summer to early autumn
Aspect Any
Pruning Light
Height or Spread 6–8ft (2–2.6m)
Flower Size 4–6in (10–15cm)

Deciduous climber. Raised, and introduced in 2005, by Raymond Evison, Guernsey, and named after his youngest daughter. The beautifully shaped double blooms are a deep, slightly purply blue and have contrasting stamens with white filaments and yellow anthers. The later blooms are usually semi-double. Suitable for growing in containers or planting in the garden. PBR: Unlicensed propagation prohibited.

'Frau Mikiko'   Early Large Flowered Group

Flowering Period Late spring to early summer and late summer to early autumn
Aspect Any
Pruning Light
Height or Spread 6–8ft (2–2.6m)
Flower Size 5–7in (12.5–17cm)

Deciduous climber. Raised in 1993 by Kozo Sugimoto, Japan, and named after his wife. The young flowers first open rosy-purple but quickly mature to a glorious rich 'royal' blue. The six to eight broad tepals overlap and taper to pointed tips. The lovely contrasting stamens have deep mauve filaments and butter yellow anthers. Suitable for growing in containers or planting in the garden.

'Frau Susanne'   Early Large Flowered Group

Flowering Period Late spring to early summer and late summer to early autumn
Aspect Any
Pruning Light
Height or Spread 6–8ft (2–2.6m)
Flower Size 5–7in (12.5–17cm)

Deciduous climber. Raised in 1996 by Mrs Masako Takeuchi, Japan and introduced to UK in 2005 by Thorncroft Clematis Nursery. These beautiful star-like blooms have a wonderful satin sheen over the surface of their eight tepals. The base colour of creamy-white has deep purply-pink radiating through the veins towards the wavy margins and pointed tips. The stamens have cream filaments with butter yellow anthers. Suitable for growing in containers or planting in the garden.

'Freckles'   Cirrhosa Group
Synonym: *C. cirrhosa* var. *purpurascens* 'Freckles'   AGM 1993

Flowering Period Mid autumn to late winter
Aspect Sunny, to encourage flowering, sheltered and free draining
Pruning Tidy after flowering
Height or Spread 12–15ft (4–5m)
Flower Size 1½–2in (4–5cm)

Evergreen climber. Selected from seed collected in the Balearic Islands and introduced in 1989 by Raymond Evison, Guernsey. The nodding bell-shaped flowers are an almost translucent pale cream with the inside very heavily freckled with rusty maroon. The stamens are pale greenish-yellow. The small glossy leaves mature mid to dark green and have serrated margins. Best suited for planting in the garden.

'Freda'

Montana Group
AGM 1993

Flowering Period Late spring to early summer
Aspect Any
Pruning Tidy after flowering
Height or Spread 15+ft (5+m)
Flower Size 2–2½in (5–6cm)

Deciduous climber. Raised by Mrs Freda Deacon, Woodbridge, Suffolk, and introduced by Jim Fisk in 1985. The deep cherry-pink blooms have paler pink bars and almost red margins that taper to rounded tips. Her four broad tepals have a satin sheen across their lightly textured surface which is enhanced by a boss of yellow anthers. The foliage is the most gorgeous bronze colour when the leaves first open and matures to purply-bronze as the season progresses. 'Freda' is not as rampant as most Montana Group cultivars, she is much more 'lady-like' and is the only one in this group that we could safely recommend to grow through a 'substantial' climbing rose, such as 'Kiftsgate' or 'Rambling Rector'. Best suited for planting in the garden.

'Fryderyk Chopin'

Early Large Flowered Group

Flowering Period Early summer to early autumn
Aspect Any
Pruning Light
Height or Spread 6–8ft (2–2.6m)
Flower Size 4–6in (10–15cm)

Deciduous climber. Raised in Poland by Brother Stefan Franczak and named after the Polish composer of music. The beautiful mid mauve-blue star-shaped flowers have a deeply textured surface and the most amazing crimped and 'frilly' margins. As the blooms mature the colour pales to a pretty light mauve-blue. The six tepals are broad, overlapping at the base and taper to very pointed, slightly recurved tips. The stamens have white filaments and cream anthers. Suitable for growing in containers or planting in the garden.

'Fujimusume'

Early Large Flowered Group
AGM 2002

Flowering Period Late spring to early summer and late summer to early autumn
Aspect Any
Pruning Light
Height or Spread 6–8ft (2–2.6m)
Flower Size 4–5in (10–12.5cm)

Deciduous climber. Raised in 1952 by Seejuuroo Arai, Japan. Blue clematis normally have an element of pink or mauve in their colouring but 'Fujimusume' is the clearest, truest mid blue clematis available today. It normally has six broad overlapping tepals which taper along gently undulating margins to pointed tips. The contrasting stamens have white filaments and pale yellow anthers. 'Fujimusume' is an excellent clematis to grow in semi-shade, but wherever you grow it, it is quite lovely! The cut blooms keep well in water. Suitable for growing in containers or planting in the garden.

'Fukuzono'   Diversifolia Group
Synonym: 'Fujizono'

Flowering Period Early summer to early autumn
Aspect Any
Pruning Hard
Height or Spread 3–5ft (1–1.6m)
Flower Size 2–3in (5–7.5cm)

Semi-herbaceous, deciduous, non-clinging, semi-climber or scrambler. Raised in 1997 by Tetsuya Hirota, Japan, its name means 'Garden of Happiness' and indeed this lovely clematis does bring pleasure to those who stop to admire it. The blooms of 'Fukuzono' begin semi-nodding, maturing to become more open, outward or upward facing. They have four to six tepals, the reverse of which has deep lavender bars with dark purple mid-ribs and paler bluish-lavender margins, the inside colouring is light bluish-lavender with a deeper bar. The undulating margins twist as they taper to pointed, gently recurved tips. The stamens have white filaments flushed with lavender and pale yellow anthers. The cut flowers keep well in water. Suitable for growing in containers or planting in the garden.

fusca   Viorna Group

Flowering Period Mid summer to early autumn
Aspect Sunny, to encourage flowering
Pruning Hard
Height or Spread 6–8ft (2–2.6m)
Flower Size 1in (2.5cm)

Semi-herbaceous, deciduous climber. A native of northern and northeastern China, Mongolia, eastern Russia, Korea and Japan, originally introduced to Britain in 1860. The nodding urn-shaped flowers are borne singly from the leaf axils, their four thick, ribbed tepals are dusky purple which is disguised by a covering of reddish-brown hairs. The tepals taper to pointed, slightly recurved tips which reveals the pale greenish-cream inside, it also has very attractive seed heads. This delightful and unusual clematis is not the one to grow if you want a stunning visual impact. We grow *C. fusca* in a pot on our terrace where it can be appreciated at close quarters; it's certainly a talking-point! The cut flowers keep well in water. Suitable for growing in containers or planting in the garden.

fusca **Lansdown Brown seedlings**   Viorna Group

Flowering Period Late spring to mid summer
Aspect Sunny, to encourage flowering
Pruning Hard
Height or Spread 1–2ft (30–60cm)
Flower Size 1in (2.5cm)

Herbaceous, deciduous, semi-erect stems. These very short 'dwarf' growing *fusca*-like clematis originated from seed of a clematis called 'Lansdown Brown' in the garden of Gill Brown, a British Clematis Society member. However, the original plant was almost impossible to propagate vegetatively and therefore has only been propagated from seed, making it incorrect to use the original cultivar name. At present it seems that there is no 'correct' way to name this seedling form. We have grown this in a pot for several years and each spring, when it bursts into bloom, it gives us enormous pleasure to see its strange mauve-brown, hairy, nodding, urn-shaped flowers – it is one of nature's little treasures! Suitable for growing in containers or planting in the garden.

'Fuyu-no-tabi'   Early Large Flowered Group

Flowering Period Late spring to early summer and late summer to early autumn
Aspect Any
Pruning Light
Height or Spread 6–8ft (2–2.6m)
Flower Size 6–7in (15–17cm)

Deciduous climber. Raised in 1994 by Mrs Masako Takeuchi, Japan and introduced to UK in 2005 by Thorncroft Clematis Nursery. The beautiful white flowers have an elegant satin sheen across their lightly textured surface. Their six to eight broad tepals overlap and taper via delicately crimped, undulating margins to blunt tips. The crown of contrasting stamens have white filaments and reddy-brown anthers. Suitable for growing in containers or planting in the garden.

GALORE 'Evipo032'   Viticella Group
Synonym: VESUVIUS

Flowering Period Early summer to early autumn
Aspect Not north
Pruning Hard
Height or Spread 8–10ft (2.6–3.3m)
Flower Size 2–3in (5–7.5cm)

Deciduous climber. Raised, and introduced in 2006, by Raymond Evison, Guernsey. The dusky amethyst-purple flowers have six broad tepals that are narrow at the base and have a deeply textured surface and recurving, somewhat twisted margins that taper to pointed, slightly recurved tips. The blooms twist and turn in a very attractive manner and are offset by butter yellow anthers that make a lovely contrast. Suitable for growing in containers or planting in the garden. PBR: Unlicensed propagation prohibited.

'General Sikorski'   Early Large Flowered Group

Flowering Period Early summer to early autumn
Aspect Any
Pruning Light
Height or Spread 6–8ft (2–2.6m)
Flower Size 5–6in (12.5–15cm)

Deciduous climber. 'General Sikorski' has a chequered history – it is widely believed to be the cultivar originally named 'Jadwiga Teresa' that was raised by Brother Stefan Franczak, Poland in 1965. It was renamed by Władysław Noll in honour of the Polish general W.E. Sikorski (1881–1943) who became Prime Minister of the Polish government in exile during the Second World War. The lovely mid mauvy-blue flowers have a small rose pink bar extending from the base of each tepal to about halfway along. It normally bears six broad tepals that taper to rounded tips via lightly crimped margins. The contrasting stamens have greeny-cream filaments and butter yellow anthers. Suitable for growing in containers or planting in the garden.

gentianoides   Forsteri Group

Flowering Period Early to late spring
Aspect Sunny, to enhance perfume, sheltered and free-draining
Pruning Tidy after flowering
Height or Spread 1–2ft (30–60cm)
Flower Size 1–1½in (2.5–4cm)

Semi-evergreen herbaceous sub-shrub, produces runners beneath the soil. A native of Tasmania that has male and female flowers on separate plants. The small white, slightly scented, star-shaped flowers have between four and eight narrow tepals. The young foliage is purply-bronze, and in mild or protected situations it remains evergreen. Suitable for growing in containers or planting in the garden.

'Geoffrey Tolver'   Diversifolia Group

Flowering Period Early summer to early autumn
Aspect Not north
Pruning Hard
Height or Spread 5–7ft (1.6–2.3m)
Flower Size 2½–3½in (6–9cm)

Semi-herbaceous, deciduous, non-clinging, semi-climber or scrambler. Raised by Geoffrey Tolver, Ruth's father, who helped establish Thorncroft Clematis Nursery. We are delighted that Mike Brown, a very knowledgeable clematarian and Holder of the National Collection of Herbaceous Clematis, suggested that this should be named in his honour. The glorious deep bluey-purple flowers have a richer, brighter purple bar. They bear four to six broad tepals that are narrow at base and taper via slightly wavy margins to blunt tips. The stamens have white filaments and dark dusky purple anthers. Suitable for growing in containers or planting in the garden.

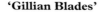

'Giant Star'   Montana Group

Flowering Period Late spring to early summer
Aspect Any
Pruning Tidy after flowering
Height or Spread 15–20ft (5–6m)
Flower Size 3–4in (7.5–10cm)

Deciduous climber. Raised in New Zealand by Robin Mitchell in 1995, 'Giant Star' is said by Val Le May Neville-Parry, the Holder of the National Collection of Clematis Montana Group, to be 'easily the best of the New Zealand (Montana) introductions'. These pretty mid-pink, lightly scented flowers have paler, almost white margins. Opening somewhat cup-shaped, the four broad tepals have crimped, almost frilly and slightly undulating margins that gently recurve as the flowers mature, and taper to blunt tips. The stamens have white filaments and butter yellow anthers. Best suited for planting in the garden.

'Gillian Blades'   Early Large Flowered Group
                                                                        AGM 1993

Flowering Period Late spring to early summer and early autumn
Aspect Any
Pruning Light
Height or Spread 6–8ft (2–2.6m)
Flower Size 6–7in (15–17cm)

Deciduous climber. Raised by Jim Fisk, Westleton, and named after one of his secretaries, introduced in 1975. This glorious, almost frilly looking star-shaped bloom has six to eight broad, lightly textured, overlapping tepals that are pure white with very pale bluey-mauve ruffled margins that taper to pointed tips. The stamens have white filaments and primrose yellow anthers. Suitable for growing in containers or planting in the garden.

'Gipsy Queen'   Late Large Flowered Group
                                                    AGM 1993

Flowering Period Mid summer to early autumn
Aspect Not north
Pruning Hard
Height or Spread 10–12ft (3.3–4m)
Flower Size 5–5½in (12.5–13cm)

Deciduous climber. Raised, and introduced in 1877, by Thomas Cripps of Tunbridge Wells. The flowers open a very dark purple and mature to bluey-purple with a velvety reddish-purple bar. The four to six broad tepals are narrow at base, giving a somewhat gappy appearance, and their lightly crimped margins taper to blunt tips. The stamens have mauve-white filaments and dark red anthers. Best suited for planting in the garden.

'Gojōgawa'   Early Large Flowered Group

Flowering Period Late spring to early summer and late summer to early autumn
Aspect Any
Pruning Light
Height or Spread 6–8ft (2–2.6m)
Flower Size 5–7in (12.5–17cm)

Deciduous climber. Raised in 2001 by Mr Hiroshi Takeuchi, Japan, and introduced to the UK by Thorncroft Clematis Nursery in 2009. This lovely clematis produces both semi-double and single blooms in spring and early summer that are pale to light mauve-pink merging out to deep mauve-pink margins and tips, with this deeper shade running through veins along the bars. The single flowers normally have eight broad and overlapping tepals which taper to pointed tips. The textured surface of the tepals has a satin sheen and the margins are slightly wavy. The stamens have white filaments and primrose yellow anthers. Suitable for growing in containers or planting in the garden.

GOLDEN TIARA 'Kugotia'   Tangutica Group
                BCS Certificate of Merit 1999 and AGM 2002

Flowering Period Mid summer to mid autumn
Aspect Any, and free-draining
Pruning Hard
Height or Spread 6–8ft (2–2.6m)
Flower Size 2–3in (5–7.5cm)

Deciduous climber. Raised by H.J.M. Kuif, The Netherlands, and introduced in 1994. The bright golden-yellow nodding lantern-shaped flowers quickly open out flat, almost slightly reflexed, to reveal the lovely contrasting stamens that have deep reddish-purple filaments and beige anthers. The four waxy, textured tepals taper to pointed, recurved tips. A lovely display of silky seedheads continues the interest right through the winter making this a good candidate for the smaller garden. Some people have suggested that there is a slight fragrance, but we have not noticed it. The cut flowers and seed heads keep well in water. Suitable for growing in containers or planting in the garden. PBR: Unlicensed propagation prohibited.

'Grace'   Tangutica Group

Flowering Period Early to mid autumn
Aspect Any, and free-draining
Pruning Hard
Height or Spread 8–10ft (2.6–3.3m)
Flower Size 1½–2in (4–5cm)

Deciduous climber. Raised, and introduced in 1939, by Dr Frank Skinner, Canada. The small, outward facing creamy-white flowers have a pretty crown of contrasting stamens with cream filaments and deep beige-pink anthers. The texture of the four broad tepals is like tissue paper and they taper to pointed, recurved tips. Best suited for planting in the garden.

'Gravetye Beauty' (pronounced Grave–tie)   Texensis Group

Flowering Period Mid summer to mid autumn
Aspect Sunny, to encourage flowering
Pruning Hard
Height or Spread 8–10ft (2.6–3.3m)
Flower Size 2–2½in (5–6cm)

Semi-herbaceous, deciduous climber. Raised by Morel in France, then named and introduced by William Robinson, Gravetye Manor, East Sussex, in 1914. The outward or upward facing, trumpet or tulip shaped flowers are a lovely deep, rich red on the outside with paler mauve-pink margins. Their four (sometimes five or six) tepals taper to pointed reflexed tips, and open out as they mature to reveal the textured inner surface which has a bright crimson bar merging to rich purply-red margins. The stamens have creamy-white filaments and deep purply-red anthers. The cut flowers keep well in water. Best suited for planting in the garden.

'Guernsey Cream'   Early Large Flowered Group

Flowering Period Late spring to early summer and late summer to early autumn
Aspect Partial shade, to preserve colour
Pruning Light
Height or Spread 6–8ft (2–2.6m)
Flower Size 5–6in (12.5–15cm)

Deciduous climber. Raised, and introduced in 1989, by Raymond Evison, Guernsey. When first open the blooms are yellowy-cream with a deeper bar but if the spring has been dull and cold you may notice the bar is pale green. As the light levels increase and the blooms mature, the colour will change to cream with a primrose-yellow bar. The six to eight broad, overlapping tepals taper via undulating margins to blunt tips. The stamens have white filaments and yellow anthers. It really benefits from dead-heading as the blooms die disgracefully. Suitable for growing in containers or planting in the garden.

'H.F. Young'   Early Large Flowered Group

Flowering Period Late spring to early summer and early autumn
Aspect Any
Pruning Light
Height or Spread 8–10ft (2.6–3.3m)
Flower Size 6–7in (15–17cm)

Deciduous climber. Raised by Walter Pennell, Lincoln, in 1954. The slightly mauvy mid, 'Wedgwood' blue flowers have six to eight broad, overlapping tepals which taper along slightly wavy margins to pointed tips. The newly opening blooms can have a soft pinkish bar that quickly fades as the flowers open fully. The stamens have white filaments and pale yellow anthers. 'H.F. Young' is a spectacular sight in late spring and early summer, producing blooms from soil level right to the top of the plant. Suitable for growing in containers or planting in the garden.

'Hagley Hybrid'
Trade designation: PINK CHIFFON in USA

Late Large Flowered Group

Flowering Period Early summer to early autumn
Aspect Partial shade, to preserve colour
Pruning Hard
Height or Spread 6–8ft (2–2.6m)
Flower Size 5–6in (12.5–15cm)

Deciduous climber. Raised by Percy Picton when he was head gardener at Hagley Hall and introduced by Jim Fisk in 1956. The star-shaped blooms open a pretty shell pink which matures to pale mauve-pink. The six broad tepals have a deeply textured surface with a satin sheen and their crimped margins incurve slightly as they taper to pointed tips. The stamens have white filaments that merge to very dark purplish-red anthers. Perfect to brighten a shady situation. Suitable for growing in containers or planting in the garden.

'Hakuookan'

Early Large Flowered Group

Flowering Period Late spring to early summer and early autumn
Aspect Any
Pruning Light
Height or Spread 6–8ft (2–2.6m)
Flower Size 6–7in (15–17cm)

Deciduous climber. Raised in Japan by Yoshio Kubota and introduced to the UK by Jim Fisk in 1971. Its name means 'The White Royal Crown', referring to the huge crown of stamens which have white filaments and primrose-yellow anthers that make a fantastic contrast to the rich 'royal' purple tepals. The seven or eight broad, overlapping tepals, that sometimes have a paler bar overlaid by dark purple veins, taper via slightly incurved and wavy margins to pointed tips. The early blooms are occasionally semi-double. Suitable for growing in containers or planting in the garden.

'Hakuree'

Integrifolia Group

Flowering Period Early summer to early autumn
Aspect Any
Pruning Hard
Height or Spread 2–3ft (60cm–1m)
Flower Size 1¾–2in (4.5–5cm)

Herbaceous, deciduous, clump-forming, semi-erect or scrambling stems. Raised in 1991 by Hiroshi Hayakawa, Japan. The outside of the nodding bell-shaped flowers have four long slightly bluish-white tepals which have quite prominent ribs down the centre. The tepals twist as they taper via lightly crimped margins to very pointed, recurved tips, thus revealing the inner surface which has a pale mauve-blue bar radiating out to bluish-white margins. The tips of the bright yellow anthers are just visible. The flowers have a delicate hawthorn-like scent. Suitable for growing in containers or planting in the garden.

'Hanaguruma'

Early Large Flowered Group

Flowering Period Late spring to early summer and late summer to early autumn
Aspect Any
Pruning Light
Height or Spread 6–8ft (2–2.6m)
Flower Size 4–5in (10–12.5cm)

Deciduous climber. Raised in 1985 by Goroo Joosha, Japan. The wonderfully rich mid-pink blooms have six to eight broad tepals with a lightly textured surface, which overlap and taper to blunt tips. The stamens have white filaments and pale yellow anthers. Suitable for growing in containers or planting in the garden.

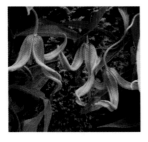

'Hanajima'   Integrifolia Group

Flowering Period Early summer to early autumn
Aspect Any
Pruning Hard
Height or Spread 1–2ft (30–60cm)
Flower Size 1½in (4cm)

Herbaceous, deciduous, clump-forming, semi-erect or scrambling stems. Raised in Japan by Kazushige Ozawa. The nodding bell-shaped flowers have four long, narrow, twisted tepals that taper to very pointed recurved tips that flare out as the flowers mature. The outer colour near the flower stalk is very deep mauve-pink which gradually pales towards the tips, and the margins are light pink. The inner colouring is very similar to the outside, again with paler margins. The tips of the yellow anthers are just visible. The cut flowers keep well in water. Suitable for growing in containers or planting in the garden.

'Hania'   Early Large Flowered Group

Flowering Period Late spring to early autumn
Aspect Partial shade, to preserve colour
Pruning Light
Height or Spread 6–8ft (2–2.6m)
Flower Size 5–6in (12.5–15cm)

Deciduous climber. Raised by Szczepan Marczyński, Poland, in 1993 and named after his mother. The six to eight broad tepals have vivid velvety purply-red bars merging to light pinky-mauve wavy margins which taper to pointed tips. As the blooms mature their margins recurve slightly. The stamens have white filaments and golden yellow anthers. Suitable for growing in containers or planting in the garden.

'Hanna'   Viticella Group
Synonym: *C. viticella* 'Hanna'

Flowering Period Mid summer to early autumn
Aspect Any
Pruning Hard
Height or Spread 6–8ft (2–2.6m)
Flower Size 1½–2½in (4–6cm)

Deciduous climber. Raised in Sweden by Sixten Widberg around 1990. The pretty nodding bell-shaped flowers have four tepals that are pale violet-blue, with three darker, very distinct ribs running down the middle of each. The crimped and wavy margins taper to pointed recurved tips. The inside is a slightly deeper shade than the outside and has a deeply textured surface. The anthers are butter yellow. Suitable for growing in containers or planting in the garden.

'Haru Ichiban'   Early Large Flowered Group

Flowering Period Late spring to early summer and late summer to early autumn
Aspect Any
Pruning Light
Height or Spread 6–8ft (2–2.6m)
Flower Size 4–6in (10–15cm)

Deciduous climber. Raised in 1992 by Mrs Masako Takeuchi, Japan, and introduced to the UK in 2005 by Thorncroft Clematis Nursery. The very deep cerise, almost red margins merge to lighter bars where the cerise overlays pale mauve giving a slightly mottled appearance. The eight tepals overlap and taper via gently incurving margins to pointed tips, giving each tepal on the young flowers a boat shape. As the blooms mature they flatten out. The stamens have white filaments and dark red anthers. These beautiful blooms keep well in water. Suitable for growing in containers or planting in the garden.

'Helen Cropper'   Early Large Flowered Group

Flowering Period Late spring to early summer and early autumn
Aspect Any
Pruning Light
Height or Spread 6–8ft (2–2.6m)
Flower Size 6–7in (15–17cm)

Deciduous climber. Raised in 1977 by Vince and Sylvia Denny, Preston, and named after their granddaughter. The very pale pink background is heavily overlaid with deep, dusky mauve-pink, deepening towards the margins and giving an elegant mottled appearance. The six to eight broad, overlapping tepals taper to blunt tips via lightly crimped, wavy margins. The reverse has three distinctive deep red ribs along the centre of each tepal. The stamens, which have white filaments merging to deep red anthers, add to the beauty of this clematis that occasionally produces semi-double blooms early in the season. Suitable for growing in containers or planting in the garden.

'Helios'   Tangutica Group

Flowering Period Early summer to early autumn *or* mid summer to mid autumn
Aspect Any, and free-draining
Pruning Light *or* Hard
Height or Spread 10ft+ (3.3m+) *or* 4–6ft (1.3–2m)
Flower Size 1½–2½in (4–6cm)

Deciduous climber. Raised at the Proefstation voor de Boomkwekerij, the Netherlands and introduced in 1988. We love this pretty clematis with its bright lemon-yellow nodding flowers whose four tepals open out flat and have pointed and somewhat twisted, swept back tips that reminds one of the roofs of oriental pagodas. The stamens have mid purplish-brown filaments and light yellow anthers. This also has a good display of silky seedheads for winter interest. Hard pruning will keep the plant more compact but will delay the flowering period by a few weeks. We have seen a magnificent specimen at the RHS garden at Wisley that was almost to the guttering of a two storey building, having only been lightly pruned. The cut flowers and seed heads keep well in water. Suitable for growing in containers if hard pruned, or planting in the garden.

'Helsingborg'   Atragene Group
                                                          AGM 1993

Flowering Period Mid to late spring
Aspect Any, with free drainage
Pruning Tidy after flowering
Height or Spread 6–8ft (2–2.6m)
Flower Size 1½–2in (4–5cm)

Deciduous climber. Raised about 1970 by Tage Lundell in Sweden. The flower buds are a deep rosy-purple which changes to deep bluey-purple as the blooms open. The four tepals of the nodding bell-shaped flowers have paler, slightly twisted margins and the staminodes are pale dusky purple, as is the inside of the tepals. The cut flowers keep well in water. Suitable for growing in containers or planting in the garden.

'Hendersonii'   Diversifolia Group
Synonym: *C.* × *diversifolia* 'Hendersonii'

Flowering Period Early summer to early autumn
Aspect Any
Pruning Hard
Height or Spread 6–8ft (2–2.6m)
Flower Size 2–3in (5–7.5cm)

Semi-herbaceous, deciduous, non-clinging, semi-climber or scrambler. Raised by J.A. Henderson and Co., Pine-Apple Nursery, St. John's Wood, London in 1835, a cross between *C. integrifolia* and *C. viticella*, it is one of the oldest clematis hybrids and was originally known as *C. hendersoni.* The dark purply-blue nodding bell-shaped flowers have four slightly twisted tepals, ribbed on the outside and a deeply textured surface on the inside. The margins which are slightly paler on the outside are crimped and wavy, and taper to pointed recurved tips. The stamens have creamy-white filaments (almost unseen due to the bell shape) and pale yellow anthers. We have a fine example of this clematis that has been in our garden for fifteen years or more – it is trained up stout canes into the branches and silver leaves of *Pyrus salicifolia* 'Pendula' (the ornamental pear), where it looks fantastic. The cut flowers keep well in water. Suitable for growing in containers or planting in the garden.

'Hendersonii'   Integrifolia Group

Flowering Period Mid to late summer
Aspect Any
Pruning Hard
Height or Spread 2–3ft (60cm–1m)
Flower Size 2½in (6cm)

Herbaceous, deciduous, clump-forming, semi-erect or scrambling stems. Of unknown origin. The deep blue nodding bell-shaped flowers have four long narrow, twisted tepals. The outside has three prominent dark blue ribs running down the centre of each tepal with slightly paler mauvy-blue towards their edges. The crimped margins twist as they taper to pointed recurved tips. The inside of the bells is the same deep blue as the outside, also with paler margins. The tips of the yellow anthers are just visible and the flowers are slightly scented. The cut flowers keep well in water. Suitable for growing in containers or planting in the garden.

'Hendryetta'   Diversifolia Group
Synonym: *C.* × *diversifolia* 'Hendryetta'

Flowering Period Early summer to early autumn
Aspect Any
Pruning Hard
Height or Spread 4–5ft (1.3–1.6m)
Flower Size 2–2½in (5–6.5cm)

Semi-herbaceous, deciduous, non-clinging, semi-climber or scrambler. Raised, and introduced in 2003, by Wim Snoeijer, The Netherlands. The very pretty mid pink semi-nodding bell-shaped flowers have four broad tepals which taper via crimped margins to pointed slightly recurved tips. The outside of the bloom has three prominent ribs down the centre of each tepal which are very deep pink with mid pink margins. The stamens have cream filaments and butter yellow anthers. We have this clematis growing beside a huge specimen of the grass *Stipa gigantea* and each summer 'Hendryetta' clambers her way up the tall spires of grass where she looks radiant and the gentle fragrance of her blooms can be appreciated. The cut flowers keep well in water. Suitable for growing in containers or planting in the garden. PBR: Unlicensed propagation prohibited.

'Henryi'   Early Large Flowered Group
AGM 1993

Flowering Period Early to late summer *or* late summer to mid autumn
Aspect Any
Pruning Light *or* Hard
Height or Spread 10–12ft (3.3–4m) *or* 6–8ft (2–2.6m)
Flower Size 7–8in (17–20cm)

Deciduous climber. Raised by Isaac Anderson-Henry, Edinburgh, in 1855, thought to have been a cross between *C. patens* and *C. lanuginosa,* 'Henryi' was one of the earliest large-flowered clematis to have been hybridized. The six to eight broad, overlapping tepals open creamy-white and mature to pure white with an elegant satin sheen and taper to blunt tips. The crown of stamens have white filaments and 'dark chocolate' brown anthers. Hard pruning will keep the plant more compact but will delay the flowering period by a few weeks. Suitable for growing in containers if hard pruned, or planting in the garden.

'Hoshi-no-flamenco'   Early Large Flowered Group

Flowering Period Late spring to early summer and late summer to early autumn
Aspect Any
Pruning Light
Height or Spread 6–8ft (2–2.6m)
Flower Size 5–7in (12.5–18cm)

Deciduous climber. Raised around 1990 by Minoru Hoshino, Japan, soon to be introduced by Thorncroft Clematis. These glorious bright carmine-red flowers have six to eight broad, overlapping tepals that taper via lightly crimped, slightly recurved margins to rounded, somewhat reflexed tips. The blooms sometimes have a paler mauve-pink bar. The stamens make a wonderful contrast to the rich red, having cream filaments and butter-yellow anthers – gorgeous! The cut flowers keep well in water. Suitable for growing in containers or planting in the garden.

'Huldine'   Late Large Flowered Group
AGM 2002

Flowering Period Late summer to mid autumn
Aspect Sunny, to encourage flowering
Pruning Hard
Height or Spread 8–10ft (2.6–3.3m)
Flower Size 3–4in (7.5–10cm)

Deciduous climber. Raised by F. Morel, France, in the early 1900s, it received the RHS Award of Merit when shown by Ernest Markham in 1934. The pearly-white blooms have a satin sheen and an almost translucent appearance as their pretty mauve reverse shows through. The reverse also has a deep dusky reddish-purple bar running along the mid-ribs, paling towards the margins. The six broad tepals have somewhat incurved margins that taper to pointed, gently recurved tips. The stamens have white filaments and butter-yellow anthers. Best suited for planting in the garden.

'Huvi'   Late Large Flowered Group

Flowering Period Mid summer to mid autumn
Aspect Not north
Pruning Hard
Height or Spread 6–8ft (2–2.6m)
Flower Size 4–5in (10–12.5cm)

Deciduous climber. Raised by Uno and Aili Kivistik, Estonia, in 1986. The glorious deep purply-red blooms have brighter velvety-red bars. Their six to eight broad, overlapping tepals have lightly crimped, slightly incurved, undulating margins that taper to pointed gently recurved tips. The stamens have pinkish-cream filaments and wine-red anthers. Suitable for growing in containers or planting in the garden.

HYDE HALL 'Evipo009'   Early Large Flowered Group

Flowering Period Late spring to early summer and early autumn
Aspect Any
Pruning Light
Height or Spread 6–8ft (2–2.6m)
Flower Size 5–6in (12.5–15cm)

Deciduous climber. Raised, and introduced in 2004, by Raymond Evison, Guernsey. The cultivar is named after the RHS garden in Essex. A beautiful, slightly creamy-white, star-shaped bloom that has a pink 'wash' down the bars of the early blooms. This pink colouring fades in the sun and does not normally appear on the later blooms. The seven or eight broad, overlapping tepals have crimped, undulating margins that taper to pointed tips. The crown of stamens have white filaments and pinkish-brown anthers. Suitable for growing in containers or planting in the garden. PBR: Unlicensed propagation prohibited.

ICE BLUE 'Evipo003'   Early Large Flowered Group

Flowering Period Late spring to early summer and late summer to early autumn
Aspect Any
Pruning Light
Height or Spread 5–6ft (1.6–2m)
Flower Size 5–7in (12.5–18cm)

Deciduous climber. Raised, and introduced in 2005, by Raymond Evison, Guernsey. The appropriately named, elegant bluish-white flowers bear a mid mauve-blue bar when first open. The six to eight broad, overlapping tepals have crimped, wavy margins that give a rather frilly look to the early blooms. The stamens have white filaments and primrose-yellow anthers. The later blooms are flatter and almost pure white. Suitable for growing in containers or planting in the garden. PBR: Unlicensed propagation prohibited.

INSPIRATION 'Zoin'   Diversifolia Group
                                                                       BCS Certificate of Merit 2003

Flowering Period Early summer to early autumn
Aspect Any
Pruning Hard
Height or Spread 5–6ft (1.6–2m)
Flower Size 2–3in (5–7.5cm)

Semi-herbaceous, deciduous, non-clinging, semi-climber or scrambler. Raised in 1993 by Wim Snoeijer, The Netherlands. The stunning vivid reddish-pink blooms have a beautiful satin sheen across the textured surface and very slightly paler mauve-pink margins. The four tepals taper via lightly crimped and undulating margins to pointed slightly recurved tips. The stamens are a pleasing contrast having white filaments and pale yellow anthers. For years we grew this scrambling in a bed that was bordered by a 'hedge' of the very dark purple lavender 'Imperial'; the clematis would drape her blooms through the lavender which looked stunning. The cut flowers keep well in water. Suitable for growing in containers or planting in the garden. PBR: Unlicensed propagation prohibited.

integrifolia   Integrifolia Group

Flowering Period Mid to late summer
Aspect Any
Pruning Hard
Height or Spread 2–3ft (60cm–1m)
Flower Size 1½in (4cm)

Herbaceous, deciduous, clump-forming, semi-erect or scrambling stems. A species from central and eastern Europe to south western Russia, also western and central Asia. Wild forms can be found with blue, pink or white flowers. The nodding bell-shaped flowers have prominent ribs on the outside. The most common cultivated form is very dark blue, graduating to light blue towards the crimped recurved margins. The four tepals are narrow and taper to pointed, recurved and slightly twisted tips. The tips of the bright yellow anthers are just visible and the flowers are very slightly scented. The cut flowers keep well in water. Suitable for growing in containers or planting in the garden.

integrifolia 'Alba'   Integrifolia Group

Flowering Period Mid to late summer
Aspect Any
Pruning Hard
Height or Spread 2–3ft (60cm–1m)
Flower Size 1½in (4cm)

Herbaceous, deciduous, clump-forming, semi-erect or scrambling stems. A selected white form of the species *C. integrifolia*. The pure white nodding bell-shaped flowers have four narrow deeply ribbed tepals that taper to recurved and slightly twisted, pointed tips. The tips of the bright yellow anthers are just visible and the flowers have a slight scent. The cut flowers keep well in water. Suitable for growing in containers or planting in the garden.

'Iola Fair'   Early Large Flowered Group

Flowering Period Late spring to early summer and late summer to early autumn
Aspect Any
Pruning Light
Height or Spread 6–8ft (2–2.6m)
Flower Size 5–6in (12.5–15cm)

Deciduous climber. Raised by Keith Fair, Lincolnshire, in 1992 and named after his daughter. The beautiful, almost luminous pale, ever so slightly pinky lavender blooms have a lovely satin sheen across the lightly textured surface of the five or six broad, overlapping tepals that taper to pointed tips. When first open there is a hint of a pink bar which quickly fades as the blooms mature. The stamens, that have white filaments and wine red anthers, make a stunning contrast to the pale tepals. Suitable for growing in containers or planting in the garden.

'Ivan Olsson'   Early Large Flowered Group

Flowering Period Late spring to early summer and early autumn
Aspect Any
Pruning Light
Height or Spread 6–8ft (2–2.6m)
Flower Size 5–6in (12.5–15cm)

Deciduous climber. Raised by Magnus Johnson, Sweden, in 1955. A most beautiful bloom with pale satin grey-blue margins radiating from a white bar. Their blooms have six to eight broad overlapping tepals tapering to pointed tips. The reverse has a broad white bar merging to very pale blue margins. The crown of stamens make a pleasing contrast with white filaments and deep wine red anthers. Suitable for growing in containers or planting in the garden.

'Jackmanii'   Late Large Flowered Group
                                                         FCC 1863 and AGM 1993

Flowering Period Mid summer to early autumn
Aspect Any
Pruning Hard
Height or Spread 8–12ft (2.6–4m)
Flower Size 3–5in (7.5–12.5cm)

Deciduous climber. Raised by George Jackman and Son, Woking, in 1858. Worldwide, this has to be one of the most well-known and widely grown clematis, which has adorned many a cottage wall over the last 150 years. The slightly nodding to outward facing blooms have four, occasionally five or six, tepals which are a good bluish-purple with a reddish flush at the base when first open. The broad tepals have a textured surface and taper via crimped margins to blunt tips. The stamens are pale beige-green. Best suited for planting in the garden.

'Jackmanii Alba'   Early Large Flowered Group

Flowering Period Early to mid summer and early autumn
Aspect Any
Pruning Light
Height or Spread 8–12ft (2.6–4m)
Flower Size 5–6in (12.5–15cm)

Deciduous climber. Raised, and introduced in 1878, by Charles Noble, Bagshot. The early blooms, produced from the old ripened wood are double and have many layers of deeply textured, pointed tepals. The outer layers are bluey-mauve with splashes of green and have green bars on the reverse, the inner layers are bluey-white and the whole bloom turns whiter as it matures. The single blooms that appear later from the current season's growth have five or six bluish-white tepals. The stamens have white filaments and light brown anthers. Best suited for planting in the garden.

Jackmanii Purpurea 'Zojapur'   Late Large Flowered Group

Flowering Period Early summer to early autumn
Aspect Any
Pruning Hard
Height or Spread 6–8ft (2–2.6m)
Flower Size 3–5in (7.5–12.5cm)

Deciduous climber. Raised in 2002 by Wim Snoeijer, The Netherlands. A glorious velvety plum-purple that is deeper at the margins and tips with paler highlights in the centre, the colour matures to bluey-purple. Normally bearing four broad tepals whose margins recurve slightly as they taper to blunt tips. The stamens have cream filaments and pale yellow anthers. We first saw this in 2009 and were most impressed. We think it would look particularly good grown through an apricot coloured climbing rose for instance. Suitable for growing in containers or planting in the garden. PBR: Unlicensed propagation prohibited.

'Jackmanii Rubra'   Early Large Flowered Group

Flowering Period Late spring to early summer and late summer to mid autumn
Aspect Sunny, to enhance colour
Pruning Light
Height or Spread 8–12ft (2.6–4m)
Flower Size 4–6in (10–15cm)

Deciduous climber. Raised in France around the early 1900s. The early blooms produced from the old ripened wood are usually semi-double, with single blooms later from the current season's growth. The purply-red textured tepals appear more crimson when grown in a sunny position and they mature to bluish-red. The single flowers have four to six broad, overlapping tepals that taper via undulating margins to blunt, recurved tips. The stamens have white filaments and yellow anthers. Best suited for planting in the garden.

'Jackmanii Superba'   Late Large Flowered Group

Flowering Period Early summer to early autumn
Aspect Any
Pruning Hard
Height or Spread 8–12ft (2.6–4m)
Flower Size 3–5in (7.5–12.5cm)

Deciduous climber. Raised, and introduced in 1882, by Thomas Cripps, Tunbridge Wells.
The blooms are a lovely rich purple with a reddish bar when first open, they gradually lose the bar and mature to a more bluish-purple. The four to six textured tepals are broad and taper to blunt tips via crimped margins. The stamens have greenish-cream filaments and beige anthers. Whilst it is very similar to 'Jackmanii' the flowers of 'Jackmanii Superba' are a somewhat stronger colour and its tepals are broader. Best suited for planting in the garden.

'Jacqueline du Pré'   Atragene Group
                                           AGM 2002

Flowering Period Mid to late spring
Aspect Any, with free drainage
Pruning Tidy after flowering
Height or Spread 6–8ft (2–2.6m)
Flower Size 2–2½in (5–6cm)

Deciduous climber. Raised in 1981 by Barry Fretwell, Devon, and named after the world
famous cellist who died in 1987. The four deep pink tepals which form a nodding bell-shaped flower have paler pink margins and the inside of the bells is very pale pink. The staminodes are creamy-white with a hint of pale pink washed over them. The cut flowers keep well in water. Suitable for growing in containers or planting in the garden.

'Jacqui'   Montana Group
                                          BCS Certificate of Merit 2001

Flowering Period Late spring to early summer
Aspect Sunny, to enhance perfume
Pruning Tidy after flowering
Height or Spread 15+ft (5+m)
Flower Size 1½–3in (4–7.5cm)

Deciduous climber. Selected and named after Jacqui Williams and introduced in 1998. The
pretty white, semi-double and single, lightly hawthorn scented blooms have a pretty satin sheen. The margins of the broad tepals both incurve and recurve towards the blunt tips making a dainty Catherine-wheel shaped flower. The prominent stamens have white filaments and pale yellow anthers. If grown in a shady situation or when the spring has been dull and cold, the tepals may have green leaf-like tips. Best suited for planting in the garden.

'James Mason'   Early Large Flowered Group

Flowering Period Late spring to early summer and late summer to early autumn
Aspect Any
Pruning Light
Height or Spread 6–8ft (2–2.6m)
Flower Size 4–6in (10–15cm)

Deciduous climber. Raised in 1984 by Barry Fretwell, Devon, and named after the famous actor (1909–1984) who was very fond of white flowers. The elegant white blooms have six to eight broad, overlapping tepals that are deeply grooved along the mid-rib and taper to blunt tips via crimped, gently undulating margins that recurve as the blooms mature. The crown of stamens make a beautiful contrast with their white filaments and dark wine-red anthers. Suitable for growing in containers or planting in the garden.

'Jan Fopma'   Diversifolia Group

Flowering Period Mid summer to early autumn
Aspect Any
Pruning Hard
Height or Spread 4–5ft (1.3–1.6m)
Flower Size 1–2in (2.5–5cm)

Semi-herbaceous, deciduous, non-clinging, semi-climber or scrambler. Raised in 1990 by Wim Snoeijer, The Netherlands, named after the nurseryman and clematarian, Jan Fopma, to celebrate his 75th birthday in 2003. The nodding bell-shaped flowers are a wonderful glossy deep purply-red with deep dusky pink margins and have deep ribbing running their length towards the very pointed recurved tips. The stamens have creamy-white filaments and yellowy-beige anthers. We use this clematis, amongst others, to add summer interest to a bed of 'flag' irises; it looks lovely clambering up their spire-like leaves and this sunny position really enhances the delicate chocolate scent and glossy flowers of the clematis – they look fabulous. The cut flowers keep well in water. Suitable for growing in containers or planting in the garden. PBR: Unlicensed propagation prohibited.

'Jan Lindmark'   Atragene Group

Flowering Period Mid to late spring
Aspect Any, with free drainage
Pruning Tidy after flowering
Height or Spread 6–8ft (2–2.6m)
Flower Size 1½–2in (4–5cm)

Deciduous climber. Raised in Sweden by our friend Jan Lindmark and introduced in 1981. The semi-double nodding bell-shaped flowers are mid rosy-lavender. The four tepals open out almost flat. The inner layers have a white flash where they join the stamens. Suitable for growing in containers or planting in the garden.

'Jan Paweł II'   Late Large Flowered Group
Synonym: 'John Paul II'

Flowering Period Late summer to mid autumn *or* early to late autumn
Aspect Partial shade, to preserve colour
Pruning Light *or* Hard
Height or Spread 10–12ft (3.3–4m) *or* 8–10ft (2.6–3.3m)
Flower Size 5–5½in (12.5–13cm)

Deciduous climber. Raised in 1966 by Brother Stefan Franczak, Poland and named in honour of the Polish born Pope John Paul II. The pearly pinkish-white blooms have a satin sheen across their textured surface, with a deeper pink bar on both sides. As the blooms mature the bar on the surface fades, but that on the reverse still gives a hint of pink through the tepal. The five or six broad, overlapping tepals taper via lightly crimped margins to pointed tips that gently recurve with age. The stamens have creamy-white filaments and purplish-red anthers. Adapt your pruning technique to suit your growing conditions to encourage a better display of flowers – in a mild climate or a sheltered garden, hard pruning may be necessary, but in colder districts light pruning will enhance flowering. Best suited for planting in the garden.

japonica

Flowering Period Late spring to early summer
Aspect Any
Pruning Tidy after flowering
Height or Spread 6–12ft (2–4m)
Flower Size 1¼in (3cm)

Deciduous climber. A clematis species from Japan, thought to have been introduced to Britain during the mid-nineteenth century. The nodding bell-shaped flowers have four thick reddish-brown tepals that have paler margins and taper to pointed gently recurved tips. The inside is greenish-cream flushed with reddish-brown and the tips of the pale yellow anthers are just visible. Years ago we grew this on both sides of an arch which spanned a regularly used path, it was lovely to see these charming flowers at such close quarters. Best suited for planting in the garden.

'Jenny'   Late Large Flowered Group

Flowering Period Mid summer to early autumn
Aspect Any
Pruning Hard
Height or Spread 8–10ft (2.6–3.3m)
Flower Size 3–3½in (7.5–9cm)

Deciduous climber. Raised in 1991 by Krister Cedergren, Sweden. A gorgeous mid violet-blue overlays pale blue to make a 'veined' bar which gradually merges across the deeply textured surface to broad mid-blue margins. Normally four, sometimes five broad tepals taper via undulating margins to pointed, gently recurved tips. The stamens have cream filaments and pale yellow anthers. Best suited for planting in the garden.

'Jenny Keay'   Montana Group

Flowering Period Late spring to early summer
Aspect Sunny, to enhance colour
Pruning Tidy after flowering
Height or Spread 10–15ft (3.3–5m)
Flower Size 2–2½in (5–6cm)

Deciduous climber. Raised in 1989 by Alister Keay, New Zealand, and named after his wife. The semi-double flowers have four narrow tepals overlaid by several layers of narrow, pointed staminodes that are almost as long as the tepals. They all have a creamy-white base with deep salmon-pink radiating out towards their crimped margins. The flowers have very little colour when first open but a few days in the sun brings them to life as their glorious deep salmon-pink develops. This is best suited to being grown in a sunny position where it will develop a really good colour, it is less vigorous than many Montana Group cultivars and can be slow to establish. This clematis brings back happy memories for our son Peter who spent several weeks with Jenny and Alister at their nursery in Christchurch. Best suited for planting in the garden.

'Jerzy Popiełuszko'
(pronounced Yearzay Popee-yo-noush-tchko)

Early Large Flowered Group

Flowering Period Late spring to mid autumn
Aspect Any
Pruning Light
Height or Spread 4–6ft (1.3–2m)
Flower Size 5–6in (12.5–15cm)

Deciduous climber. Raised in 1993 by Szczepan Marczyński, Poland, and named after the Roman Catholic priest (1947–84) chaplain of the Independent Trade Union 'Solidarność' (Solidarity), who in his patriotic sermons called for respect for human rights, and was kidnapped and murdered by the Polish Secret Police. The beautiful satin white flowers have six to eight broad, overlapping tepals that taper to blunt tips. The contrasting crown of stamens have white filaments and coffee coloured anthers. An excellent free-flowering clematis. Suitable for growing in containers or planting in the garden.

'Jingle Bells'
Synonym: *C. cirrhosa* var. *purpurascens* 'Jingle Bells'

Cirrhosa Group

Flowering Period Mid winter to early spring
Aspect Sunny, to encourage flowering, sheltered and free draining
Pruning Tidy after flowering
Height or Spread 12–15ft (4–5m)
Flower Size 1½–2in (4–5cm)

Evergreen climber. Raised in 1992 by Robin Savill, Essex. The creamy-white nodding bell-shaped flowers have four tepals with deeply textured surfaces, their crimped margins taper to rounded, lightly recurved tips. The stamens have lime greeny-cream filaments and creamy-beige anthers and there is a hint of citrus scent. Best suited for planting in the garden.

'Joe'
Synonym: *C.* × *cartmanii* 'Joe'

Forsteri Group

Flowering Period Mid to late spring
Aspect Sheltered, free draining and winter protection
Pruning Tidy after flowering
Height or Spread Prostrate, 3–6ft (1–2m)
Flower Size 1–1½in (2.5–4cm)

Evergreen, prostrate habit. Raised in 1983 by Henry and Margaret Taylor, Scotland, from seed sent to them by Joe Cartman, New Zealand. The white, male flowers normally produce six (sometimes five, seven or eight) broad, overlapping tepals that taper to blunt tips, their margins gently recurve as the flowers mature. The evergreen foliage is dark green and similar to a coarse parsley. The stamens are pale yellow. Best grown in containers (*see* Forsteri Group notes on page 130).

JOHN HOWELLS 'Zojohnhowells'

Viticella Group

Flowering Period Early summer to early autumn
Aspect Any
Pruning Hard
Height or Spread 8–10ft (2.6–3.3m)
Flower Size 2½–3in (6–7.5cm)

Deciduous climber. Raised in 1999 by Wim Snoeijer, the Netherlands, and named after a founding member and past chairman of the British Clematis Society who died in 2008. The elegant, rich carmine red flowers have a brighter red bar along the centre of their four to six broad, overlapping, textured tepals whose crimped margins taper to pointed tips. The stamens have greenish-cream filaments and wine-red anthers. We have no doubt that this relatively new clematis will become a favourite in many gardens. Best suited for planting in the garden. PBR: Unlicensed propagation prohibited.

'John Huxtable'   Late Large Flowered Group
                                                      AGM 2002

Flowering Period Mid summer to mid autumn
Aspect Any
Pruning Hard
Height or Spread 6–8ft (2–2.6m)
Flower Size 4½–5in (11–12.5cm)

Deciduous climber. A seedling, probably from 'Comtesse de Bouchaud', discovered in the Devon garden of John Huxtable in the 1960s, its beautiful satin white flowers are identical in size and shape to those of its suspected parent. The four to six deeply textured tepals have a wonderful satin sheen and taper to blunt, slightly recurved tips. The stamens have white filaments and yellow anthers. Suitable for growing in containers or planting in the garden.

'John Treasure'   Viticella Group

Flowering Period Mid summer to early autumn
Aspect Any
Pruning Hard
Height or Spread 8–10ft (2.6–3.3m)
Flower Size 2–2½in (5–6.5cm)

Deciduous climber. Introduced by Treasures of Tenbury, Worcestershire, in 1999, named after their well-known clematarian. The nodding mid bluey-purple flowers have four narrow tepals with slightly paler margins and recurved tips. The margins also have the merest hint of rose-pink shading and have the deeper bluey-purple colouring in veins running through the deeply textured surface. The stamens have white filaments and pale yellow anthers. The reverse is mid bluey-purple with mauve margins. Best suited for planting in the garden.

'John Warren'   Early Large Flowered Group

Flowering Period Early to late summer
Aspect Sheltered
Pruning Light
Height or Spread 6–8ft (2–2.6m)
Flower Size 6–8in (15–20cm)

Deciduous climber. Raised by Walter Pennell, Lincoln, in the 1960s, John Warren was a Principal of Lincoln College of Agriculture. The large star-shaped flowers have six to eight overlapping, long pointed tepals whose base colour is an unusual grey-white which is overlaid by deep pinky-red along the bars and margins. The lovely crown of stamens have white filaments and wine-red anthers. Suitable for growing in containers or planting in the garden.

JOLLY GOOD 'Zojogo'   Late Large Flowered Group

Flowering Period Early to late summer
Aspect Any
Pruning Hard
Height or Spread 5–6ft (1.6–2m)
Flower Size 2–3in (5–7.5cm)

Deciduous climber. Raised in 1997 by Wim Snoeijer, the Netherlands. The four to six broad, overlapping and deeply textured tepals are a deep pinkish-mauve and have brighter rose-pink bars. Their crimped margins incurve slightly and taper to blunt tips. The stamens have white filaments and butter yellow anthers. Exceptionally free flowering, this certainly lives up to its name! Suitable for growing in containers or planting in the garden. PBR: Unlicensed propagation prohibited.

JOSEPHINE 'Evijohill'   Early Large Flowered Group
                                                                        AGM 2002

Flowering Period Early summer to early autumn
Aspect Sunny, to enhance colour
Pruning Light
Height or Spread 6–8ft (2–2.6m)
Flower Size 4–5in (10–12.5cm)

Deciduous climber. Discovered by Mrs Josephine Hill in 1980 and introduced by Raymond
Evison in 1998. This unique clematis produces extremely double, rosette-like blooms of
light mauvy-pink with each tepal bearing a deeper pink bar. The six to eight outer tepals
are broad and taper to rounded tips; the inner layers are narrow and taper to pointed tips.
The early blooms can have greenish markings on the outer tepals which will disappear as the light levels increase.
Growing it in a sunny position will also improve the colour. It always produces double flowers. Suitable for growing in
containers or planting in the garden. PBR: Unlicensed propagation prohibited.

'Julka' (pronounced Youlka)   Early Large Flowered Group

Flowering Period Early to late summer
Aspect Any
Pruning Light
Height or Spread 6–8ft (2–2.6m)
Flower Size 5–6in (12.5–15cm)

Deciduous climber. Raised in Poland in 1993 by Szczepan Marczyński and named after his
youngest daughter Julianna. The rich velvety violet-purple blooms have deep, yet bright,
purply-red bars. The six broad tepals overlap and taper via ruffled margins to blunt tips. The stamens have white filaments and reddy-chocolate anthers. Suitable for growing in containers or planting in the garden.

'June Pyne'   Early Large Flowered Group

Flowering Period Late spring to early summer and late summer to early autumn
Aspect Not north
Pruning Light
Height or Spread 5–6ft (1.6–2m)
Flower Size 5–6in (12.5–15cm)

Deciduous climber. Raised in 1990 by Ken Pyne, Chingford, and named after his wife. The
pretty star-shaped flowers have deep rose-pink bars that merge to paler mauve-pink
margins. Their six to eight broad, overlapping and lightly textured tepals have crimped,
somewhat undulating margins that taper to pointed tips. The stamens have creamy-white filaments and primrose
yellow anthers. The early blooms from the old ripened wood are often semi-double. Suitable for growing in containers
or planting in the garden.

'Juuli' (pronounced Yoolee)   Diversifolia Group

Flowering Period Mid summer to early autumn
Aspect Any
Pruning Hard
Height or Spread 5–6ft (1.6–2m)
Flower Size 3–3½in (7.5–9cm)

Semi-herbaceous, deciduous, non-clinging, semi-climber or scrambler. Raised in 1984 by Uno
and Aili Kivistik, Estonia. The open, semi-nodding to outward facing flowers are mid to
light lavender-blue with a deeper pinkish-lavender bar. Normally bearing six (occasion-
ally four or five) tepals which taper to pointed, gently recurved tips. The stamens have cream filaments and butter
yellow anthers. The cut flowers keep well in water. Suitable for growing in containers or planting in the garden.

'Kacper' (pronounced Kasper)   Early Large Flowered Group

Flowering Period Late spring to early summer and late summer to early autumn
Aspect Any
Pruning Light
Height or Spread 6–8ft (2–2.6m)
Flower Size 6–8in (15–20cm)

Deciduous climber. Raised in 1970 by Brother Stefan Franczak, Poland, and named after his father and one of the Three Wise Men (Casper). When first open the large, elegant blooms are reddy-purple but gradually mature to bluey-purple, whilst retaining a deeper bar. The six to eight broad tepals taper via lightly crimped margins to pointed, slightly recurved tips. The stamens have pinkish-white filaments and red anthers. The cut blooms keep well in water. Suitable for growing in containers or planting in the garden.

'Kaen'   Early Large Flowered Group

Flowering Period Late spring to early summer and late summer to mid autumn
Aspect Sunny, to enhance colour
Pruning Light
Height or Spread 6–8ft (2–2.6m)
Flower Size 3–5in (7.5–12.5cm)

Deciduous climber. Raised by Hiroyasu Shinzawa, Japan, before 2003. This very unusual multi-layered double has very deep pink, almost red tepals which have pale to light pink bars with occasional pale green mottling. The outer tepals of these shaggy blooms have green leaf-like markings. The stamens have deep pink filaments and butter yellow anthers. The early blooms are fully double, the later blooms are semi-double. Suitable for growing in containers or planting in the garden.

'Kaiu'   Viticella Group
Synonym: *C. texensis* 'Kaiu'   BCS Commended Certificate 2007

Flowering Period Mid summer to early autumn
Aspect Any
Pruning Hard
Height or Spread 8–10ft (2.6–3.3m)
Flower Size 1in (2.5cm)

Deciduous climber. Raised in 1982 by Erich Pranno, Estonia. The pearly white nodding urn-shaped flowers have a pinky-mauve blush over the crown of their four waxy textured tepals whose crimped margins taper to pointed recurved tips. The stamens which are hidden from view have creamy white filaments and pale yellow anthers. The cut blooms keep well in water. Best suited for planting in the garden.

'Kalina'   Early Large Flowered Group

Flowering Period Late spring to early summer and late summer to early autumn
Aspect Any
Pruning Light
Height or Spread 6–8ft (2–2.6m)
Flower Size 5–7in (12.5–17cm)

Deciduous climber. Raised in 1978 by Brother Stefan Franczak, Poland. A beautiful star-shaped bloom that has six to eight broad tepals which overlap and taper to pointed tips. Upon opening the margins are frilly and the colour is bright rose-pink along the bars radiating towards deep rosy-mauve margins and as the blooms mature the colouring pales slightly. Whichever, they have a certain elegance that is enhanced by their lovely stamens which have cream filaments and dark purply-pink anthers. Suitable for growing in containers or planting in the garden.

'Kardynał Wyszyński'   Late Large Flowered Group
(pronounced Cardinow Vi-shin-ski) Synonym: 'Cardinal Wyszyński'

Flowering Period Early summer to early autumn
Aspect Any
Pruning Hard
Height or Spread 8–10ft (2.6–3.3m)
Flower Size 5–6in (12.5–15cm)

Deciduous climber. Raised in Poland in 1974 by Brother Stefan Franczak and named after the
the Polish Cardinal (1901–1981) who was head of the Catholic Church in Poland for
over 30 years, calling for justice and freedom and subsequently imprisoned in 1953 for three years by the communist
authorities. The rich 'cardinal' red blooms produce between six and eight broad and overlapping tepals. The vibrant red
is most intense along the bars, merging to velvety slightly purply-red at the undulating margins as they taper to blunt
tips. The stamens have white filaments and dark wine red anthers. Best suited for planting in the garden.

'Kermesina'   Viticella Group
                                                                                  AGM 2002

Flowering Period Mid summer to early autumn
Aspect Any
Pruning Hard
Height or Spread 8–10ft (2.6–3.3m)
Flower Size 2–2½in (5–6cm)

Deciduous climber. Raised, and introduced in 1883, by Lemoine et fils, France. This lovely old clematis has glorious
deep crimson flowers that have a white spot at the base of each of its four or five textured tepals. The margins of the
semi-nodding to outward facing blooms recurve and the tepal tips are strongly recurved. The stamens have greenish
filaments and dark brown anthers. The cut blooms keep well in water. Best suited for planting in the garden.

Kingfisher 'Evipo037'   Early Large Flowered Group

Flowering Period Late spring to early summer and late summer to early autumn
Aspect Any
Pruning Light
Height or Spread 6–8ft (2–2.6m)
Flower Size 6–7in (15–17cm)

Deciduous climber. Raised, and introduced in 2007, by Raymond Evison, Guernsey. The
rich velvety 'royal' blue flowers have eight broad, overlapping tepals whose undulating margins taper to pointed tips.
They have a wonderful crown of contrasting stamens with bluey-white filaments and pale yellow anthers. Suitable for
growing in containers or planting in the garden. PBR: Unlicensed propagation prohibited.

'Kinju Atarashi'   Early Large Flowered Group

Flowering Period Late spring to early summer and late summer to early autumn
Aspect Any
Pruning Light
Height or Spread 6–8ft (2–2.6m)
Flower Size 4–6in (10–15cm)

Deciduous climber. Raised in 1999 by Mr C.W. Welch, Norfolk, and named after the
husband of a Japanese friend of his. Introduced in 2010 by Thorncroft Clematis Nursery.
The elegant blooms open a rich deep rosy-lilac which matures to mid mauvy-blue that is further enhanced by a rose-
pink half-bar. The very 'full' flowers are made up of six to eight broad overlapping tepals that taper via somewhat undulating margins to rounded tips. The crown of stamens have creamy-white filaments and rich coffee coloured anthers.
The mature plant blooms from top to bottom. Suitable for growing in containers or planting in the garden.

'Kiri Te Kanawa'   Early Large Flowered Group

Flowering Period Late spring to early summer and late summer to early autumn
Aspect Not north
Pruning Light
Height or Spread 6–8ft (2–2.6m)
Flower Size 4–5in (10–12.5cm)

Deciduous climber. Raised in 1986 by Barry Fretwell, Devon, and named after the opera singer from New Zealand who sang at the wedding of H.R.H. Prince Charles and Lady Diana Spencer. The pretty double blooms are deep lavender-blue with many layers of broad, ruffle edged tepals tapering to rounded tips. It produces double blooms from both the old ripened wood and the new growth made in the current season. The stamens have white filaments and cream anthers. Suitable for growing in containers or planting in the garden.

'Kommerei'   Late Large Flowered Group

Flowering Period Mid summer to early autumn
Aspect Any
Pruning Hard
Height or Spread 6–8ft (2–2.6m)
Flower Size 4–5in (10–12.5cm)

Deciduous climber. Raised in 1985 by Uno and Aili Kivistik, Estonia. The very deep reddish-pink flowers have five or six broad, overlapping tepals that have a textured surface and their slightly undulating margins taper to gently recurved blunt tips. The stamens have white filaments and purply-red anthers. Suitable for growing in containers or planting in the garden.

'Königskind'   Early Large Flowered Group
Trade designations: CLIMADOR and KÖNIGSSHON

Flowering Period Late spring to early summer and late summer to mid autumn
Aspect Any
Pruning Light
Height or Spread 4–6ft (1.3–2m)
Flower Size 3½–4½in (9–11.5cm)

Deciduous climber. Raised in 1982 by Manfred Westphal, Germany. The mid violet-blue star-shaped blooms have slightly paler bars and their six to eight broad, lightly textured tepals, overlap and taper via undulating margins to pointed tips. The stamens have white filaments and very dark purplish-red anthers. Suitable for growing in containers or planting in the garden.
PBR: Unlicensed propagation prohibited.

'Küllus' (pronounced Kooloose)   Early Large Flowered Group

Flowering Period Early to late summer *or* mid summer to early autumn
Aspect Any
Pruning Light *or* Hard
Height or Spread 6–8ft (2–2.6m) *or* 4–6ft (1.3–2m)
Flower Size 5–6in (12.5–15cm)

Deciduous climber. Raised in 1980 by Uno and Aili Kivistik, Estonia. The gorgeous ice-blue star-shaped flowers have a pink blush when first open which fades as the blooms mature. Their six to eight broad, deeply textured tepals, overlap and have crimped, almost frilly undulating margins with pointed, gently recurved tips. The stamens have white filaments and pinkish-brown anthers. Hard pruning will keep the plant more compact but will delay the flowering period by a few weeks. Suitable for growing in containers or planting in the garden.

ladakhiana
Tangutica Group

Flowering Period Late summer to mid autumn
Aspect Sunny and free draining
Pruning Hard
Height or Spread 10–12ft (3.3–4m)
Flower Size 1in (2.5cm)

Deciduous climber. A native of north western India and Tibet. Like many in this group, its 'correct' name continues to be debated. Current opinion suggests this to be *C. tibetana;* however we feel that this could cause further confusion so we therefore feel that we should retain the commonly used name for the time being. These unusual open, semi-nodding to outward facing flowers have a slightly greenish-yellow base that matures to a more orange-yellow which is heavily over-laid by brown mottling. The four narrow tepals have somewhat recurved margins and pointed, twisted and recurved tips. The stamens have purply-brown filaments and yellowy-beige anthers. We are very fond of this charming clematis that also has lovely glaucous foliage which is an added bonus. Best suited for planting in the garden.

'Lady Betty Balfour'
Late Large Flowered Group

Flowering Period Late summer to early autumn *or* early to mid autumn
Aspect Sunny, to encourage flowering
Pruning Light *or* Hard
Height or Spread 12–15ft (4–5m) *or* 8–10ft (2.6–3.3m)
Flower Size 4–6in (10–15cm)

Deciduous climber. Raised, and introduced in 1912, by George Jackman and Son, Woking. The very deep lavender-blue flowers have mid blue shading along their bar. Normally bearing six broad, overlapping tepals that taper via slightly crimped margins to blunt tips. The crown of contrasting stamens have white filaments and pale yellow anthers. A lovely late flowering clematis that really needs a warm sunny position to flourish. Adapt your pruning technique to suit your growing conditions to encourage a better display of flowers – in a mild climate or a sheltered garden, hard pruning may be necessary, but in colder districts light pruning and a sunny position will enhance flowering. Best suited for planting in the garden.

'Lady Northcliffe'
Early Large Flowered Group

Flowering Period Early summer to early autumn
Aspect Any
Pruning Light
Height or Spread 5–6ft (1.6–2m)
Flower Size 4–6in (10–15cm)

Deciduous climber. Raised and introduced in 1906 by George Jackman and Son, Woking. This lovely old cultivar opens a rich 'royal' blue and gradually matures to a slightly lighter lavender-blue. The six broad, overlapping tepals have wavy margins tapering to blunt tips. The stamens have creamy-white filaments and pale greenish-yellow anthers. Suitable for growing in containers or planting in the garden.

'Lagoon'
Atragene Group
Synonym: *C. macropetala* 'Lagoon'
AGM 2002

Flowering Period Mid to late spring
Aspect Any, with free drainage
Pruning Tidy after flowering
Height or Spread 8–10ft (2.6–3.3m)
Flower Size 1½–2¼in (4–5.5cm)

Deciduous climber. Selected by George Jackman and Son, Woking and introduced in 1959. The deep rich (yet slightly greyish) blue semi-double nodding bell-shaped flowers have inner layers of the same colour bearing occasional white markings. In our garden we have this clambering over the pergola and allow a few stems to drape themselves across a neighbouring rich red rhododendron which makes quite a spectacular sight in spring. The cut flowers keep well in water. Best suited for planting in the garden.

'Lambton Park'   Tangutica Group
                                                     AGM 2002

Flowering Period Early summer to early autumn
Aspect Sunny, to enhance perfume and free-draining
Pruning Hard
Height or Spread 10–12ft (3.3–4m)
Flower Size 2in (5cm)

Deciduous climber. Discovered in 1985 by Tom Bennett at the Lambton Park Garden
Centre in Co. Durham. This glorious clematis has bright buttercup-yellow nodding
lantern-shaped flowers that have a really good coconut-like perfume. The strongly recurved margins and pointed,
recurved tips of the four waxy, deeply textured tepals reveal the greenish, yellow-brown stamens. The flowers are
followed by a superb display of silky seedheads and both are lovely to use in flower arrangements. This vigorous grower
requires plenty of space in a sunny position to enhance its lovely perfume. Best suited for planting in the garden.

'Lasurstern'   Early Large Flowered Group
                                                     AGM 1993

Flowering Period Late spring to early summer and early autumn
Aspect Any
Pruning Light
Height or Spread 8–10ft (2.6–3.3m)
Flower Size 5–7in (12.5–18cm)

Deciduous climber. Raised, and introduced in 1905, by Goos and Koenemann, Germany.
The glorious star-shaped flowers are a rich, slightly mauve mid blue with the central bar paling as the bloom matures.
The six to eight overlapping tepals taper to pointed tips via somewhat wavy margins. The stamens have white filaments
and yellow anthers. Best suited for planting in the garden.

'Laura Denny'   Early Large Flowered Group

Flowering Period Late spring to early summer and early autumn
Aspect Any
Pruning Light
Height or Spread 6–8ft (2–2.6m)
Flower Size 4–6in (10–15cm)

Deciduous climber. Raised in 1977 by Vince and Sylvia Denny, Preston, and named after
their granddaughter. These beautiful flowers open creamy-white and clear to almost pure
white as they mature, their seven or eight broad, overlapping tepals taper to blunt tips. The stamens have creamy-white
filaments and pinkish-beige anthers. Suitable for growing in containers or planting in the garden.

'Lech Wałęsa'   Early Large Flowered Group

Flowering Period Early summer to mid autumn
Aspect Any and free draining
Pruning Light
Height or Spread 6–8ft (2–2.6m)
Flower Size 6–8in (15–20cm)

Deciduous climber. Raised in 1993 by Szczepan Marczyński, Poland, and named after the
first chairman of the Independent Trade Union 'Solidarność' (Solidarity), who became
President of Poland 1990–95 and was awarded the Nobel Peace Prize in 1983. These
fabulous star-shaped flowers have six broad, overlapping tepals that are light bluish-violet
merging towards an almost white bar. They have a lightly textured surface and wavy, almost frilly, slightly incurved
margins tapering to pointed and gently reflexed tips. The stamens have white filaments and yellow-beige anthers. Suitable for growing in containers or planting in the garden.

'Lemon Bells'   Atragene Group
Synonym: *C. chiisanensis* 'Lemon Bells'

Flowering Period Mid spring to mid summer
Aspect Any, with free drainage
Pruning Tidy after flowering
Height or Spread 6–8ft (2–2.6m)
Flower Size 2–2½in (5–6cm)

Deciduous climber. Selected from seed originally collected in South Korea in 1988. The light citrus-yellow, nodding, bell-shaped flowers have a 'rusty' red wash at their base and deep ridges running down the outside of their four tepals, whose margins taper to very pointed recurved tips. The staminodes are yellowy-white at base gradually deepening to limey citrus yellow with a hint of rusty-red at their tips. The shiny flower buds are shaped like tear-drops and hang like jewels in the spring sunshine. The cut flowers keep well in water. Suitable for growing in containers or planting in the garden.

'Lemon Chiffon'   Early Large Flowered Group

Flowering Period Late spring to early summer and late summer to early autumn
Aspect Shaded, to preserve colour
Pruning Light
Height or Spread 6–8ft (2–2.6m)
Flower Size 4–6in (10–15cm)

Deciduous climber. Raised by Ed Philips, Kent, and introduced in 1993. When first open the pretty blooms are a pale 'primrose' yellow with a satin sheen that matures to creamy-white. If the spring has been cold and light levels have been low then the early flowers may have a hint of a pink bar. The six to eight broad, overlapping tepals taper via gently undulating margins to blunt, almost rounded tips. The stamens have cream filaments with pale yellow anthers that turn brown with age, so this lovely clematis benefits visually from dead-heading. Suitable for growing in containers or planting in the garden.

'Lilactime'   Early Large Flowered Group

Flowering Period Late spring to early summer and early autumn
Aspect Not north
Pruning Light
Height or Spread 6–8ft (2–2.6m)
Flower Size 6–7in (15–17cm)

Deciduous climber. Raised in 1983 by Ken Pyne, Chingford. The light bluish-lilac semi-double and single star-shaped blooms are slightly deeper in colour around the wavy margins which taper to pointed tips. There is a very slight hint of rose-pink at the base of the tepals near the stamens. The large crown of stamens have white filaments and wine red anthers. Suitable for growing in containers or planting in the garden.

'Little Nell'   Viticella Group

Flowering Period Mid summer to early autumn
Aspect Any
Pruning Hard
Height or Spread 8–10ft (2.6–3.3m)
Flower Size 2–2½in (5–6cm)

Deciduous climber. Raised in France by Morel and introduced to Britain in 1939 by Jackman's of Woking. These delicate looking semi-nodding flowers have four to six textured tepals with white bars that merge to broad, pale mauve-pink margins. The crimped edges of the tepals recurve as they taper to blunt, gently recurved and sometimes twisted tips. The stamens have greenish-cream filaments and pale yellow anthers. We have grown this with the bright red climbing rose 'Paul's Scarlet Climber', they looked charming together. The cut blooms keep well in water. Best suited for planting in the garden.

'Lord Herschell'   Diversifolia Group

Flowering Period Late spring to mid autumn
Aspect Sunny, to enhance colour
Pruning Hard
Height or Spread 1½–3ft (45cm–1m)
Flower Size 2–2½in (5–6cm)

Herbaceous, deciduous, clump-forming, semi-erect stems. Raised, and introduced in 1998, by Barry Fretwell, Exeter. The rich velvety, purply-red nodding to outward facing bell-shaped flowers, mature and open to reddy-purple and have paler outside margins. The four tepals taper to pointed, recurved tips revealing the greenish-yellow anthers. A little gem to grow near the front of a border, it flowers for such a long time. The cut flowers keep well in water. Suitable for growing in containers or planting in the garden.

'Louise Rowe'   Early Large Flowered Group

Flowering Period Early to mid summer and early autumn
Aspect Any
Pruning Light
Height or Spread 4–6ft (1.3–2m)
Flower Size 5–6in (12.5–15cm)

Deciduous climber. Raised by Mrs Jean Rowe, Norfolk, and named after her daughter, introduced in 1983 by Jim Fisk. Said to probably be a cross between 'Marie Boisselot' and 'William Kennett', although we suspect that a double flowered clematis such as 'Countess of Lovelace' was involved in this liason. This beautiful clematis is quite unusual in that it flowers double, semi-double and single all at the same time. The colour is essentially pale mauve but the shade varies from delicate mauve to pinky-mauve and grey-mauve, depending upon the light at different times of the day – whichever, it is absolutely gorgeous! The single blooms have six to eight broad, overlapping tepals that taper via undulating margins to blunt tips. The inner layers of the double and semi-double blooms have rather more pointed and twisted tepals, making an almost frilly looking flower. The stamens have white filaments and primrose-yellow anthers. This is Jon's favourite clematis! Suitable for growing in containers or planting in the garden.

'Love Jewelry'   Early Large Flowered Group

Flowering Period Late spring to early summer and late summer to early autumn
Aspect Any
Pruning Light
Height or Spread 4–5ft (1.3–1.6m)
Flower Size 4–5in (10–12.5cm)

Deciduous climber. Raised in Japan by Kozo Sugimoto. The pretty star-shaped blooms bear very bright cerise-pink bars that merge through deep purply-pink to pinkish-mauve margins, as they mature the colour changes to rose-pink at the bar with bluey-mauve margins. The six to eight broad, overlapping tepals taper via lightly crimped wavy margins to pointed and somewhat twisted tips and as the flowers age they tend to flatten out. Early in the season the blooms are often semi-double with beautiful, yet rather irregular shaped flowers. The stamens have white filaments and dark red anthers. Suitable for growing in containers or planting in the garden.

LOVING MEMORY 'Izumi'   Early Large Flowered Group

Flowering Period Late spring to early summer and late summer to early autumn
Aspect Any
Pruning Light
Height or Spread 6–8ft 2–2.6m)
Flower Size 4½–5in (11–12.5cm)

Deciduous climber. Raised in 1993 by Mrs Masako Takeuchi, Japan, and named in memory
of her brother. Soon to be introduced by Thorncroft Clematis. The six or seven broad
tepals taper via crimped, undulating margins to pointed recurved tips. The textured
surface has a pretty satin sheen and its colour is light to mid blue with mottling over a white half bar. The stamens have
white filaments and butter yellow anthers. Suitable for growing in containers or planting in the garden.

'Lunar Lass'   Forsteri Group

Flowering Period Mid to late spring
Aspect Sheltered, free draining and winter protection
Pruning Tidy after flowering
Height or Spread Prostrate, 1½–2ft (45–60cm)
Flower Size ¾–1in (2–2.5cm)

Evergreen, prostrate habit. Raised by Graham Hutchins, Essex, before 1990. The delightful
little star-shaped female flowers are a pretty greeny-cream and have the most gorgeous
citrus perfume. The tiny, finely cut evergreen leaves are very dark green. Best grown in
containers (*see* Forsteri Group notes on page 130).

macropetala   Atragene Group

Flowering Period Mid to late spring
Aspect Any, with free drainage
Pruning Tidy after flowering
Height or Spread 8–10ft (2.6–3.3m)
Flower Size 1½–2in (4–5cm)

Deciduous climber. This 'wild' clematis from northern China has light to mid-blue semi-
double nodding bell-shaped flowers. The outside has a slight rosy flush at the base of the
tepals near the flower stalk. The inside of the tepals is pale blue flecked with white and the
staminodes are of the same colouring. A fabulous garden plant! The cut flowers keep well
in water. Best suited for planting in the garden.

'Madame Julia Correvon'   Viticella Group
                                                               AGM 1993

Flowering Period Early summer to early autumn
Aspect Any
Pruning Hard
Height or Spread 6–8ft (2–2.6m)
Flower Size 2½–3½in (6.5–9cm)

Deciduous climber. Raised, and introduced in 1900, by Morel, France. The gorgeous rich,
vibrant red flowers are offset beautifully by their contrasting yellow stamens. The four to
six textured tepals are gappy at the base and taper via gently crimped, undulating and
somewhat twisted margins to pointed, recurved tips. If you like irregular shaped flowers,
look no further, it is reliable, very free-flowering and a spectacular sight when in full bloom. Suitable for growing in
containers or planting in the garden.

'Maidwell Hall'   Atragene Group
Synonym: *C. macropetala* 'Maidwell Hall'

Flowering Period Mid to late spring
Aspect Any, with free drainage
Pruning Tidy after flowering
Height or Spread 6–8ft (2–2.6m)
Flower Size 1½–2in (4–5cm)

Deciduous climber. Selected, and introduced by George Jackman and Son, Woking, in 1956. The deep to mid greyish (or french navy blue) semi-double nodding, bell-shaped flowers have irregular grey markings. There is also purple colouring on the outside of the tepals near their base. The inner layers occasionally have white markings. This is similar to 'Lagoon' but slightly paler and smaller. The cut flowers keep well in water. Suitable for growing in containers or planting in the garden.

mandschurica   Flammula Group

Flowering Period Mid summer to early autumn
Aspect Sunny, to enhance perfume
Pruning Hard
Height or Spread 3–5ft (1–1.6m)
Flower Size ¾–1in (2–2.5cm)

Herbaceous, deciduous, clump-forming, semi-erect or scrambling stems. A native of north eastern China, Mongolia, south eastern Russia and Korea. We love to grow this pretty clematis in a mixed border, where it is allowed to scramble naturally, taking its own course and displaying its many clusters of white star-like flowers to perfection. The five, sometimes four or six, narrow tepals taper to blunt or pointed tips and their crown of stamens have white filaments and primrose-yellow anthers. Their perfume is like spicy lilac. Suitable for growing in containers or planting in the garden.

'Margaret Hunt'   Late Large Flowered Group

Flowering Period Mid summer to mid autumn
Aspect Any
Pruning Hard
Height or Spread 8–10ft (2.6–3.3m)
Flower Size 3½–4½in (9–11.5cm)

Deciduous climber. Raised by Mrs Margaret Hunt, Norwich, and introduced by Jim Fisk in 1969. When first open the four to six broad textured tepals are deep dusky mauve-pink with an even deeper shade forming a half-bar near the centre of the flower. This colour is carried along the crimped margins and through veins across the entire surface. The blooms mature to pale dusky mauve-pink whilst retaining a slightly deeper shade at the margins and the bar turns pinky-white. The stamens have pale yellow filaments and red anthers. Even in poor conditions, this clematis flowers extremely well and looks wonderful when grown with a cream rose such as 'Albéric Barbier'. Best suited for planting in the garden.

'Margot Koster'   Viticella Group
Synonym: 'M. Koster'

Flowering Period Mid summer to early autumn
Aspect Any
Pruning Hard
Height or Spread 8–10ft (2.6–3.3m)
Flower Size 3–4in (7.5–10cm)

Deciduous climber. Raised, and introduced around 1895, by Marinus Koster, the Netherlands. This lovely old clematis has unusual, rather dishevelled-looking semi-nodding flowers that are deep mauve-pink and this rich colouring is maintained up to tepal fall, even if grown in full sun. Their four to six tepals have recurved margins that twist as they taper to the blunt, recurved tips. The stamens have greenish-white filaments and pale yellow anthers. Best suited for planting in the garden.

'Maria Cornelia'   Viticella Group
Synonym: 'Zomacor'

Flowering Period Early summer to early autumn
Aspect Any
Pruning Hard
Height or Spread 6–8ft (2–2.6m)
Flower Size 2–2½in (5–6cm)

Deciduous climber. Raised in 2001 by Willem Straver, Germany, and named in honour of his mother. The semi-nodding or outward facing flowers are a slightly creamy white, becoming pure white and have four or five broad tepals that taper via lightly crimped margins to rounded tips. The contrasting stamens have pale green filaments and purple anthers. Suitable for growing in containers or planting in the garden. PBR: Unlicensed propagation prohibited.

'Marie Boisselot'   Early Large Flowered Group
                                                                     AGM 1993

Flowering Period Early to late summer *or* mid summer to early autumn
Aspect Any
Pruning Light *or* Hard
Height or Spread 10–12ft (3.3–4m) *or* 6–8ft (2–2.6m)
Flower Size 5–7in (12.5–18cm)

Deciduous climber. Raised in France by A. Boisselot and introduced in 1890. These elegant flowers open creamy-white and gradually mature to pure white, whilst their golden stamens can still give a slightly creamy appearance to the blooms. The six to eight broad, overlapping tepals gently twist as the blooms mature and they taper to blunt or rounded tips; their lightly textured surface has a lovely satin sheen and deep grooves along the mid-rib. Hard pruning will keep the plant more compact but will delay the flowering period by a few weeks. Suitable for growing in containers if hard pruned, or planting in the garden.

'Marjorie'   Montana Group

Flowering Period Late spring to early summer
Aspect Sunny, to enhance colour
Pruning Tidy after flowering
Height or Spread 10–15ft (3.3–5m)
Flower Size 2½in (6cm)

Deciduous climber. Discovered by Miss Marjorie Free, Westleton, Suffolk and introduced by Jim Fisk in 1980. Unfortunately, the semi-double flowers can be a rather 'grubby' white when first open, but after a few days in the sun a glorious deep salmon-pink colouring spreads through veins across the tepals. This colour is much more pronounced along the margins as the base colour turns to cream. The four narrow tepals are blunt tipped and the shorter inner layers of staminodes stand almost erect. Plant this in a sunny position where the blooms can be seen to their best advantage. The cut flowers keep well in water. Best suited for planting in the garden.

'Markham's Pink'   Atragene Group
Synonym: *C. macropetala* 'Markham's Pink'   AGM 1993

Flowering Period Mid to late spring
Aspect Any, with free drainage
Pruning Tidy after flowering
Height or Spread 8–10ft (2.6–3.3m)
Flower Size 2–2½in (5–6cm)

Deciduous climber. Raised by Ernest Markham, East Grinstead, and introduced in 1935. The light to mid pink semi-double nodding, bell-shaped flowers have deep purply-rose pink at the base of each tepal. This deep colouring radiates into the tepals along the veins. The inside of the tepals and the staminodes are light candy pink. An old cultivar that is still one of the best! The cut flowers keep well in water. Best suited for planting in the garden.

'Marmori'   Late Large Flowered Group

Flowering Period Mid summer to early autumn
Aspect Any
Pruning Hard
Height or Spread 4–6ft (1.3–2m)
Flower Size 4–5in (10–12.5cm)

Deciduous climber. Raised in Estonia by Uno and Aili Kivistik in 1986. The pale candy-pink, star-shaped flowers have dusky-rose shading at the base of their six broad, over-lapping tepals. They have a satin sheen across their deeply textured surface and taper via almost frilly margins to pointed tips. The crown of stamens are a very prominent feature of this clematis. The filaments are white at the base merging to very deep pink with dark coffee coloured anthers. Suitable for growing in containers or planting in the garden.

'Mary Rose'   Viticella Group
Synonym: *C. viticella* 'Flore Pleno'

Flowering Period Mid summer to early autumn
Aspect Sunny, to enhance colour
Pruning Hard
Height or Spread 8–10ft (2.6–3.3m)
Flower Size 1½in (4cm)

Deciduous climber. The 'Double Purple Virgin's Bower' was seemingly lost to cultivation until it was thankfully found and reintroduced by Barry Fretwell, Devon, in 1982. This was the same year that Henry Vlll's flagship Mary Rose was raised from the sea-bed having been sunk in 1545. It is believed that this lovely old clematis dates from the same period. The small semi-nodding fully double flowers have many layers of spiky tepals or petaloid stamens that are a gorgeous dusky-amethyst colour. We are particularly fond of this clematis and grow it against the cream colour washed walls of our house where it looks magnificent. Best suited for planting in the garden.

'Mayleen'   Montana Group
                                                            AGM 2002

Flowering Period Late spring to early summer
Aspect Any
Pruning Tidy after flowering
Height or Spread 20–30ft (6–10m)
Flower Size 2–3in (5–7.5cm)

Deciduous climber. Given to Jim Fisk who introduced it in 1984. The four broad, light to mid mauvy-pink tepals have a textured surface and satin sheen. Their paler margins recurve and are slightly ruffled, tapering to rounded recurved tips. The stamens have white filaments with butter yellow anthers and the foliage has a distinctive bronze colour-ing. The cut flowers keep well in water. A gorgeous montana, 'Mayleen' has a wonderful spicy, clove-like scent. Best suited for planting in the garden.

'Mazury'
Early Large Flowered Group

Flowering Period Late spring to early summer and late summer to early autumn *or* mid summer to early autumn
Aspect Not north
Pruning Light *or* Hard
Height or Spread 8–10ft (2.6–3.3m) *or* 6–8ft (2–2.6m)
Flower Size 5–7in (12.5–17cm)

Deciduous climber. Raised in 1994 by Szczepan Marczyński, Poland, and introduced to the UK by Thorncroft Clematis Nursery in 2010. The double blooms, which are borne from both the old and current season's growth, are mid mauve-blue flushed with pale purply-blue and have white mottling across their lightly textured surface. The outer tepals, that also have green mottling, are broad and taper to pointed tips. The inner layers are rather more blunt tipped and have wavy margins. The stamens are cream. Hard pruning will keep the plant more compact but will delay the flowering period by a few weeks. Suitable for growing in containers if hard pruned, or planting in the garden.

'Mercury'
Early Large Flowered Group

Flowering Period Late spring to early summer and late summer to early autumn
Aspect Any
Pruning Light
Height or Spread 6–8ft (2–2.6m)
Flower Size 6–7in (15–17cm)

Deciduous climber. Raised in Essex by Ken Pyne in 1987. When they are first open, the stunning white star-shaped blooms are washed with palest silvery-mauve blue, the later blooms are usually pure white. The eight broad, overlapping tepals taper to pointed tips via frilly margins. The stamens have creamy-white filaments and butter yellow anthers. The cut blooms keep well in water. Occasionally the early blooms are semi-double. Suitable for growing in containers or planting in the garden.

Mienie Belle 'Zomibel'
Texensis Group

Flowering Period Early summer to early autumn
Aspect Sunny, to encourage flowering
Pruning Hard
Height or Spread 5–6ft (1.6–2m)
Flower Size 1½–2in (4–5cm)

Semi-herbaceous, deciduous climber. Raised in The Netherlands by Wim Snoeijer and introduced in 2007. The upward or outward facing, trumpet or tulip shaped flowers are deep rose pink with pale mauve-pink margins on the outside. The inside has mid mauve-pink margins with a clearer pink bar. The five or six tepals have pointed tips that recurve slightly. A lovely compact plant which is very free-flowering. The cut flowers keep well in water. Suitable for growing in containers or planting in the garden. PBR: Unlicensed propagation prohibited.

'Minister'
Early Large Flowered Group
Synonym: 'Pastel Princess'

Flowering Period Late spring to early summer and late summer to early autumn *or* early summer to early autumn
Aspect Any
Pruning Light *or* Hard
Height or Spread 6–8ft (2–2.6m) *or* 5–6ft (1.6–2m)
Flower Size 5–6in (12.5–15cm)

Deciduous climber. Raised, and introduced in 1982, by Uno and Aili Kivistik, Estonia. The light bluey-mauve textured surface has a hint of a rose-pink bar with glorious contrasting stamens whose white filaments merge through shades of red to very dark red anthers. The five or six broad tepals overlap and taper via crimped, slightly incurved margins to pointed and gently recurved tips. Hard pruning will keep the plant more compact but will delay the flowering period by a few weeks. Suitable for growing in containers or planting in the garden.

'Minuet'

Viticella Group
AGM 1993

Flowering Period Mid summer to early autumn
Aspect Any
Pruning Hard
Height or Spread 8–10ft (2.6–3.3m)
Flower Size 2½in (6cm)

Deciduous climber. Raised in France by Morel and introduced to Britain by Jackman's of Woking in 1952. The pretty semi-nodding flowers have four textured tepals with dusky purply-red margins radiating from white bars. The margins are crimped, recurved and taper to rounded tips and as the blooms mature the tepals twist slightly. The stamens have pale greenish-yellow filaments and cream anthers. Best suited for planting in the garden.

'Miss Bateman'

Early Large Flowered Group
FCC 1869, AGM 1993

Flowering Period Late spring to early summer
Aspect Any
Pruning Light
Height or Spread 6–8ft (2–2.6m)
Flower Size 5½–6in (13–15cm)

Deciduous climber. Raised, and introduced in 1869, by Charles Noble, Bagshot. It is understood to have been named after one of the Batemans from Biddulph Grange, Staffordshire. The pure white blooms have a delicate satin sheen and often the early flowers bear pale green bars. The eight broad tepals overlap and taper to somewhat rounded tips via gently undulating margins. The beautifully contrasting crown of stamens have white filaments and dark red anthers. Suitable for growing in containers or planting in the garden.

'Miss Christine'

Montana Group

Flowering Period Late spring to early summer
Aspect Sunny, to enhance perfume
Pruning Tidy after flowering
Height or Spread 15–20ft (5–6m)
Flower Size 2–3in (5–7.5cm)

Deciduous climber. Raised by Sheila Chapman, Essex, who named it after one of her daughters, introduced in 2001. The single, pure white, scented flowers appear creamy-white when first open and they bear broad purply-pink margins on their reverse. The four broad, rounded tipped tepals have lightly crimped, gently undulating margins. The stamens have white filaments and yellow anthers. Best suited for planting in the garden.

montana 'Grandiflora'
Synonym: *C. montana* var. *grandiflora*

Montana Group
AGM 1993

Flowering Period Late spring to early summer
Aspect Any
Pruning Tidy after flowering
Height or Spread 30–40ft (10–13m)
Flower Size 3–4in (7.5–10cm)

Deciduous climber. A native of west and south China, Tibet and the Himalaya. Moore and Jackman, describing *C. montana* in their book of 1872 wrote: 'A variety called grandiflora, with flowers twice the size of the original, has also been introduced by Messrs. Veitch and Son'. The beautiful satin white flowers have four broad tepals with lightly ruffled margins that taper to rounded tips. The stamens have white filaments and bright yellow anthers. Best suited for planting in the garden.

montana 'Rubens'   Montana Group
Synonym: *C. montana* var. *rubens*

Flowering Period Late spring to early summer
Aspect Sunny, to enhance perfume
Pruning Tidy after flowering
Height or Spread 20–30ft (6–10m)
Flower Size 2½–3in (6–7.5cm)

Deciduous climber. For the past few decades, the clematis sold under this name do not appear to be from the original stock that was introduced to England from China by E.H. Wilson in 1901. Today's plants do not follow an early description of 'rosy-red, as large as 'Grandiflora''. However, the one we describe here is commonly grown worldwide as 'Rubens'. The single, light candy-pink flowers have a pretty satin sheen across the four broad, textured tepals which have slightly ruffled margins and rounded tips. The stamens have white filaments and pale yellow anthers and there is a lovely vanilla scent. The foliage is tinged with bronze. Best suited for planting in the garden.

montana 'Wilsonii'   Montana Group
Synonym: *C. montana* var. *wilsonii*

Flowering Period Late spring to early summer
Aspect Sunny, to enhance perfume
Pruning Tidy after flowering
Height or Spread 20–30ft (6–10m)
Flower Size 2½in (6cm)

Deciduous climber. It is widely believed that the original *C. montana* var. *wilsonii*, introduced by E.H. Wilson from central China in the early 1900s (also, at the time, known as 'the autumn-flowering montana') is no longer in commercial production. Therefore, what is described here is the form that is currently sold worldwide under this name; it fits the original description except that it only begins blooming just a couple of weeks later than other Montana Group cultivars. The single, satin-white flowers are sweetly scented. Their four narrow tepals have slightly wavy margins which taper to blunt, recurved tips. The stamens have white filaments and greeny-cream anthers. Best suited for planting in the garden.

'Monte Cassino'   Early Large Flowered Group

Flowering Period Early to late summer *or* mid summer to early autumn
Aspect Any
Pruning Light *or* Hard
Height or Spread 8–10ft (2.6–3.3m) *or* 6–8ft (2–2.6m)
Flower Size 5–6in (12.5–15cm)

Deciduous climber. Raised in 1975 by Brother Stefan Franczak, Poland, and named to commemorate the battle near the abbey of Monte Cassino, Italy, in 1944. The vivid purply-red blooms have six broad, overlapping, textured tepals that taper, via crimped margins, to rounded tips. The stamens are a lovely contrast having pinkish-cream filaments and pale yellow anthers. Hard pruning will keep the plant more compact but will delay the flowering period by a few weeks. Suitable for growing in containers if hard pruned, or planting in the garden.

'Moonman'   Forsteri Group

Flowering Period Mid to late spring
Aspect Sheltered, free draining and winter protection
Pruning Tidy after flowering
Height or Spread Prostrate, 1½–2 ft (45–60cm)
Flower Size 1½in (4cm)

Evergreen, prostrate habit. Raised by Graham Hutchins, Essex, before 1990. The greenish-cream tepals of the male flowers incurve along the margins making a very attractive boat shape. The stamens are very pale yellow and the foliage is evergreen. Best grown in containers (*see* Forsteri Group notes on page 130).

MORNING STAR 'Zoklako'   Early Large Flowered Group

Flowering Period Late spring to early autumn
Aspect Any
Pruning Light
Height or Spread 6–8ft (2–2.6m)
Flower Size 4–6in (10–15cm)

Deciduous climber. Raised, and introduced in 2007, by Wim Snoeijer, The Netherlands. The beautiful star-shaped flowers have broad, deep plumy-pink margins and a white bar which is overlaid with veins of rose-pink. The six to eight tepals are broad, overlapping and taper to pointed tips. The stamens have deep plumy-pink filaments and bright yellow anthers. Suitable for growing in containers or planting in the garden. PBR: Unlicensed propagation prohibited.

'Mrs Cholmondeley' (pronounced Chumley)   Early Large Flowered Group
                                                   FCC 1873, AGM 1993

Flowering Period Late spring to late summer *or* mid summer to mid autumn
Aspect Any
Pruning Light *or* Hard
Height or Spread 10–12ft (3.3–4m) *or* 6–8ft (2–2.6m)
Flower Size 5–7in (12.5–18cm)

Deciduous climber. Raised, and introduced in 1873, by Charles Noble, Bagshot. The light mauvy-blue flowers have a slightly paler bar that is overlaid with mauve-blue veins. Their six broad tepals are slightly gappy at base and taper via lightly crimped and gently recurved margins to rounded tips. The stamens have white filaments flushed with blue and pale coffee-coloured anthers. Hard pruning will keep the plant more compact but will delay the flowering period by a few weeks. A very reliable old cultivar. Best suited for planting in the garden.

'Mrs George Jackman'   Early Large Flowered Group
                                              AGM 1993

Flowering Period Late spring to early summer and late summer to early autumn
Aspect Any
Pruning Light
Height or Spread 6–8ft (2–2.6m)
Flower Size 5–6in (12.5–15cm)

Deciduous climber. Raised in 1873 by George Jackman and Son, Woking, this is another very old clematis that has stood the test of time. The single blooms have eight broad, overlapping tepals that open the palest cream, quickly maturing to white and with a gorgeous satin sheen. Their gently undulating margins taper to rounded tips. The stamens have creamy-white filaments and coffee-coloured anthers. Some early blooms are semi-double. Suitable for growing in containers or planting in the garden.

'Mrs N. Thompson'   Early Large Flowered Group

Flowering Period Late spring to early summer and early autumn
Aspect Any
Pruning Light
Height or Spread 6–8ft (2–2.6m)
Flower Size 4–6in (10–15cm)

Deciduous climber. Raised in 1954 by Walter Pennell, Lincoln. The striking deep purply-blue flowers have a rich purply-cerise bar that extends out towards the margins. Their four to six broad, overlapping tepals taper to a point and have slightly twisted, undulating margins. The stamens have pale pink filaments and dark red anthers. This was one of the first clematis Ruth's family had in their garden when she was a child. Suitable for growing in containers or planting in the garden.

'Mrs Robert Brydon'   Heracleifolia Group

Flowering Period Mid summer to early autumn
Aspect Sunny, to encourage flowering and free draining
Pruning Hard
Height or Spread 8–10ft (2.6–3.3m)
Flower Size 1–1½in (2.5–4cm)

Semi-herbaceous, deciduous, vigorous semi-climber or scrambler. Raised by Robert Brydon, USA, around the mid 1930s. The clusters of small white, delicately scented flowers are tinged with grey-mauve, in some conditions pale blue. Their four or five narrow tepals roll right back on themselves to reveal a crown of prominent stamens that have white filaments and creamy-beige anthers. The woody, non-clinging stems will scramble across the ground unless given support, but look lovely when allowed to clamber up through a large open shrub. Best suited for planting in the garden.

'Mrs Spencer Castle'   Early Large Flowered Group

Flowering Period Late spring to early summer and late summer to early autumn
Aspect Any
Pruning Light
Height or Spread 6–8ft (2–2.6m)
Flower Size 5–6in (12.5–15cm)

Deciduous climber. Raised by George Jackman and Son, Woking, about 1913. This lovely old semi-double clematis has blooms which are various shades of mauve-pink. The larger outer tepals are quite a deep mauve-pink whilst the inner layers are slightly paler and smaller. All the tepals are narrow and taper to very pointed, often twisted tips and have a textured surface and satin sheen. The stamens have white filaments and cream anthers. The early blooms produced from the old ripened wood are semi-double, with single blooms later from the current season's growth. Suitable for growing in containers or planting in the garden.

'Mrs T. Lundell'   Viticella Group

Flowering Period Mid summer to early autumn
Aspect Any
Pruning Hard
Height or Spread 8–10ft (2.6–3.3m)
Flower Size 3–3½in (7.5–9cm)

Deciduous climber. Discovered in the nursery of Tage Lundell, Sweden, and named after his wife by K. Cedergren. The mid mauve-pink blooms have a slightly clearer rose-pink bar and the surface of the four tepals is heavily textured. The crimped, recurved margins taper to pointed, recurved and twisted tips making a very pretty Catherine-wheel shaped bloom. The stamens have white filaments and pale yellow anthers. A 'good-doer' that thrives in our garden despite its unfavourable position! Best suited for planting in the garden.

'Multi Blue'   Early Large Flowered Group

Flowering Period Late spring to early summer and late summer to early autumn
Aspect Sunny, to enhance colour
Pruning Light
Height or Spread 6–8ft (2–2.6m)
Flower Size 4½–5in (11–12.5cm)

Deciduous climber. Raised in 1983 by Bouter and Zoon, the Netherlands, as a sport from 'The President'. The attractive spiky double blooms are a light french navy-blue. Their six to eight broad outer tepals have slightly paler bars, they overlap and taper via gently undulating margins to pointed tips. The huge crown of 'spiky' narrow, inner tepals or petaloid stamens have pale greenish-cream tips and are often lightly tinted with rose-pink. Suitable for growing in containers or planting in the garden.

napaulensis   Cirrhosa Group

Flowering Period Late autumn to early spring
Aspect Sheltered and free-draining
Pruning Tidy after flowering
Height or Spread 15–20ft (5–6m)
Flower Size ¾–1in (2–2.5cm)

Winter-green climber. A native of Nepal, Tibet and Northern India. This unusual clematis has small, slightly greenish-cream nodding bell-shaped flowers. Their four tepals taper to blunt, strongly recurved tips and it bears very distinctive, long reddish-pink anthers. The attractive foliage is winter-green rather than evergreen as it usually has a period of dormancy in the summer when it can lose its leaves. Best suited for planting in the garden.

'Nelly Moser'   Early Large Flowered Group
                                                                        AGM 1993

Flowering Period Late spring to early summer and early autumn
Aspect Shaded, to preserve colour
Pruning Light
Height or Spread 8–10ft (2.6–3.3m)
Flower Size 7–8in (17–20cm)

Deciduous climber. Raised, and introduced in 1897 by Moser, France. This lovely old cultivar has sadly been much scorned over the years, mainly we feel, because of its inability to cope with bright sunlight which fades the colour quickly. Please don't let this put you off growing it as it is one of the very best early large-flowered hybrids to grow on a north-facing wall or in any shady or semi shady position. The lovely star-shaped blooms have light cerise-pink bars radiating out towards the pale mauve-pink margins. The six to eight broad tepals overlap, yet are slightly gappy at their base and they have lightly crimped, wavy margins tapering to pointed, gently recurved tips. The stamens have white filaments merging through pink towards dark burgundy-red anthers. Suitable for growing in containers or planting in the garden.

'New Love'   Heracleifolia Group

Flowering Period Mid summer to mid autumn
Aspect Sunny, to enhance perfume and free draining
Pruning Hard
Height or Spread 2–2½ft (60–75cm)
Flower Size 1¼in (3cm)

Herbaceous, deciduous, clump-forming, erect woody stems. Selected by Jan Fopma, the Netherlands and introduced in 1997. The large clusters of mid to deep violet-blue hyacinth shaped flowers are beautifully scented. The four tepals taper via crimped margins to strongly recurved pointed tips. The reverse is a silvery mid-blue and the stamens have white filaments with primrose yellow anthers. The woody stems are self-supporting. Suitable for growing in containers or planting in the garden. PBR: Unlicensed propagation prohibited.

'Night Veil'   Viticella Group

Flowering Period Early summer to early autumn
Aspect Sunny, to enhance colour
Pruning Hard
Height or Spread 6–8ft (2–2.6m)
Flower Size 3–3½in (7.5–9cm)

Deciduous climber. Raised in 1997 by Mr Masashi Iino, Japan. The upright or outward facing flowers are a rich slightly reddy purple with a hint of deep red at the bar and tips. The four to six tepals have a textured surface, are broad, overlap and taper via slightly recurved crimped margins to rounded tips. There is the merest hint of white at the base of each tepal close to the stamens. The stamens have creamy-white filaments and dark purple, almost black, anthers. The cut flowers keep well in water. Suitable for growing in containers or planting in the garden.

'Nikolai Rubtsov'   Late Large Flowered Group

Flowering Period Mid summer to early autumn
Aspect Any
Pruning Hard
Height or Spread 6–8ft (2–2.6m)
Flower Size 4–6in (10–15cm)

Deciduous climber. Raised in 1962 by Alexander Volosenko-Valenis at the Nikitsky State Botanic Garden, Ukraine. This is such a pretty clematis, a glorious mish-mash of colours which makes it quite difficult to describe. The four to six tepals are narrow at base, broadening out and then tapering to blunt tips making a spoon-shaped tepal. The colour is light reddish-violet over pale mauve-blue, the reddish-violet deeper along the bars and wavy margins. The stamens have white filaments and butter yellow anthers. A lovely clematis which deserves to be more widely grown. Suitable for growing in containers or planting in the garden.

'Niobe'   Early Large Flowered Group
                                                               AGM 1993

Flowering Period Early to late summer *or* mid summer to early autumn
Aspect Any
Pruning Light *or* Hard
Height or Spread 6–8ft (2–2.6m) *or* 4–6ft (1.3–2m)
Flower Size 4–5in (10–12.5cm)

Deciduous climber. Raised by Władysław Noll in Poland about 1970 and introduced to Britain by Jim Fisk in 1975. 'Niobe' is named after the legendary tragic figure in Greek mythology. The gorgeous, deep wine-red star-shaped flowers are so dark as to be almost black, when first open. The six broad tepals taper to pointed tips via lightly crimped and gently undulating margins. The stamens are a wonderful contrast against the dark tepals, having white filaments with shadings of reddish-purple and butter-yellow anthers. Hard pruning will keep the plant more compact but will delay the flowering period by a few weeks. Suitable for growing in containers or planting in the garden.

'Nunn's Gift'   Forsteri Group

Flowering Period Mid to late spring
Aspect Sheltered, free draining and winter protection
Pruning Tidy after flowering
Height or Spread Prostrate, 1½–2ft (45–60cm)
Flower Size 1–1½in (2.5–4cm)

Evergreen, prostrate habit. Raised by Roy Nunn, Cambridge about 1995. The pale creamy-yellow male flowers have a hint of green at their base near the stamens. The six or seven tepals recurve along gently undulating margins and taper to blunt, slightly twisted tips. The dark evergreen foliage is finely cut. An outstanding, free-flowering member of this Forsteri Group. Best grown in containers (*see* Forsteri Group notes on page 130).

'Ocean Pearl'   Atragene Group

Flowering Period Mid to late spring
Aspect Any, with free drainage
Pruning Tidy after flowering
Height or Spread 8–10ft (2.6–3.3m)
Flower Size 1½–2in (4–5cm)

Deciduous climber. Selected by New Leaf Plants, Evesham, in 1998. 'Ocean Pearl' is quite unique in this group of clematis as it bears double, semi-double and single nodding bell-shaped flowers all at the same time. The four tepals are a light to mid, slightly mauvy-blue, the double blooms then have many layers of narrow petaloid stamens of the same colour inside, which gives them a rather spiky appearance. The single and semi-double blooms have a creamy-white inner skirt of staminodes. Best suited for planting in the garden.

'Odoriba'   Viticella Group

Flowering Period Early summer to mid autumn
Aspect Any
Pruning Hard
Height or Spread 8–10ft (2.6–3.3m)
Flower Size 1½–2in (4–5cm)

Deciduous climber. Raised in 1990 by Kazushige Ozawa, Japan. These gorgeous nodding, bell-shaped flowers have four deeply ribbed tepals with recurved margins tapering to pointed recurved tips. They are pale mauvy-pink on the outside merging to a deeper pink at the margins and tips. The inside which has a textured glistening surface has white bars with bright rose pink margins. The stamens have creamy-white filaments and pale yellow anthers. 'Odoriba' has such pretty blooms and, due to the way the plant presents its flowers, the inside of the bells can be seen quite clearly. We would therefore recommend using this clematis to climb over an arch or pergola where the blooms can be seen close to, or growing through a creamy-white climbing rose such as 'Albéric Barbier' would be lovely. The cut flowers keep well in water. Best suited for planting in the garden.

'Omoshiro'   Early Large Flowered Group

Flowering Period Late spring to early summer and late summer to early autumn
Aspect Any
Pruning Light
Height or Spread 6–8ft (2–2.6m)
Flower Size 5–7in (12.5–17cm)

Deciduous climber. Raised in 1988 by Hiroshi Hayakawa, Japan. The white textured surface of the eight broad, overlapping tepals has a beautiful satin sheen and is outlined around the crimped margins and pointed tips by deep purply-pink. This deep colouring covers the whole of the reverse which gives the upper surface a slightly pinkish hue. A huge crown of complementary stamens have white filaments and very deep purply-pink anthers that match the borders of the bloom beautifully. Suitable for growing in containers or planting in the garden.

OOH LA LA 'Evipo041'   Early Large Flowered Group

Flowering Period Early summer to early autumn
Aspect Partial shade, to preserve colour
Pruning Hard
Height or Spread 3–4ft (1–1.3m)
Flower Size 4–5in (10–12.5cm)

Deciduous climber. Raised, and introduced in 2009, by Raymond Evison, Guernsey. The light mauvy-pink blooms have a deeper, brighter pink bar that emphasizes their star-shape. The six to eight broad, overlapping tepals have a textured surface and their crimped margins taper to pointed tips. The crown of stamens have white filaments, and dark red anthers that help to make a very flamboyant and appropriately named clematis! Hard pruning will keep this very compact. Suitable for growing in containers or planting in the garden. PBR: Unlicensed propagation prohibited.

'Orange Peel'   Tangutica Group

Synonyms: *C. tibetana* subsp. *vernayi* var. *vernayi* 'Orange Peel', and L & S 13342

Flowering Period Late summer to late autumn
Aspect Sunny, to encourage flowering and free-draining
Pruning Hard
Height or Spread 8–12ft (2.6–4m)
Flower Size 1½–1¾in (4–4.5cm)

Deciduous climber. A charming clematis that was brought back from an expedition to Tibet by Ludlow, Sherriff and Elliott in 1947 and given their collection number L & S 13342. It was exhibited by Messrs Ingwersen in 1950 and since then has generally been known as 'Orange Peel'. The nodding bell-shaped flowers have four very thick, deep golden yellow tepals that take on a deep rusty-orange hue as they mature. The contrasting stamens are dark purplish-brown and there is a very good display of seed heads throughout the autumn and winter. The finely cut foliage is also very attractive. The cut flowers and seed heads keep well in water. Best suited for planting in the garden.

'Ourika Valley'   Cirrhosa Group

Synonym: *C. cirrhosa* 'Ourika Valley'

Flowering Period Mid winter to early spring
Aspect Sunny, to encourage flowering, sheltered and free draining
Pruning Tidy after flowering
Height or Spread 10–12ft (3.3–4m)
Flower Size 1½–2in (4–5cm)

Evergreen climber. Grown from seed collected in Ourika Valley, Morocco, in 1986 by Capt. Peter Erskine. The nodding bell-shaped flowers are a pale lime green when first open, then mature to a lovely yellowy-cream. They have a slight primrose scent and are beautifully presented against their glossy mid to dark green foliage. Best suited for planting in the garden.

'Ozawa's Blue'   Integrifolia Group

Flowering Period Early summer to early autumn
Aspect Any
Pruning Hard
Height or Spread 2–3ft (60cm–1m)
Flower Size 1¾–2in (4.5–5cm)

Herbaceous, deciduous, clump-forming, semi-erect or scrambling stems. A form of the species *C. integrifolia* selected by Kazushige Ozawa, Japan, and subsequently named in his honour. The beautiful rich mid blue open, nodding bell-shaped flowers have a satin sheen and prominent dark blue ribs running down the centre of each of the four twisted tepals. The light mauve-blue margins are crimped, slightly incurved and taper to pointed, recurved tips. The inside is light satin blue with pale blue margins. The stamens have pale yellow filaments and butter yellow anthers. The cut flowers keep well in water. Suitable for growing in containers or planting in the garden.

'Pagoda'   Viticella Group
                                                                      AGM 2002

Synonym: *C. texensis* 'Pagoda'

Flowering Period Mid summer to early autumn
Aspect Sunny, to enhance colour
Pruning Hard
Height or Spread 6–8ft (2–2.6m)
Flower Size 2–2½in (5–6cm)

Deciduous climber. Raised in 1980 by John Treasure, Tenbury Wells, the result of a cross between 'Étoile Rose' and *C. viticella*. The reverse of the open nodding bell-shaped flowers is very deep purply-pink, merging to pale pinkish-cream margins, the inside is white merging to mauve-pink margins and tips. The crimped margins of the four deeply textured tepals taper to pointed, strongly recurved tips. Their shape is reminiscent of the roof-line of a Chinese pagoda, so it is very appropriately named. The cut flowers keep well in water. Suitable for growing in containers or planting in the garden.

'Pamela'   Flammula Group

Flowering Period Early to late summer
Aspect Sunny, to enhance perfume
Pruning Hard
Height or Spread 3–5ft (1–1.6m)
Flower Size 1–1½in (2.5–4cm)

Herbaceous, deciduous, clump-forming, semi-erect stems. Raised in 1962 by Dr Frank Skinner,
Canada. The cream buds open to satin-white, slightly scented flowers bearing four to six
narrow, lightly textured tepals that taper to rounded, reflexed tips. The prominent crown
of stamens have creamy-white filaments and pale yellow anthers. Suitable for growing in containers or planting in the
garden.

'Pamela Jackman'   Atragene Group
                                                                              AGM 2005

Flowering Period Mid to late spring
Aspect Any, with free drainage
Pruning Tidy after flowering
Height or Spread 8–10ft (2.6–3.3m)
Flower Size 1½in (4cm)

Deciduous climber. A selection from *C. alpina* raised by Jackman's of Woking 1960 and named after Rowland Jackman's
daughter. The deep, slightly purply, blue nodding bell-shaped flowers mature to light violet-blue with an inner skirt of
creamy-white staminodes. The cut flowers keep well in water. Suitable for growing in containers or planting in the
garden.

'Pamiat Serdtsa' (pronounced Palm-yat Saird-tsa)   Diversifolia Group

Flowering Period Mid summer to early autumn
Aspect Any
Pruning Hard
Height or Spread 4–6ft (1.3–2m)
Flower Size 2½–3in (6–7.5cm)

Semi-herbaceous, deciduous, non-clinging, semi-climber or scrambler. Raised in Russia by M.A. Beskaravainaya in 1967. The
name translates as 'Memory of the Heart'. The elegant dusky amethyst semi-nodding bell-shaped flowers have a deeper
bar and dark, pronounced mid-ribs. The four broad tepals taper via crimped margins to pointed and twisted tips. The
textured inside of the bells is a deeper shade of dusky amethyst. The barely visible stamens have white filaments and
butter yellow anthers. We first saw this clematis, many years ago, in the garden of Jan Lindmark in Sweden; it looked
stunning growing beside an Astilbe of the same colour. The cut flowers keep well in water. Suitable for growing in
containers or planting in the garden.

'Pamina'   Early Large Flowered Group

Flowering Period Late spring to early summer and late summer to early autumn
Aspect Any
Pruning Light
Height or Spread 6–8ft (2–2.6m)
Flower Size 5–7in (12.5–18cm)

Deciduous climber. Raised by Mr and Mrs C. Terry, Hampshire, before 1993 and introduced by Thorncroft Clematis Nursery in 2004. The striking blooms have a glorious rich
deep purply-red bar that merges out to mauvy-white crimped margins. The six to eight broad, overlapping tepals taper
via slightly incurved margins to blunt tips. The splendid crown of stamens have white filaments and blood-red anthers.
The early blooms are occasionally semi-double. Suitable for growing in containers or planting in the garden.

'Pangbourne Pink'

Integrifolia Group
AGM 2002

Flowering Period Mid to late summer
Aspect Any
Pruning Hard
Height or Spread 2–3ft (60cm–1m)
Flower Size 1½–2in (4–5cm)

Herbaceous, deciduous, clump-forming, semi-erect or scrambling stems. Raised by Bill Baker at Tidmarsh near Pangbourne, Berkshire, and introduced by Busheyfields Nursery, Kent in 1992. The open nodding bell-shaped flowers are rich deep rose-pink with slightly paler mauvy-pink margins. Their four narrow tepals have three prominent ribs on the outside, running down the centre. The tepals taper along slightly incurved margins to pointed, recurved tips that gently twist as the blooms mature. The stamens have pale yellow filaments, shaded with pink, and yellow anthers. The cut flowers keep well in water and have a slight scent. Suitable for growing in containers or planting in the garden.

paniculata

Forsteri Group

Flowering Period Mid to late spring
Aspect Sheltered, free draining and winter protection
Pruning Tidy after flowering
Height or Spread 10–15ft (3.3–5m)
Flower Size Male 1–2in (2.5–5cm)

Evergreen climber. This is a native of New Zealand where, in Maori folklore, it is considered a sacred plant. This evergreen clematis has clusters of delicately scented creamy-white flowers that are borne with male and female flowers on separate plants; the male flowers are larger than the female. The overlapping tepals taper via slightly undulating margins to blunt, gently recurved tips. Best grown in containers (*see* Forsteri Group notes on page 130).

Parisienne 'Evipo019'

Early Large Flowered Group

Flowering Period Early to mid summer and early to mid autumn
Aspect Any
Pruning Hard
Height or Spread 3–4ft (1–1.3m)
Flower Size 4–6in (10–15cm)

Deciduous climber. Raised, and introduced in 2002, by Raymond Evison, Guernsey. The six to eight broad, overlapping tepals open a lovely rich mid violet-blue with a satin sheen and occasionally have a hint of pink along the central bar. They mature to a light mauvy-blue and lose the pink bar. Their crimped, gently undulating margins taper to pointed tips. The stamens have white filaments and wine-red anthers. Hard pruning will keep this very compact. Suitable for growing in containers or planting in the garden. PBR: Unlicensed propagation prohibited.

'Pastel Blue'

Integrifolia Group

Flowering Period Mid to late summer
Aspect Any
Pruning Hard
Height or Spread 2–3ft (60cm–1m)
Flower Size 1¾–2in (4.5–5cm)

Herbaceous, deciduous, clump-forming, semi-erect or scrambling stems. Introduced by Barry Fretwell, Devon, in 1986. The pretty nodding bell-shaped flowers have four light blue tepals that have a deeper blue running down the mid-ribs. The pastel blue lightly crimped margins incurve as they taper to pointed recurved tips that reveal the light blue interior. The anthers are yellow and it is very slightly scented. The cut flowers keep well in water. Suitable for growing in containers or planting in the garden.

'Pastel Pink'
Integrifolia Group

Flowering Period Mid to late summer
Aspect Any
Pruning Hard
Height or Spread 2–3ft (60cm–1m)
Flower Size 1¾–2in (4.5–5cm)

Herbaceous, deciduous, clump-forming, semi-erect or scrambling stems. Introduced by Barry Fretwell, Devon, in 1986. The pale pink nodding bell-shaped flowers have four deeply ribbed tepals which taper via pastel pink crimped incurved and twisted margins to pointed recurved tips. The interior is pastel pink. The stamens have pale yellow filaments with bright yellow anthers and it is very slightly scented. The cut flowers keep well in water. Suitable for growing in containers or planting in the garden.

'Pat Coleman'
Early Large Flowered Group

Flowering Period Late spring to early summer and early autumn
Aspect Any
Pruning Light
Height or Spread 8–10ft (2.6–3.3m)
Flower Size 6–7in (15–17cm)

Deciduous climber. A seedling discovered by Pat Coleman, a knowledgeable plantswoman from Hingham, Norfolk, growing at the base of 'Lasurstern' with 'Miss Bateman' close by. Introduced by Thorncroft Clematis Nursery in 1996. One of the most beautiful white clematis, whose star-shaped blooms have six to eight broad textured tepals with a satin sheen which overlap and taper, along crimped margins, to pointed tips. When the early flowers first open they often have a pale pink bar along the centre of each tepal although this quickly fades if the plant is growing in full sun. It has a glorious crown of contrasting stamens which have white filaments and dark wine red anthers. An excellent free-flowering cultivar that's worthy of space in any garden. (Note: We have just dead-headed our 'Pat Coleman' and counted 299 seedheads!) Suitable for growing in containers or for planting in the garden.

'Paul Farges'
Vitalba Group
AGM 2002
Synonym: *C. × fargesioides.* Trade designation: Summer Snow

Flowering Period Late spring to late summer *or* early summer to early autumn
Aspect Any
Pruning Light *or* Hard
Height or Spread 15–20ft (5–6m) *or* 10–15ft (3.3–5m)
Flower Size 1½in (4cm)

Deciduous climber. Raised in 1962 by M.A. Beskaravainaya and A.N. Volosenko-Valenis at the Nikitsky State Botanic Garden, Ukraine, a cross between two species clematis *C. potaninii* and *C. vitalba.* Named after the French missionary and plant collector who was apparently murdered by Tibetan monks in 1912. This pretty creamy-white clematis produces myriad clusters of three to seven small flowers. The blooms, borne on long flower stalks, normally have six tepals with a lightly textured surface and crimped, slightly recurved margins that taper to blunt recurved tips. The huge crown of stamens have white filaments and primrose-yellow to cream anthers. Hard pruning will keep the plant more compact but will delay the flowering period by a few weeks. Best suited for planting in the garden.

'Pauline'   Atragene Group
                                                                AGM 2005

Flowering Period Mid to late spring
Aspect Any, with free drainage
Pruning Tidy after flowering
Height or Spread 8–10ft (2.6–3.3m)
Flower Size 2–2½in (5–6cm)

Deciduous climber. Raised and introduced by Washfield Nursery, Kent, about 1966. The rich, deep blue semi-double nodding bell-shaped flowers have a rosy-purple flush on the outside. The staminodes are creamy-white and the cut flowers keep well in water. Best suited for planting in the garden.

'Perle d'Azur'   Late Large Flowered Group

Flowering Period Mid summer to mid autumn
Aspect Any
Pruning Hard
Height or Spread 8–12ft (2.6–4m)
Flower Size 4–5in (10–12.5cm)

Deciduous climber. Raised, and introduced in 1885, by Morel, France. Still as popular today as it has ever been and a favourite with garden designers. The semi-nodding blooms first open a good mid-blue with a hint of rose-pink along the bar towards the stamens and as they mature, the flowers fade to light, slightly pinkish-blue and lose their pink bar. They have four to six broad tepals with a textured surface and taper via crimped, somewhat wavy margins to blunt reflexed tips. The stamens have pale greenish-cream filaments and pale yellow anthers. This lovely old cultivar only produces flowers at the top of its rather long stems, it is therefore best grown through another plant such as a climbing rose to disguise its bare legs, then it's fantastic! Best suited for planting in the garden.

'Perrin's Pride'   Early Large Flowered Group

Flowering Period Early to late summer *or* mid summer to early autumn
Aspect Sunny, to enhance colour
Pruning Light *or* Hard
Height or Spread 8–10ft (2.6–3.3m) *or* 6–8ft (2–2.6m)
Flower Size 4–6in (10–15cm)

Deciduous climber. Raised, and introduced in 1987, by Arthur 'Bing' Steffen, USA. The lovely dusky light plum-purple blooms have the merest hint of a cerise bar when first open which fades as the bloom matures. The six broad, overlapping tepals have rounded margins tapering to blunt, recurving tips, making a very round flower. The cream stamens age to pinkish-beige. Hard pruning will keep the plant more compact but will delay the flowering period by a few weeks. We love the colour of this clematis – it is particularly good with apricot or yellow climbing roses. Suitable for growing in containers if hard pruned, or planting in the garden.

PETIT FAUCON 'Evisix'   Diversifolia Group
                                      BCS Certificate of Merit 1998, AGM 2002

Flowering Period Early summer to mid autumn
Aspect Any
Pruning Hard
Height or Spread 4–6ft (1.3–2m)
Flower Size 1½–2in (4–5cm)

Semi-herbaceous, deciduous, non-clinging, semi-climber or scrambler. Raised, and introduced in 1995, by Raymond Evison, Guernsey. The gorgeous, semi-nodding to outward facing flowers have four tepals with strongly recurved margins that reveal the rich bluey-purple inner colouring. The outside has deep, slightly-rosy purple bars bearing three prominent ribs running down the centre with paler mauve undulating margins. The eye-catching stamens have rosy-purple filaments and golden yellow anthers. A wonderful plant that blooms all summer and justly deserves its awards. The cut flowers keep well in water. Suitable for growing in containers or planting in the garden. PBR: Unlicensed propagation prohibited.

'Peveril Pearl'   Early Large Flowered Group

Flowering Period Late spring to early summer and early autumn
Aspect Partial shade, to preserve colour
Pruning Light
Height or Spread 6–8ft (2–2.6m)
Flower Size 5–7in (12.5–18cm)

Deciduous climber. Raised in 1979 by Barry Fretwell, Devon. The colour of 'Peveril Pearl' is quite difficult to describe because it seems to change depending upon the time and light of the day. Imagine the palest shades of mauve, blue, pink and silvery-grey mixed together and highlighted by a delicate satin sheen. It is further enhanced with the merest hint of a rose-pink bar when the bloom first opens. Normally bearing eight broad tepals that taper to pointed tips. The large crown of stamens have white filaments and dark coffee-coloured anthers. It is quite beautiful, particularly when grown through a purply-bronze leaved shrub. Suitable for growing in containers or planting in the garden.

PICARDY 'Evipo024'   Early Large Flowered Group

Flowering Period Early summer to early autumn
Aspect Any
Pruning Hard
Height or Spread 3–4ft (1–1.3m)
Flower Size 3–4in (7.5–10cm)

Deciduous climber. Raised, and introduced in 2002, by Raymond Evison, Guernsey. The pretty star-shaped flowers are a dusky purply-red with a brighter red bar when first open, and then gradually mature to mauve-red, whilst retaining the bar. The six to eight broad, overlapping tepals have undulating margins that taper to pointed tips. The stamens have mauve-white filaments and reddy-brown anthers. Hard pruning will keep this very compact. Suitable for growing in containers or planting in the garden. PBR: Unlicensed propagation prohibited.

'Piilu' (pronounced Peeloo)   Early Large Flowered Group

Flowering Period Early to mid summer and early autumn
Aspect Any
Pruning Light
Height or Spread 5–6ft (1.6–2m)
Flower Size 2–4in (5–10cm)

Deciduous climber. Raised in Estonia by Uno and Aili Kivistik in 1984 (the name means 'Little Duckling'). The pretty mid mauvy-pink flowers have deep rose pink along the central bar and irregular white markings with a delicate satin sheen across their lightly textured surface. The outer tepals are broad and overlapping and those, plus the inner layers, taper along frilly margins to pointed tips. The stamens have white filaments and pale yellow anthers. The early blooms produced from the old ripened wood are double, with single blooms later from the current season's growth. Suitable for growing in containers or planting in the garden.

'Pink Celebration'   Early Large Flowered Group

Flowering Period Late spring to early summer and late summer to early autumn
Aspect Any
Pruning Light
Height or Spread 6–8ft (2–2.6m)
Flower Size 4–6in (10–15cm)

Deciduous climber. Introduced by Caddick's Clematis Nursery in 2000. These gorgeous blooms are a wonderful mid pink when first open and gradually mature to pale candy-pink, yet as the colour pales it seems to retain the deeper shade along the three deep grooves of the mid-ribs. Their seven or eight broad, overlapping tepals have a textured surface and crimped undulating, almost wavy margins that taper to blunt tips. The stamens have white filaments and butter-yellow anthers. Suitable for growing in containers or planting in the garden.

PINK CHAMPAGNE 'Kakio'   Early Large Flowered Group

Flowering Period Late spring to early summer and late summer to early autumn
Aspect Any
Pruning Light
Height or Spread 6–8ft (2–2.6m)
Flower Size 6–7in (15–17cm)

Deciduous climber. Raised in 1971 by Kazushige Ozawa, Japan. It was named 'Kakio' after a district in Japan, but when it was introduced to Britain by Raymond Evison it was given the name 'Pink Champagne', presumably to suit the Western market. The beautiful blooms are bright purply-cerise and have pale lilac-mauve bars. The six to ten broad, overlapping tepals have slightly incurved, gently undulating margins that taper to pointed tips. The stamens have white filaments and bright yellow anthers. One of the earliest large flowered clematis to bloom in the late spring, making a stunning sight in the garden. Suitable for growing in containers or planting in the garden.

'Pink Dwarf'   Heracleifolia Group

Flowering Period Mid summer to mid autumn
Aspect Sunny, to encourage flowering and free-draining
Pruning Hard
Height or Spread 1–1½ft (30–45cm)
Flower Size ¾–1in (2–2.5cm)

Herbaceous, deciduous, clump-forming, erect woody stems. We believe that this was originally selected by Kozo Sugimoto, Japan, in the late 1990s. The pretty hyacinth-shaped flowers are pale to light, slightly silvery pink, with yellow anthers. This has the same dwarf growing habit as 'Blue Dwarf' with short woody stems that are self-supporting, making it a perfect front of border plant. Suitable for growing in containers or planting in the garden.

'Pink Fantasy'   Early Large Flowered Group

Flowering Period Early to late summer *or* mid summer to early autumn
Aspect Any
Pruning Light *or* Hard
Height or Spread 6–8ft (2–2.6m) *or* 4–6ft (1.3–2m)
Flower Size 4½–6in (11–15cm)

Deciduous climber. Introduced to Britain from Canada in 1975 by Jim Fisk. The pretty
star-shaped blooms open a light peachy-pink with rose-pink bars which gradually fade as
the flowers mature to pale pink. The six broad, overlapping tepals have a textured surface and their ruffled margins
taper to pointed tips that gently reflex as the blooms mature. The stamens have white filaments and wine red anthers.
The cut blooms keep well in water. Hard pruning will keep the plant more compact but will delay the flowering period
by a few weeks. Suitable for growing in containers or planting in the garden.

'Pink Flamingo'   Atragene Group
                                                      AGM 2002

Flowering Period Mid to late spring +
Aspect Any, with free drainage
Pruning Tidy after main flowering
Height or Spread 6–8ft (2–2.6m)
Flower Size 1½–1¾in (4–4.5cm)

Deciduous climber. Raised by Elizabeth Jones and introduced in the early 1990s by Raymond Evison, Guernsey. The pale
pink, semi-double, nodding, bell-shaped flowers have deep rose pink at the base of the tepals which runs through the
veins on the outside. The margins of the four tepals recurve slightly. The inside of the tepals and the staminodes are
pinky-white. The cut flowers keep well in water. Suitable for growing in containers or planting in the garden.

PISTACHIO 'Evirida'   Florida Group

Flowering Period Early summer to early autumn +
Aspect Sheltered, free draining and winter protection
Pruning Hard
Height or Spread 6–8ft (2–2.6m)
Flower Size 3–4in (7.5–10cm)

Deciduous climber. Raised, and introduced in 1999, by Raymond Evison, Guernsey. The
pretty blooms are creamy-white with a lightly textured surface and satin sheen. Their six broad, overlapping tepals taper
via gently undulating margins to points that are occasionally tipped with green. They have an unusual crown of stamens
with white filaments, pinkish-grey inward curled anthers and a prominent tuft of green stigmas at their centre. The
reverse has a distinctive lime green bar. In early summer, or when light levels are lower, the tepals will be greeny-cream.
Best grown in containers (*see* Florida Group notes on page 130). PBR: Unlicensed propagation prohibited.

pitcheri   Viorna Group

Flowering Period Mid summer to early autumn
Aspect Sunny, to encourage flowering
Pruning Hard
Height or Spread 6–8ft (2–2.6m)
Flower Size 1–1¼in (2.5–3cm)

Semi-herbaceous, deciduous climber. A species originating from Colorado, USA, and northern Mexico. The glossy deep purply-red nodding urn-shaped flowers have four tepals with pointed, strongly recurved
tips and a deeply ribbed surface. The inside is very dark wine red which contrasts well with the tips of the yellow
anthers that are just visible. This clematis never fails to please in our garden and the cut flowers keep well in water. Suitable for growing in containers or planting in the garden.

'Pixie'   Forsteri Group

Flowering Period Mid to late spring
Aspect Sheltered, free draining and winter protection
Pruning Tidy after flowering
Height or Spread Prostrate, 3–4ft (1–1.3m)
Flower Size 1½in (4cm)

Evergreen, prostrate habit. Raised in Essex by Graham Hutchins in 1986. The masses of
pale greeny-cream, star-shaped male flowers have the most gorgeous citrus-like perfume.
The nodding buds open to semi-nodding or outward facing flowers, each with six round
tipped tepals. The attractive crown of stamens have green filaments and cream anthers.
For years we have grown 'Pixie' in a dark blue glazed pot which makes an eye-catching
contrast to the pretty flowers, and its perfume on our sunny south-facing terrace is lovely.
Best grown in containers (*see* Forsteri Group notes on page 130).

'Polish Spirit'   Viticella Group
                                                                              AGM 1993

Flowering Period Mid summer to mid autumn
Aspect Any
Pruning Hard
Height or Spread 8–10ft (2.6–3.3m)
Flower Size 3–3½in (7.5–9cm)

Deciduous climber. Raised in 1984 by Brother Stefan Franczak, Poland. When first open,
the textured surface of the dark purple flowers has a hint of a reddish-purple bar which
fades as the colour matures to a rather more bluey-purple. The four or five broad tepals
are narrow at base and taper via crimped and wavy margins to pointed, recurved and
slightly twisted tips. The stamens have greenish-white filaments and wine-red anthers.
Best suited for planting in the garden.

'Praecox'   Heracleifolia Group
Synonym: *C.* × *jouiniana* 'Praecox'   AGM 1993

Flowering Period Mid summer to early autumn *or* late summer to mid autumn
Aspect Sunny, to encourage flowering and free draining
Pruning Light *or* Hard
Height or Spread 8–10ft (2.6–3.3m) *or* 6–8ft (2–2.6m)
Flower Size 1½in (4cm)

Semi-herbaceous, deciduous, vigorous semi-climber or scrambler. The origin of this clematis is
unclear but its name was published in Stanley B. Whitehead's book *Garden Clematis*
published in 1959, where he suggested it was introduced around 1900. The clusters of star-shaped flowers each bear
four narrow tepals that are white with deep bluey-mauve tips. The prominent stamens have white filaments and pale
yellow anthers. The woody stems have a relaxed habit that, together with its dense foliage, makes excellent ground
cover or it can be tied up and trained against a wall. Hard pruning will keep the plant more compact but will delay the
flowering period by a few weeks. Best suited for planting in the garden.

PRETTY IN BLUE 'Zopre'   Flammula Group

Flowering Period Early summer to early autumn
Aspect Sunny, to enhance perfume
Pruning Hard
Height or Spread 3–5ft (1–1.6m)
Flower Size 1½–2in (4–5cm)

Herbaceous, deciduous, clump-forming, semi-erect stems. Raised in 1992 by Wim Snoeijer, the Netherlands. The clusters of scented violet-blue, star-shaped flowers have a slightly reddy-purple blush along the central bar. Their four narrow tepals taper via strongly recurved margins to blunt tips. The crown of stamens are an excellent contrast having creamy-white filaments and primrose-yellow anthers. Grow this in a sunny border with support, or through a small silver or golden leaved shrub, which would make a lovely contrast to its dark flowers. Suitable for growing in containers or planting in the garden. PBR: Unlicensed propagation prohibited.

'Prince Charles'   Viticella Group
                                                                       AGM 2002

Flowering Period Early summer to early autumn
Aspect Any
Pruning Hard
Height or Spread 6–8ft (2–2.6m)
Flower Size 3–4in (7.5–10cm)

Deciduous climber. The exact history of this lovely clematis is unknown, other than it was obtained by Alister Keay, New Zealand, who named and introduced it in 1976. Whilst others have this clematis placed in the Late Large-flowered or Jackmanii Groups, we feel justified in placing this within the Viticella Group as its habit and flower size are so similar to others in this group. The light to mid-blue colouring of this charming clematis varies during the course of the day, sometimes appearing almost greenish, azure blue while at other times having a hint of pink becoming a more mauve-blue. The four to six broad tepals have a deeply ribbed surface and a lovely satin sheen, their undulating margins taper to pointed, recurved and slightly twisted tips. The stamens have greenish-yellow filaments and butter-yellow anthers. The cut flowers keep well in water. This is a fantastic clematis and worthy of space in any garden! Suitable for growing in containers or planting in the garden.

'Prince Philip'   Early Large Flowered Group

Flowering Period Late spring to early summer and late summer to early autumn
Aspect Any
Pruning Light
Height or Spread 8–10ft (2.6–3.3m)
Flower Size 5–7in (12.5–18cm)

Deciduous climber. Raised, and introduced in 1977, by Steffen's Clematis Nursery, USA, and named after the husband of Queen Elizabeth II. The six to eight tepals are a rich mid mauvy-blue with a rose-pink bar and luminous satin sheen. They are broad and taper via crimped, wavy margins to pointed tips. The stamens have white filaments merging through pink to chocolate coloured anthers. Best suited for planting in the garden.

'Princess Diana'
Synonym: *C. texensis* 'The Princess of Wales'

Texensis Group
AGM 2002

Flowering Period Mid summer to mid autumn
Aspect Sunny, to enhance colour
Pruning Hard
Height or Spread 6–8ft (2–2.6m)
Flower Size 2–2½in (5–6cm)

Semi-herbaceous, deciduous climber. Raised by Barry Fretwell, Devon, and introduced in 1984. This was originally named 'The Princess of Wales', however it was renamed in 1996 to save confusion with a large flowered clematis of that name which dated from 1875. The trumpet or tulip shaped flowers are upward or outward facing, the outside of which is a very rich deep salmon pink with paler mauve-pink margins. The textured inside of the four or five tepals has deep vibrant salmon pink bars which merge to deep mauve-pink margins, tapering to pointed, reflexed tips. The stamens have creamy-white filaments and butter yellow anthers. This is a stunning clematis that is probably the best in this group. The cut flowers keep well in water. Suitable for growing in containers or planting in the garden.

'Prinsesse Alexandra'

Early Large Flowered Group

Flowering Period Late spring to early summer and late summer to early autumn
Aspect Any
Pruning Light
Height or Spread 6–8ft (2–2.6m)
Flower Size 4–6in (10–15cm)

Deciduous climber. Raised in 1991 by Flemming Hansen, Denmark, and named after Prinsesse Alexandra of Denmark. The gorgeous semi-double blooms produced from the old ripened wood are various shades of pink. The base colour is pinky-white, and then either side of the bar and merging towards the margins is a lovely light peachy-pink that is flushed with mid rose-pink giving an attractive mottled appearance. The eight to ten outer tepals have ruffled slightly incurved margins that taper to pointed, gently reflexed tips, the inner layers are much shorter. The single blooms produced later from the current season's growth normally have six to eight tepals. The stamens are creamy-yellow. Suitable for growing in containers or planting in the garden. PBR: Unlicensed propagation prohibited.

'Propertius'

Atragene Group

Flowering Period Mid to late spring and mid to late summer
Aspect Any, with free drainage
Pruning Tidy after first flush of flowers
Height or Spread 6–8ft (2–2.6m)
Flower Size 2½–3in (6–7.5cm)

Deciduous climber. Raised by Magnus Johnson in Sweden, 1979. The four tepals of the semi-double nodding bell-shaped flowers are a very deep pink with creamy-white margins. The narrower inner layers of staminodes are also creamy-white flushed with light pink. The blooms are held out on long flower stalks, ideal to admire the beauty of these exquisite flowers. Sadly our description does not seem to do justice to this very pretty clematis! The cut flowers keep well in water. Suitable for growing in containers or planting in the garden.

'Prosperity' Montana Group

Flowering Period Late spring to early summer +
Aspect Any
Pruning Tidy after main flowering
Height or Spread 15–20ft (5–6m)
Flower Size 2½–3½in (6–9cm)

Deciduous climber. A sport from 'Continuity' discovered in the garden of Caroline Todhunter and introduced by Sheila Chapman in 2007. The single, pure white flowers have a lovely satin sheen across their four, occasionally five, broad tepals that taper via lightly crimped margins to rounded or squarish tips. The crown of stamens have white filaments with butter yellow anthers. The mid-green leaves appear somewhat silvery due to the covering of fine hairs and the flowers are borne on long stalks. Whilst the main flowering period is late spring and early summer, there is a good display of flowers from late summer to early autumn. Best suited for planting in the garden.

'Proteus' Early Large Flowered Group

Flowering Period Late spring to early summer and early autumn
Aspect Any
Pruning Light
Height or Spread 6–8ft (2–2.6m)
Flower Size 5½–6in (13–15cm)

Deciduous climber. Raised, and introduced in 1876, by Charles Noble, Bagshot. The early blooms produced from the old ripened wood are double and a lovely deep dusky purply-pink with a textured surface. The outer layer of six to eight broad tepals taper to blunt tips, whereas the inner layers tend to have more pointed tips with frilly and somewhat twisted margins. If the spring has been dull and cold, the early blooms can have a green tint which usually disappears as the light levels increase. The single blooms produced later from the current season's growth are rather paler in colour than the double blooms and have slightly paler bars. The stamens have white filaments flushed with pink and butter-yellow anthers. A lovely old cultivar that combines well with cream-coloured climbing roses. Suitable for growing in containers or planting in the garden.

'Purple Spider' Atragene Group

Flowering Period Mid to late spring
Aspect Any, with free drainage
Pruning Tidy after flowering
Height or Spread 6–8ft (2–2.6m)
Flower Size 2½–3in (6–7.5cm)

Deciduous climber. Discovered in 1992 by Wim Snoeijer in the clematis collection of Jan Fopma, the Netherlands. The semi-double nodding bell-shaped blooms are a very dark purple, almost black, when first open, which is quite unusual in this group of clematis. This deep colouring shows well against the light green foliage – it is quite lovely. The cut flowers keep well in water. Suitable for growing in containers or planting in the garden.

'Purpurea Plena Elegans'

Viticella Group
AGM 1993

Flowering Period Mid summer to early autumn
Aspect Any
Pruning Hard
Height or Spread 8–10ft (2.6–3.3m)
Flower Size 1½–2½in (4–6cm)

Deciduous climber. Raised in France by Morel in the late 1800s, this gorgeous clematis has double dusky-magenta rosette-shaped flowers. The four to six broad tepals have a textured surface and their crimped margins taper to blunt tips. The many inner layers of petaloid staminodes are narrow, somewhat twisted and taper to pointed recurved tips. This looks wonderful when grown with creamy-white or apricot coloured climbing roses and its attractive flowers keep well in water. We have seen this clematis growing along rope 'swags' in the RHS gardens at Hyde Hall in Essex – it looked lovely. Best suited for planting in the garden.

QUEEN MOTHER 'Zoqum'

Viticella Group

Flowering Period Early summer to early autumn
Aspect Any
Pruning Hard
Height or Spread 4–6ft (1.3–2m)
Flower Size 1¼–1½in (3–4cm)

Deciduous climber. Raised by Willem Straver, Germany in 2003. The very 'regal' looking nodding bell-shaped flowers are light mauve-pink on the outside with paler margins and a deeply ribbed surface. The four tepals taper via crimped margins to pointed, strongly recurved tips revealing the inner textured surface of deep purply-pink. The anthers are yellow. A unique new clematis which, we are sure, will fast become much sought after! Suitable for growing in containers or planting in the garden. PBR applied for.

'Rahvarinne'

Early Large Flowered Group

Flowering Period Early summer to mid autumn
Aspect Any
Pruning Light
Height or Spread 6–8ft (2–2.6m)
Flower Size 4–5in (10–12.5cm)

Deciduous climber. Raised by Uno and Aili Kivistik, Estonia, in 1985. The wonderful reddish-purple flowers, which mature to dusky plum, have a deeply textured surface. Their six very broad tepals overlap and taper via undulating margins to blunt, slightly recurved tips. The stamens have white filaments and reddy-brown anthers. A lovely free-flowering clematis. Suitable for growing in containers or planting in the garden.

REBECCA 'Evipo016'

Early Large Flowered Group

Flowering Period Late spring to early summer and late summer to early autumn
Aspect Any
Pruning Light
Height or Spread 6–8ft (2–2.6m)
Flower Size 5–7in (12.5–18cm)

Deciduous climber. Raised, and introduced in 2008, by Raymond Evison, Guernsey and named after one of his daughters. The display of glorious rich velvety red blooms is an absolute 'show stopper'. In the sun they look almost crimson, whereas in partial shade or in the evening light they take on a much deeper tone. The six to eight broad, overlapping tepals taper via crimped margins to blunt, gently reflexed tips. The stamens have creamy-white filaments and coffee coloured anthers. Suitable for growing in containers or planting in the garden. PBR: Unlicensed propagation prohibited.

recta   Flammula Group

Flowering Period Early to late summer
Aspect Sunny, to enhance perfume
Pruning Hard
Height or Spread 3–5ft (1–1.6m)
Flower Size ¾in (2cm)

Herbaceous, deciduous, clump-forming, semi-erect stems. A native of central and southern Europe, introduced to Britain in 1597. This dainty clematis has long been a favourite of garden designers, with its clouds of small white star-shaped flowers that have a hawthorn-like perfume. The clusters of flowers display well with their bluey-green foliage. Suitable for growing in containers or planting in the garden.

recta 'Purpurea'   Flammula Group

Flowering Period Early to late summer
Aspect Sunny, to enhance perfume
Pruning Hard
Height or Spread 3–5ft (1–1.6m)
Flower Size ¾in (2cm)

Herbaceous, deciduous, clump-forming, semi-erect stems. A selected form of *C. recta* that has purply-bronze foliage; otherwise it is identical, with its clusters of small white star-shaped flowers that have a hawthorn-like perfume. We are particularly fond of this clematis as its glorious rich foliage is such a good addition to herbaceous borders long before their flowers open. Give it some support to keep its stems erect and it will repay you! Suitable for growing in containers or planting in the garden.

'Red Beetroot Beauty'   Atragene Group
Synonym: 'Betina'

Flowering Period Mid to late spring
Aspect Any, with free drainage
Pruning Tidy after flowering
Height or Spread 8–10ft (2.6–3.3m)
Flower Size 1½in (4cm)

Deciduous climber. Raised by Magnus Johnson, Sweden, 1980. The original name 'Betina' was not accepted under the ICNCP rules, so Magnus Johnson renamed it 'Red Beetroot Beauty' which actually describes the colour of this clematis very well, although the name 'Betina' tends to be most widely used. It is a deep purply-red almost the same colour as cooked beetroot. The single nodding bell-shaped blooms are brighter in colour on the inside. The cream staminodes are streaked with purply-red. The cut flowers keep well in water. Suitable for growing in containers or planting in the garden.

'Red Pearl'   Early Large Flowered Group

Flowering Period Late spring to early summer and late summer to early autumn
Aspect Partial shade, to preserve colour
Pruning Light
Height or Spread 4–5ft (1.3–1.6m)
Flower Size 5–6in (12.5–15cm)

Deciduous climber. Raised, and introduced about 1992, by Kozo Sugimoto, Japan. The pretty star-shaped flowers have broad purply-cerise margins and a bright crimson bar when first open and mature to light purply-cerise, losing their bar and taking on a rather mottled appearance. Their six to eight broad, overlapping tepals taper to pointed tips via ruffled margins. The contrasting stamens have white filaments and butter-yellow anthers. Suitable for growing in containers or planting in the garden.

REFLECTIONS 'Evipo035'   Late Large Flowered Group

Flowering Period Early summer to early autumn
Aspect Any
Pruning Hard
Height or Spread 4–6ft (1.3–2m)
Flower Size 4–6in (10–15cm)

Deciduous climber. Raised, and introduced in 2010, by Raymond Evison, Guernsey. The attractive semi-double flowers open lilac-blue with a hint of pink at their base, and they mature to pale lilac-blue. The six outer tepals are broad, overlapping and taper to blunt tips via slightly undulating margins. There is an inner layer of somewhat smaller tepals, or petaloid staminodes, that are beautifully offset by a crown of contrasting stamens. Suitable for growing in containers or planting in the garden. PBR: Unlicensed propagation prohibited.

rehderiana   AGM 1993

Flowering Period Early to late autumn
Aspect Sunny, to enhance perfume and free-draining
Pruning Hard
Height or Spread 10–15ft (3.3–5m)
Flower Size ³⁄₄in (2cm)

Deciduous climber. A native of western China and Tibet. This lovely clematis makes a fantastic garden plant, given a sunny position and a fair bit of space. We used to grow ours over a huge viburnum that stood around ten feet tall (3.3m). The dainty pale yellow nodding bell-shaped flowers are borne in clusters and have a cowslip-like perfume. Each little flower has four 'ribbed' tepals whose tips roll back. The tips of the pale yellow anthers are just visible inside the bells. Its leaves have five to nine small leaflets, hairy on both sides and with coarsely toothed margins. Sometimes slow to establish, *C. rehderiana* will eventually become a vigorous climber. The cut flowers keep well in water, bringing their delicate perfume into the house. Best suited for planting in the garden.

'Remembrance'   Late Large Flowered Group

Flowering Period Mid summer to early autumn
Aspect Any
Pruning Hard
Height or Spread 6–8ft (2–2.6m)
Flower Size 4–5in (10–12.5cm)

Deciduous climber. The pretty light raspberry-red flowers mature to a very deep pink and have a crown of contrasting stamens with white filaments and bright yellow anthers. The six tepals have a deeply textured surface and their crimped margins taper to rounded, recurved tips. Suitable for growing in containers or planting in the garden.

'Rhapsody' (Fretwell)   Early Large Flowered Group

Flowering Period Late spring to late summer *or* early summer to early autumn
Aspect Any
Pruning Light *or* Hard
Height or Spread 6–8ft (2–2.6m) *or* 4–5ft (1.3–1.6m)
Flower Size 4–5¹⁄₂in (10–13cm)

Deciduous climber. Raised by Barry Fretwell, Devon, and introduced in 1991. 'Rhapsody' has the most beautiful bright sapphire-blue star-shaped flowers with six deeply textured tepals tapering along crimped and undulating margins to pointed tips. The crown of stamens are an excellent contrast, having white filaments and primrose yellow anthers. This is one of the very few large flowered clematis to have a noticeable sweet scent. Hard pruning will keep the plant more compact but will delay the flowering period by a few weeks. Suitable for growing in containers or planting in the garden.

'Richard Pennell'

Early Large Flowered Group
AGM 1993

Flowering Period Early to late summer
Aspect Any
Pruning Light
Height or Spread 8–10ft (2.6–3.3m)
Flower Size 5–7in (12.5–18cm)

Deciduous climber. Raised in 1962 by Walter Pennell, Lincoln, and named after his son. The elegant blooms are dark pinkish-lavender with a hint of deep rose-pink down the centre of each tepal and radiating in veins through the textured surface towards the margins. The six to eight broad tepals taper to pointed tips via crimped and wavy margins. The beautiful crown of stamens have deep rose-pink filaments and creamy-yellow anthers. Best suited for planting in the garden.

'Roko-Kolla'

Late Large Flowered Group

Flowering Period Early summer to early autumn
Aspect Any
Pruning Hard
Height or Spread 6–8ft (2–2.6m)
Flower Size 6–7in (15–17cm)

Deciduous climber. Raised in 1982 by Uno and Aili Kivistik, Estonia. The beautiful white star-shaped flowers have a glorious satin sheen across their lightly textured surface. The four to eight broad tepals have pale green bars when first open which gradually fade as the blooms mature. The lightly crimped, slightly undulating margins taper to pointed tips that gently recurve as the flowers age. The stamens have white filaments and pale yellow anthers. Suitable for growing in containers or planting in the garden.

'Romantika'

Late Large Flowered Group
BCS Certificate of Merit 1998

Flowering Period Mid summer to early autumn
Aspect Any
Pruning Hard
Height or Spread 6–8ft (2–2.6m)
Flower Size 4–5in (10–12.5cm)

Deciduous climber. Raised in 1983 by Uno and Aili Kivistik, Estonia. The very dark, velvety purple flowers, which are almost black when first open, have a lovely satin sheen and a slightly paler bar. The four to six broad tepals have undulating margins tapering to blunt tips. The pale yellow stamens make an excellent contrast to the dark tepals. For years this clematis has survived, against all the odds, on a very dry bank in our garden, growing amongst mature shrubs. It looks stunning clambering up into a double flowered Philadelphus as they bloom at the same time, while some stems cascade down over the variegated foliage of *Abelia* 'Francis Mason'. Suitable for growing in containers or planting in the garden.

'Rooguchi'

Diversifolia Group

Flowering Period Early summer to mid autumn
Aspect Any
Pruning Hard
Height or Spread 6–8ft (2–2.6m)
Flower Size 2–2½in (5–6cm)

Herbaceous, deciduous, non-clinging, semi-climber or scrambler. Raised in Japan by Mr. Kazushige Ozawa in 1988. The rich, glossy deep purple bell-shaped flowers have paler silvery-purple margins that taper to pointed recurved tips. Each of the four tepals has very prominent ribs down the centre. The purple interior of the bell has shiny reddy-purple bars and the butter yellow anthers are just visible. The long, rigid flower stalks makes these blooms ideal for flower-arranging, they last for over a week in water. Suitable for growing in containers or planting in the garden.

'Rooran'   Early Large Flowered Group

Flowering Period Late spring to early summer and late summer to early autumn
Aspect Any
Pruning Light
Height or Spread 6–8ft (2–2.6m)
Flower Size 5–6in (12.5–15cm)

Deciduous climber. Raised in 1995 by Mrs Masako Takeuchi, Japan, and introduced to the UK in 2005 by Thorncroft Clematis Nursery. The pale pink background is overlaid with deep rose-pink around the broad margins and along the outer half of the bar, which gives a somewhat mottled appearance. The eight broad tepals overlap and taper to blunt tips via attractive, wavy margins. The stamens have yellowy-white filaments with reddy-brown anthers. The cut flowers keep well in water. Suitable for growing in containers or planting in the garden.

'Rosa Königskind'   Early Large Flowered Group

Flowering Period Late spring to early summer and late summer to early autumn
Aspect Any
Pruning Light
Height or Spread 4–6ft (1.3–2m)
Flower Size 4–5in (10–12.5cm)

Deciduous climber. Raised in 1994 by Manfred Westphal, Germany. 'Rosa Königskind' has a profusion of very pretty light mauve-pink star-shaped flowers which it produces on a neat, compact plant. The six to eight broad, overlapping tepals are lightly textured and taper via crimped and undulating margins to pointed tips. The stamens have white filaments and dark wine red anthers, and are an excellent contrast to the tepals. Suitable for growing in containers or planting in the garden. PBR: Unlicensed propagation prohibited.

'Rose Supreme'   Early Large Flowered Group

Flowering Period Late spring to early summer and late summer to early autumn
Aspect Any
Pruning Light
Height or Spread 6–8ft (2–2.6m)
Flower Size 5–7in (12.5–18cm)

Deciduous climber. Raised by Frank Watkinson, Doncaster, around the early 1980s, it was given to us in 1991 by his wife. These gorgeous pale satin pink star-shaped flowers have deeper lilac-pink running through veins across the surface of their six to eight tepals that taper to pointed tips, the later blooms are more light mauve-pink. The stamens have cream filaments and butter yellow anthers. Suitable for growing in containers or planting in the garden.

'Rosea'   Integrifolia Group

Flowering Period Mid to late summer
Aspect Any
Pruning Hard
Height or Spread 2–3ft (60cm–1m)
Flower Size 1½in (4cm)

Herbaceous, deciduous, clump-forming, semi-erect or scrambling stems. Unfortunately, it has become obvious in recent years that the clematis currently grown and sold as 'Rosea' are somewhat variable in shade and shape of flower. However, they are all a mid mauvy-pink with open nodding bell-shaped flowers, and their four tepals taper to pointed, recurved tips. The original 'Rosea' received an Award of Garden Merit but due to the uncertainty of which was actually the original form, we have not included the award in these details. Suitable for growing in containers or planting in the garden.

ROSEMOOR 'Evipo002'

Early Large Flowered Group

Flowering Period Early summer to early autumn
Aspect Any
Pruning Light
Height or Spread 6–8ft (2–2.6m)
Flower Size 5–6in (12.5–15cm)

Deciduous climber. Raised, and introduced in 2004, by Raymond Evison, Guernsey and named after the RHS garden in Devon. The glorious rich velvety-red blooms have six to eight broad, overlapping tepals that taper via crimped, undulating margins to blunt tips. Their contrasting crown of stamens have purply-red filaments and butter-yellow anthers. Suitable for growing in containers or planting in the garden. PBR: Unlicensed propagation prohibited.

'Rosy O'Grady'

Atragene Group
AGM 2002

Flowering Period Mid to late spring
Aspect Any, with free drainage
Pruning Tidy after flowering
Height or Spread 8–10ft (2.6–3.3m)
Flower Size 2½–3in (6–7.5cm)

Deciduous climber. Raised by Dr F.L. Skinner, Canada, around the early 1960s. The large mid mauvy-pink semi-double bell-shaped flowers have deeper pink veining on the outside. The margins of the four tepals recurve to reveal the pale pink on their underside and creamy-white staminodes. The blooms have a very delicate appearance which belies their tough nature. Best suited for planting in the garden.

'Rouge Cardinal'

Late Large Flowered Group

Flowering Period Early to late summer
Aspect Any
Pruning Hard
Height or Spread 6–8ft (2–2.6m)
Flower Size 4–5in (10–12.5cm)

Deciduous climber. Raised in France by A. Girault and introduced to Britain by Jim Fisk in the 1960s. This lovely clematis opens a very dark burgundy-wine red and has a wonderful velvety sheen that adds depth to its colouring. As the blooms mature the colour changes to a deep purply-cerise and their six broad tepals taper to blunt, recurved tips. The stamens have creamy-white filaments and coffee-coloured anthers. A lovely old, reliable clematis. Suitable for growing in containers or planting in the garden.

'Royal Velours'

Viticella Group
AGM 1993

Flowering Period Mid summer to early autumn
Aspect Any
Pruning Hard
Height or Spread 8–10ft (2.6–3.3m)
Flower Size 2½–3in (6–7.5cm)

Deciduous climber. Raised in France by Morel, probably around the early 1900s. The elegant, semi-nodding to outward facing flowers are a rich, velvety purply-red, or reddy-purple depending upon how you see colours! As the flowers mature the colour gently fades and appears to have mauve mottling across the four or five, occasionally six, broad, overlapping tepals that taper via crimped, undulating margins to blunt, recurved tips. Best suited for planting in the garden.

ROYAL VELVET 'Evifour'   Early Large Flowered Group

Flowering Period Late spring to early summer and late summer to early autumn
Aspect Any
Pruning Light
Height or Spread 6–8ft (2–2.6m)
Flower Size 5–6½in (12.5–16cm)

Deciduous climber. Raised, and introduced in 1993, by Raymond Evison, Guernsey. The rich velvety reddy-purple blooms have a brighter purply-red bar enhancing their star-like shape. The six to eight broad, overlapping tepals have a lightly textured surface and crimped, gently undulating margins that taper to blunt tips. The stamens have pink filaments and dark red anthers. Suitable for growing in containers or planting in the garden. PBR: Unlicensed propagation prohibited.

'Ruby'   Atragene Group
Synonym: *C. alpina* 'Ruby'

Flowering Period Mid to late spring and late summer
Aspect Any, with free drainage
Pruning Tidy after first flush of flowers
Height or Spread 6–8ft (2–2.6m)
Flower Size 1½–2in (4–5cm)

Deciduous climber. Raised by Ernest Markham, East Grinstead, in 1937. 'Ruby' has very deep reddy-pink nodding bell-shaped flowers that open to reveal creamy-white staminodes which have a flush of mauve-pink at their tips. We prefer to see 'Ruby' growing in full sun where her colour is so much better than when grown in a shady position. Suitable for growing in containers or planting in the garden.

'Rüütel' (pronounced Rootle)   Late Large Flowered Group

Flowering Period Early summer to early autumn
Aspect Any
Pruning Hard
Height or Spread 6–8ft (2–2.6m)
Flower Size 6–7in (15–17cm)

Deciduous climber. Raised in 1982 by Uno and Aili Kivistik, Estonia. The deep, slightly purplish, red star-shaped flowers are lightly mottled with white and have a rich, almost luminous red bar. The six or seven broad tepals have a textured surface and crimped, gently recurved margins that taper to pointed slightly recurved tips. The stamens have purply-pink filaments and wine red anthers. Suitable for growing in containers or planting in the garden.

'Saalomon' (pronounced Solomon)   Late Large Flowered Group

Flowering Period Mid summer to early autumn
Aspect Any
Pruning Hard
Height or Spread 6–8ft (2–2.6m)
Flower Size 5–6in (12.5–15cm)

Deciduous climber. Raised in 1985 by Uno and Aili Kivistik, Estonia. The pure white blooms have a deeply textured surface and their six broad, overlapping tepals have crimped and wavy margins that taper to pointed tips. The stamens have white filaments and butter yellow anthers. Suitable for growing in containers or planting in the garden.

'Sander'

Heracleifolia Group

Flowering Period Mid summer to early autumn
Aspect Sunny to enhance perfume, and free-draining
Pruning Hard
Height or Spread 3–6ft (1–2m)
Flower Size 1½–2in (4–5cm)

Herbaceous, deciduous, semi-erect woody stems. Raised in 1989 by R. Zwijnenburg, the Netherlands. Borne in clusters, the pretty satin-white star-like flowers have a bluish tinge when first open. Each bloom has four to six narrow tepals which taper via recurved margins to blunt slightly recurved tips. The stamens have white filaments and pale yellow anthers, and it has a delicate cowslip scent. The woody stems are almost self-supporting but may benefit from support as summer progresses. Suitable for growing in containers or planting in the garden.

'Semu'

Late Large Flowered Group

Flowering Period Mid summer to early autumn
Aspect Any
Pruning Hard
Height or Spread 6–8ft (2–2.6m)
Flower Size 4–5½in (10–13cm)

Deciduous climber. Raised, and introduced in 1981, by Uno and Aili Kivistik, Estonia. The lovely light lavender-blue semi-nodding to outward facing flowers have six broad, overlapping tepals that taper via undulating margins to pointed tips. The reverse is dusky lavender-blue with a pale mauve bar and three deep lavender-blue ribs. The stamens have creamy-white filaments, dark coffee coloured anthers and prominent cream stigma. Suitable for growing in containers or planting in the garden.

serratifolia

Tangutica Group

Flowering Period Late summer to early autumn
Aspect Sunny to encourage flowering, and free-draining
Pruning Hard
Height or Spread 8–10ft (2.6–3.3m)
Flower Size 1½in (4cm)

Deciduous climber. A native of north eastern China, south eastern Russia, North Korea and northern Japan introduced to Britain around 1918. The pretty pale to light, slightly greenish-yellow nodding bell-shaped flowers open out as they mature to reveal their contrasting reddish-purple stamens. Grown in a sunny position its lovely citrus-like perfume will be quite noticeable. We grow ours over a purply-bronze leaved berberis which perfectly displays the interesting leaves, charming flowers and silky seed heads of the clematis. The cut flowers and seed heads keep well in water. Best suited for planting in the garden.

'Sheila Thacker'

Early Large Flowered Group

Flowering Period Late spring to early summer and late summer to mid autumn
Aspect Any
Pruning Light
Height or Spread 8–10ft (2.6–3.3m)
Flower Size 6–7in (15–17cm)

Deciduous climber. Raised from naturally or 'open' pollinated seed of 'Marie Boisselot' by Mr. Charles Thacker, a respected Norfolk clematarian, and named after his wife. Introduced by Thorncroft Clematis Nursery in 1996. The beautiful pale mauvy-blue flowers are slightly deeper along the bar, bearing six to eight broad tepals that overlap and taper via undulating margins to blunt tips. The stamens have white filaments and coffee coloured anthers. An excellent free-flowering cultivar. Best suited for planting in the garden.

'Shikoo'   Early Large Flowered Group

Flowering Period Late spring to early summer and late summer to early autumn
Aspect Not north
Pruning Light
Height or Spread 6–8ft (2–2.6m)
Flower Size 4–6in (10–15cm)

Deciduous climber. A sport of 'The President' discovered by Mr Teruo Isogai, Japan, in 1985, and soon to be introduced by Thorncroft Clematis. The very double rosette-like blooms are rich purply-blue with a slightly paler bar. They have eight broad and overlapping outer tepals that taper to pointed tips via slightly undulating margins. The many inner layers of tepals are narrower with very pointed tips. Very similar to the already widely grown clematis 'Multi Blue', but we have found 'Shikoo' to be the better of the two cultivars. Suitable for growing in containers or planting in the garden.

SHIMMER 'Evipo028'   Late Large Flowered Group

Flowering Period Early summer to early autumn
Aspect Any
Pruning Hard
Height or Spread 4–6ft (1.3–2m)
Flower Size 5–7in (12.5–17cm)

Deciduous climber. Raised, and introduced in 2010, by Raymond Evison, Guernsey. The deep lilac-blue flowers have a paler bar and a hint of rose-pink near the crown of contrasting stamens, the tepal colour matures to light blue. The broad, overlapping tepals taper to pointed tips via undulating margins. Suitable for growing in containers or planting in the garden. PBR: Unlicensed propagation prohibited.

'Silver Moon'   Early Large Flowered Group

Flowering Period Late spring to early summer and late summer to early autumn
Aspect Any
Pruning Light
Height or Spread 6–8ft (2–2.6m)
Flower Size 5–7in (12.5–17cm)

Deciduous climber. Raised by Percy Picton in Worcestershire and introduced by Jim Fisk in 1971. The pretty silvery-mauve-grey flowers have a satin sheen across their six to eight broad, overlapping tepals. Their lightly crimped margins taper to rounded, gently recurved tips. The stamens have white filaments with pale yellow anthers. A super clematis that never fails to please the eye. The cut flowers keep well in water. Suitable for growing in containers or planting in the garden.

'Sir Eric Savill'   Montana Group

Flowering Period Late spring to early summer
Aspect Any
Pruning Tidy after flowering
Height or Spread 15+ft (5+m)
Flower Size 2½in (6cm)

Deciduous climber. Sadly, the history of this beautiful clematis is at present unknown, although it is thought to have originated at the Savill Gardens, Windsor. The deep-pink buds open to a pretty mid-pink with slightly paler margins and gradually mature to light pink – this range of shades makes for a really lovely display of flowers. Their four broad tepals have a lightly textured surface whose crimped, almost ruffled margins taper to rather square 'notched' tips that gently recurve as the blooms mature. The stamens have greenish-cream filaments with golden yellow anthers and the foliage is an elegant purply-bronze. Best suited for planting in the garden.

'Sir Trevor Lawrence'   Texensis Group

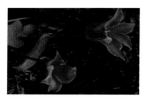

Flowering Period Early summer to early autumn
Aspect Sunny, to encourage flowering
Pruning Hard
Height or Spread 8–10ft (2.6–3.3m)
Flower Size 2–2½in (5–6cm)

Semi-herbaceous, deciduous climber. Raised by Arthur Jackman, Woking, in 1890 and named after the gentleman who was at the time President of the Royal Horticultural Society. The upward or outward facing trumpet or tulip shaped flowers are a dusky purply-red on the outside. Their four to six pointed tepals reflex to reveal the inner surface that has bright scarlet-red bars merging to light reddy-purple margins. The stamens have creamy-white filaments and butter-yellow anthers. Best suited for planting in the garden.

'Sizaia Ptitsa' (pronounced Sisia Feetsa)   Diversifolia Group

Flowering Period Early summer to mid autumn
Aspect Any
Pruning Hard
Height or Spread 5–8ft (1.6–2.6m)
Flower Size 3–5in (7.5–12.5cm)

Semi-herbaceous, deciduous, non-clinging, semi-climber or scrambler. Raised in 1967 by M.A. Beskaravainaya at the Nikitsky State Botanic Garden, Ukraine. The open, semi-nodding flowers are dusky violet-purple on the inside with a deeper violet bar. The four to six tepals have margins that both incurve and recurve towards the pointed recurved tip making an attractive, slightly twisted bloom. The reverse is dusky violet with dark glossy violet along the three mid-ribs. The stamens have violet-white filaments and dark reddy-brown anthers. The cut flowers keep well in water. Suitable for growing in containers or planting in the garden.

'Snowdrift'   Armandii Group

Flowering Period Early to late spring
Aspect Sunny to enhance perfume, sheltered and free draining
Pruning Tidy after flowering
Height or Spread 15–20ft (5–6m)
Flower Size 2in (5cm)

Evergreen climber. The individual white flowers of 'Snowdrift' are larger than those of the species *C. armandii*, however, they have the same gorgeous vanilla-like perfume and long oval evergreen leaves that are a glossy dark green, borne in threes. Best suited for planting in the garden.

'Snow Queen'   Early Large Flowered Group

Flowering Period Late spring to early summer and late summer to early autumn
Aspect Any
Pruning Light
Height or Spread 6–8ft (2–2.6m)
Flower Size 6–7in (15–17cm)

Deciduous climber. Selected by W.S. Callick, New Zealand, in 1956 and introduced there in 1960 by Alister Keay. The early blooms open bluey-white, which changes to pure white as they mature. Then later in the season the blooms open pinky-white with a hint of a pink bar, but again as the blooms mature they clear to pure white. The six to eight broad, overlapping tepals have a textured and deeply ribbed surface with crimped and somewhat wavy margins tapering to blunt tips. The contrasting stamens have pale pink filaments and dark burgundy-red anthers. We have grown this elegant clematis with a very dark red climbing rose called 'Étoile de Hollande' – they looked magnificent together. Suitable for growing in containers or planting in the garden.

'Södertälje' (pronounced Sir-da-tarlia)   Viticella Group

Flowering Period Mid summer to early autumn
Aspect Any
Pruning Hard
Height or Spread 8–10ft (2.6–3.3m)
Flower Size 2–3in (5–7.5cm)

Deciduous climber. Introduced in Sweden by Magnus Johnson in the mid 1950s. The dusky pinkish-red semi-nodding flowers have four, sometimes five tepals which taper via crimped margins to rounded recurved tips. The stamens have greeny-yellow filaments and anthers. It looks gorgeous grown with apricot coloured climbing roses such as 'Climbing Lady Hillingdon' or 'Alchymist'. Best suited for planting in the garden.

'Sokojiro'   Early Large Flowered Group

Flowering Period Late spring to early summer and late summer to early autumn
Aspect Any
Pruning Light
Height or Spread 6–8ft (2–2.6m)
Flower Size 6–9in (15–22cm)

Deciduous climber. Bred in Japan by Mr Hiroshi Takeuchi and soon to be introduced by Thorncroft Clematis. The elegant star-shaped blooms are light to mid mauvy-blue with paler, often creamy-white bars. They have a lovely satin sheen across their six or seven broad, overlapping tepals which taper to pointed tips. The crown of contrasting stamens have creamy-white filaments and wine red anthers. It has proven to be an excellent new cultivar in our trials. Suitable for growing in containers or planting in the garden.

'Solidarność'   Early Large Flowered Group

Flowering Period Late spring to early summer and late summer to early autumn
Aspect Any
Pruning Light
Height or Spread 4–6ft (1.3–2m)
Flower Size 5–6in (12.5–15cm)

Deciduous climber. Raised in 1993 by Szczepan Marczyński, Poland, and named after Solidarity, the Polish Independent Trade Union that was formed in 1980 and instigated the collapse of the Communist system in central and eastern Europe. The beautiful, dark velvety red blooms mature to a rich mid-red with a slightly lighter bar. Their six broad, overlapping tepals have lightly crimped, undulating margins tapering to blunt tips that gently recurve as the blooms mature. The stamens have pinky-white filaments and dark red anthers. Suitable for growing in containers or planting in the garden.

'Special Occasion'   Early Large Flowered Group

Flowering Period Late spring to early summer and late summer to early autumn
Aspect Any
Pruning Light
Height or Spread 6–8ft (2–2.6m)
Flower Size 6–7in (15–17cm)

Deciduous climber. Raised in 1987 by Ken Pyne, Chingford. The pretty blooms are a very pale pearly bluey-mauve with a slightly deeper bar and they have a delicate satin sheen across their surface. The six broad, overlapping tepals taper via undulating margins to blunt tips. The stamens have white filaments and dark coffee-coloured anthers. Suitable for growing in containers or planting in the garden.

stans   Heracleifolia Group

Flowering Period Mid summer to mid autumn
Aspect Sunny to enhance perfume, and free draining
Pruning Hard
Height or Spread 3–4ft (1–1.3m)
Flower Size ½–1in (1.3–2.5cm)

Herbaceous, deciduous, clump-forming, erect woody stems. A species originating from Japan
that has woody, largely self-supporting stems, and clusters of small hyacinth shaped flowers whose crimped margins taper to strongly recurved tips. Because seed was collected in
different areas, both the colour of the flowers, which range from a bluish-white to pale blue, and the strength of the
perfume varies. But whatever, they are very pretty and worthy of space in the garden. Suitable for growing in containers
or planting in the garden.

'Star of India'   Late Large Flowered Group
                                                              FCC 1867

Flowering Period Mid summer to early autumn
Aspect Any
Pruning Hard
Height or Spread 8–12ft (2.6–4m)
Flower Size 4–5in (10–12.5cm)

Deciduous climber. Raised in 1864 by Thomas Cripps, Tunbridge Wells. This lovely reliable
old clematis has four to six rounded-edged tepals that taper to blunt tips. They open a
rich reddish-purple which matures to deep bluey-purple with cerise bars running down their centre and radiating out
in veins across their textured surface. The stamens have creamy-white filaments and beige anthers. This looked fantastic growing through our rose hedge of *Rosa rugosa* 'Alba' and 'Roseraie de l'Hay'. Best suited for planting in the garden.

STILL WATERS 'Zostiwa'   Early Large Flowered Group

Flowering Period Late spring to late summer
Aspect Any
Pruning Light
Height or Spread 5–6ft (1.6–2m)
Flower Size 3–4in (7.5–10cm)

Deciduous climber. Raised in the Netherlands in 1999 by Wim Snoeijer. The pale mauvy-
blue flowers have a pretty satin sheen. The six to eight broad overlapping tepals taper to
blunt tips via crimped, slightly incurved margins that flatten out as the bloom matures. The beautifully contrasting
stamens have white filaments and wine red anthers. This lovely clematis is compact and very free-flowering. Suitable
for growing in containers or planting in the garden. PBR: Unlicensed propagation prohibited.

'Stolwijk Gold'   Atragene Group

Flowering Period Mid to late spring
Aspect Any, with free drainage
Pruning Tidy after flowering
Height or Spread 6–8ft (2–2.6m)
Flower Size 1½–2in (4–5cm)

Deciduous climber. Discovered by Hans Stolwijk in 2001, introduced by G.C. Stolwijk and
Co., The Netherlands, in 2006. This has fabulous golden-yellow foliage which is at its
most striking in the spring, especially when grown in a sunny situation. The leaves contrast particularly well with the
dark red stems. The deep purply-blue nodding bell-shaped flowers have a white inner skirt that has violet-blue shadings
and display themselves well against the bright foliage. The cut flowers keep well in water. Suitable for growing in
containers or planting in the garden. PBR: Unlicensed propagation prohibited.

'Swedish Bells'

Diversifolia Group

Flowering Period Mid summer to early autumn
Aspect Sunny, to encourage flowering
Pruning Hard
Height or Spread 5–6ft (1.6–2m)
Flower Size 1½–2¼in (4–6cm)

Herbaceous, deciduous, non-clinging, semi-climber or scrambler. Raised by Magnus Johnson in Sweden, it was introduced to the UK by Thorncroft Clematis Nursery in 2005. The nodding bell-shaped flowers have four deeply ribbed tepals which taper via ruffled margins to pointed recurved tips. The outside is lavender-blue with a gorgeous satin sheen and has paler matt, bluey-white margins. The inside of the bells is pale lavender-blue with a glistening textured surface. The tips of the butter yellow anthers are just visible. The cut flowers keep well in water. Suitable for growing in containers or planting in the garden.

'Sylvia Denny'

Early Large Flowered Group

Flowering Period Late spring to early summer and late summer to early autumn
Aspect Any
Pruning Light
Height or Spread 8–10ft (2.6–3.3m)
Flower Size 4–5in (10–12.5cm)

Deciduous climber. Raised in 1974 by Stephen Denny, Preston, and named after his mother. The early blooms produced from the old ripened wood are double or semi-double, with single blooms later from the current season's growth. They are pure white with a satin sheen and have a textured surface. The outer tepals of the semi-double blooms are broad, overlap and taper to blunt, gently recurved tips, the inner layers taper to pointed tips and all have lightly crimped and wavy margins. The stamens have white filaments and primrose-yellow anthers. An exceptionally good double white and a far better garden plant than the well-known clematis 'Duchess of Edinburgh'! Best suited for planting in the garden.

'Tae'

Early Large Flowered Group

Flowering Period Late spring to early summer and late summer to early autumn
Aspect Any
Pruning Light
Height or Spread 6–8ft (2–2.6m)
Flower Size 6–8in (15–20cm)

Deciduous climber. Raised by Mr. Ren Tanaka, Japan, and named after his late first wife. Introduced to Britain in 2009 by Thorncroft Clematis Nursery. An amazing star-like bloom whose eight tepals taper to very pointed tips. The shape is enhanced as the bloom matures because the edges of the tepals recurve and twist slightly giving an almost Catherine wheel-like appearance. The base colour of the tepals is white, which is overlaid with very deep purply-pink from halfway along the tepal towards the tips. The margins are also outlined with this deep colouring and the whole surface has a beautiful satin sheen. The crown of stamens have white filaments and dark purply-pink anthers. The cut blooms keep well in water. Suitable for growing in containers or planting in the garden. PBR applied for.

TEMPTATION 'Zotemp'

Early Large Flowered Group

Flowering Period Late spring to early summer and late summer to early autumn
Aspect Sunny, to enhance colour
Pruning Light
Height or Spread 4–5ft (1.3–1.6m)
Flower Size 4–5in (10–12.5cm)

Deciduous climber. Raised by Willem Straver, Germany, in 2002 and introduced to the UK by Thorncroft Clematis Nursery in 2009. TEMPTATION produces gloriously unusual, very neat, double and semi-double blooms early, with single flowers later. The seven or eight broad tepals of the early flowers are a deep purply-red maturing to deep purply-pink; they have slightly incurving margins which are deeply crimped, and a green and white bar on the reverse is apparent on the surface when lit from behind. The multi-layered rosette-like centre of petaloid stamens are light pinkish-purple, green and mauve and the stamens have cream filaments with dark purply-red anthers. The single flowers have bright cerise-pink bars that merge to deep pinky-mauve margins which tend to recurve and are not as crimped as those of the double flowers. Suitable for growing in containers or planting in the garden. PBR: Unlicensed propagation prohibited.

terniflora
Synonym: *maximowicziana*

Flammula Group

Flowering Period Early to late autumn
Aspect Sunny to enhance perfume, and free draining
Pruning Hard
Height or Spread 15–18ft (5–5.8m)
Flower Size 1in (2.5cm)

Deciduous climber. A native of Japan, central and eastern China, Korea and Taiwan. The many clusters of small white star-shaped flowers appear as a huge white cloud in the autumn and give a gorgeous hawthorn, or almond-like fragrance to the garden, hence its common name of 'sweet autumn clematis'. Their four narrow tepals taper to blunt, gently recurved tips and the crown of stamens have white filaments and cream anthers. A lovely addition to the autumn garden. Best suited for planting in the garden.

'Tetrarose'
Synonym: *C. montana* var. *rubens* 'Tetrarose'

Montana Group
AGM 1993

Flowering Period Late spring to early summer
Aspect Sunny, to enhance perfume
Pruning Tidy after flowering
Height or Spread 15–20ft (5–6m)
Flower Size 3in (7.5cm)

Deciduous climber. This lovely clematis was the result of experiments using colchicine on *C. montana* 'Rubens' at Proefstation voor de Boomkwekerij in the Netherlands, and was introduced in the early 1960s. The single blooms have four broad, very deep mauvy-pink textured tepals whose margins incurve slightly as they taper to round or squarish tips, giving an almost bowl-shaped flower. The stamens have white filaments with cream anthers, and the bronze-tinted foliage and delicate spicy scent adds to the charm of this lovely montana. The cut flowers keep well in water. Best suited for planting in the garden.

texensis   Texensis Group

Flowering Period Mid summer to mid autumn
Aspect Sunny, to enhance flowering.
Pruning Hard
Height or Spread 4–6ft (1.3–2m)
Flower Size 1in (2.5cm)

Semi-herbaceous, deciduous climber. A native of Texas, USA. In cultivation, this rare North American species is commonly grown from seed as it is notoriously difficult to propagate vegetatively; therefore no two plants are identical. The two forms most often seen are described here. Both have semi-nodding to outward facing small urn-shaped flowers, each bearing four fleshy tepals with a wax-like texture. One form is a very bright, slightly orangey, scarlet on the outside and as the pointed tips to the tepals recurve the cream inside is clearly visible. They look like lips pouting for a kiss! The other form is a rather deeper scarlet on both the outside and inside. The stamens of both forms have cream anthers that are barely visible being deep inside the tight urn-shaped flower. The flowering stems die down completely each winter, and new shoots appear from below the soil in the spring which carry the new season's flowers. One of nature's gems! Suitable for growing in containers or planting in the garden. Best in a pot and given protection in winter.

'The Bride'   Early Large Flowered Group

Flowering Period Late spring to late summer
Aspect Any
Pruning Light
Height or Spread 6–8ft (2–2.6m)
Flower Size 3–4in (7.5–10cm)

Deciduous climber. Raised by George Jackman and Son around 1920. The 'bridal' white flowers have a lovely satin sheen, with six to eight broad tepals which overlap and taper to rounded tips. The stamens have white filaments and pale yellow anthers. Suitable for growing in containers or planting in the garden. An ideal wedding gift!

'The First Lady'   Early Large Flowered Group

Flowering Period Late spring to early summer and late summer to early autumn
Aspect Any
Pruning Light
Height or Spread 6–8ft (2–2.6m)
Flower Size 6–8in (15–20cm)

Deciduous climber. Raised in the USA in 1978 by Arthur (Bing) Steffen Jr. The gorgeous bluey-mauve star-shaped flowers have a textured surface with a satin sheen and, on opening, a hint of deep rose-pink bar that gradually fades as the blooms mature. The six to eight broad tepals have crenulated, wavy margins tapering to pointed, slightly recurved tips. The rather irregularly shaped stamens have white filaments merging to deep raspberry-red anthers. A good garden partner to 'The President' (see below) – try growing the two together, they would make a wonderful combination of colours. Suitable for growing in containers or planting in the garden.

'The President'   Early Large Flowered Group
                                                         FCC 1876 and AGM 1993

Flowering Period Late spring to early summer and late summer to early autumn
Aspect Any
Pruning Light
Height or Spread 8–10ft (2.6–3.3m)
Flower Size 6–7in (15–17cm)

Deciduous climber. Raised and introduced before 1873 by Charles Noble, Bagshot. The wonderful rich deep purply-blue star-shaped flowers of this lovely old cultivar have very slightly paler bars, and their six to eight broad, overlapping tepals taper to pointed tips via somewhat wavy margins. The stamens have white filaments with deep pink shading and dark red anthers. Best suited for planting in the garden.

'The Vagabond'

Early Large Flowered Group

Flowering Period Late spring to mid summer and early to mid autumn
Aspect Any
Pruning Light
Height or Spread 4–6ft (1.3–2m)
Flower Size 5–6in (12.5–15cm)

Deciduous climber. Raised in 1984 by Ken Pyne, Chingford. The velvety bluey-purple star-shaped blooms have reddy-purple bars. Their six to eight broad tepals taper to pointed tips via crimped margins. The stamens have creamy-white filaments and yellow anthers. Suitable for growing in containers or planting in the garden.

'Tie Dye'

Late Large Flowered Group

Flowering Period Early summer to early autumn
Aspect Any
Pruning Hard
Height or Spread 8–10ft (2.6–3.3m)
Flower Size 4–6in (10–15cm)

Deciduous climber. Selected by James van Laeken, USA in 2000 and introduced to UK by Thorncroft Clematis Nursery in 2010. The strikingly unusual violet-blue flowers are liberally marbled with mauve and white, making a most eye-catching display of these gorgeous blooms. The four to six deeply textured tepals are broad and taper to a point at both ends via toothed, undulating and slightly recurved margins. Their stamens have greenish-white filaments and pinky-beige anthers. The clematis was very cleverly named – it reminds us exactly of our 'tie dyed' tee shirts in the 1960s and 70s! This would look great combined with our single flowered, apricot-coloured climbing rose 'Meg', we must try it. Best suited for planting in the garden.

'Toki'

Early Large Flowered Group

Flowering Period Late spring to early summer and late summer to early autumn
Aspect Any
Pruning Light
Height or Spread 6–8ft (2–2.6m)
Flower Size 5–7in (12.5–18cm)

Deciduous climber. Raised in 1989 by Kozo Sugimoto, Japan, and named after a district in Gifu Prefecture. The beautiful rich satin-white blooms first open a creamy-white with cream bars; however, as the blooms mature the cream tint disappears leaving it pure white. The gently undulating margins of the eight broad tepals recurve slightly as they taper towards blunt tips. The stamens have cream filaments and pale yellow anthers. Suitable for growing in containers or planting in the garden.

'Triternata Rubromarginata'
Synonyms: *C. flammula* 'Rubromarginata' and
C. × triternata 'Rubromarginata'

Flammula Group
FCC 1863 and AGM 1993

Flowering Period Mid summer to early autumn
Aspect Sunny, to enhance perfume
Pruning Hard
Height or Spread 10–15ft (3.3–5m)
Flower Size 1–2in (2.5–5cm)

Deciduous climber. Raised by Thomas Cripps, Tunbridge Wells, before 1863. This is a cross between *C. flammula* and *C. viticella*. The clusters of small star-like flowers are borne in such profusion that there is an absolute mass of their almond-scented blossom creating a gorgeous perfume across the garden. The individual flowers have four narrow tepals that are white at base merging to rich red halfway along their length to their blunt, recurved tips. As the flowers mature their tepals twist slightly and the margins recurve, their stamens are pale yellow. Although it can be a little 'tricky' to establish, given patience it is fantastic and is a favourite in our garden. Best suited for planting in the garden.

'Tsuzuki'   Early Large Flowered Group

Flowering Period Late spring to early summer and late summer to early autumn
Aspect Any
Pruning Light
Height or Spread 6–8ft (2–2.6m)
Flower Size 5–7in (12.5–17cm)

Deciduous climber. Raised in 1982 by Kazushige Ozawa, Japan. When first open the white blooms have pale greeny-cream bars, however, these quickly fade leaving a clear, pure white with a satin sheen and an almost transparent appearance. The seven or eight overlapping tepals taper to blunt tips. The stamens have white filaments and primrose yellow anthers. The reverse has greeny-cream bars which can be reflected through the tepals; this combined with the cream anthers can give the bloom a pale cream appearance. Suitable for growing in containers or planting in the garden.

tubulosa   Heracleifolia Group
Synonym: *C. heracleifolia* var. *davidiana*

Flowering Period Mid summer to mid autumn
Aspect Sunny to enhance perfume, and free draining
Pruning Hard
Height or Spread 3ft (1m)
Flower Size ³⁄₄–1in (2–2.5cm)

Herbaceous, deciduous, clump-forming, erect woody stems. A native of north western China, there is a wonderful description in Moore and Jackman's book *The Clematis as a Garden Flower* published in 1872: 'A stout-growing herbaceous perennial, with stiff erect slightly branched stems, somewhat woody at the base, bearing large long-stalked ternate bright-green leaves, the leaflets of which are rhombeo-ovate and mucronately-toothed, the middle one being largest. The flowers are numerous, in terminal and axillary corymbs, and individually bear considerable resemblance to those of a single blue hyacinth; they, however, consist of four distinct sepals recurved at the top, and so closely convergent for the greater part of their length that the blossoms appear tubular.' We would simplify the description of the leaves as heart-shaped (or vine-like) with serrated edges and the flowers, hyacinth-shaped and borne in clusters. The shade of the flowers can vary from pale to light blue, but they all have the most gorgeous perfume. There remains much debate as to the distinction between the species *C. tubulosa* and *C. heracleifolia* and their correct form of nomenclature. Plants of this popular clematis can be found with either label and we await further research to establish an acceptable conclusion. Suitable for growing in containers or planting in the garden.

'Twilight'   Early Large Flowered Group

Flowering Period Late spring to late summer
Aspect Any
Pruning Light
Height or Spread 6–8ft (2–2.6m)
Flower Size 4–5¹⁄₂in (10–13cm)

Deciduous climber. Raised in 1971 by Percy Picton, Worcestershire. These pretty flowers first open a deep mauve-pink with a splash of bright pink along their central bars which is offset beautifully by a crown of cream stamens. As the blooms mature their colour changes to light mauve-pink and the bar disappears. The six to eight broad, overlapping tepals taper via gently undulating margins to blunt, recurved tips. Suitable for growing in containers or planting in the garden.

'Valge Daam' (pronounced Volga Darm)   Early Large Flowered Group

Flowering Period Late spring to early summer and late summer to early autumn *or* mid summer to early autumn
Aspect Any
Pruning Light *or* Hard
Height or Spread 6–8ft (2–2.6m) *or* 4–6ft (1.3–2m)
Flower Size 5–6in (12.5–15cm)

Deciduous climber. Raised in 1980 by Uno and Aili Kivistik, Estonia, its name translates as White Lady. The blooms have six, occasionally seven, broad, overlapping tepals that are a slightly bluey-white with pure white bars and the gently undulating margins taper to pointed tips. Their crown of contrasting stamens have creamy-white filaments and deep pinky-beige anthers. Hard pruning will keep the plant more compact but will delay the flowering period by a few weeks. Suitable for growing in containers or planting in the garden.

'Veitch'   Montana Group
Synonym: *C. montana* var. *rubens* 'Veitch'

Flowering Period Late spring to early summer
Aspect Any
Pruning Tidy after flowering
Height or Spread 8–10ft (2.6–3.3m)
Flower Size 2½–3in (6–7.5cm)

Deciduous climber. Introduced from China by Messrs. Veitch in the early 1900s and originally named *C. montana* 'Veitch's Form'. The four, occasionally five, broad tepals of the deep-pink flowers have slightly incurved margins and as they mature to mid-pink the margins and tips gently recurve. The foliage has a nice bronze tint and, together with the lovely crown of stamens that have white filaments and pale yellow anthers, adds to the charm of this pretty flower. A reasonably compact montana which is therefore ideal for the smaller garden. Best suited for planting in the garden.

'Velvet Night'   Flammula Group
Synonym: *C. recta* 'Velvet Night'

Flowering Period Early to late summer
Aspect Sunny, to enhance perfume
Pruning Hard
Height or Spread 3–5ft (1–1.6m)
Flower Size ¾in (2cm)

Herbaceous, deciduous, clump-forming, semi-erect stems. Selected by R. Brown, Evesham, and introduced about 1995. A much sought-after form of *C. recta* that has the best dark purply-bronze foliage; otherwise its clusters of small white star-shaped, hawthorn-scented flowers are identical to *C. recta* 'Purpurea'. Sadly, rarely available – get it if you can, as it is very good! Suitable for growing in containers or planting in the garden.

'Venosa Violacea'   Viticella Group
     AGM 1993

Flowering Period Early summer to early autumn
Aspect Any
Pruning Hard
Height or Spread 8–10ft (2.6–3.3m)
Flower Size 3–4in (7.5–10cm)

Deciduous climber. Raised, and introduced in 1883, by Lemoine et fils, France. From the central white bars of this pretty clematis, purple radiates out towards the margins in veins, increasing in depth of colour as it goes so that the broad margins are a very deep purple. The five or six broad, slightly overlapping tepals taper to blunt tips. The stamens have cream filaments and black anthers. Best suited for planting in the garden.

'Vera'

Montana Group

Flowering Period Late spring to early summer
Aspect Sunny, to enhance perfume
Pruning Tidy after flowering
Height or Spread 20–30ft (6–10m)
Flower Size 3–3½in (7.5–9cm)

Deciduous climber. Thought to have been raised in Cornwall in the 1900s. 'Vera' has one of the largest blooms in the Montana Group. The single blooms have four mid-pink tepals with a lovely satin sheen across their lightly textured surface and their crimped margins taper to rounded tips. She has a lovely vanilla-like perfume and bears a glorious crown of very long stamens which have white filaments and yellow anthers. Best suited for planting in the garden.

'Victoria'

Late Large Flowered Group
FCC 1870 and AGM 2002

Flowering Period Mid summer to early autumn
Aspect Any
Pruning Hard
Height or Spread 8–12ft (2.6–4m)
Flower Size 4–5½in (10–13cm)

Deciduous climber. Raised in 1867 by Thomas Cripps of Tunbridge Wells. These gorgeous deep pinky-mauve semi-nodding to outward facing flowers have a rose-pink flush along their central bars which fades as the blooms mature to light pinkish-mauve. Their four to six broad tepals have a deeply textured surface and the crimped margins undulate as they taper to blunt tips. One of our favourite clematis which we have grown on our pergola with the pinky-white climbing rose 'Madame Alfred Carrière' – they made a fantastic combination. She was also perfectly suited to scrambling over a huge prostrate conifer we used to have in the garden, where we could look down onto her flowers. Best suited for planting in the garden.

Viennetta 'Evipo006'

Florida Group

Flowering Period Early summer to early autumn +
Aspect Sheltered, free-draining and winter protection
Pruning Hard
Height or Spread 6–8ft (2–2.6m)
Flower Size 3–4in (7.5–10cm)

Deciduous climber. Raised, and introduced in 2002, by Raymond Evison, Guernsey. These exotic looking blooms have cream tepals with a dramatic dome-shaped central boss of purple staminodes which are mottled with cream. At their very centre are further layers of purple tipped green staminodes. The six tepals are broad and taper to pointed tips via slightly incurved margins. In early summer, or when light levels are lower, the tepals will be greeny-cream. Best grown in containers (*see* Florida Group notes on page 130). PBR: Unlicensed propagation prohibited.

'Ville de Lyon'

Late Large Flowered Group

Flowering Period Early summer to early autumn
Aspect Any
Pruning Hard
Height or Spread 8–10ft (2.6–3.3m)
Flower Size 4–6in (10–15cm)

Deciduous climber. Raised, and introduced in 1899, by Morel, France. This lovely old clematis has vibrant cherry-red flowers with a broad pinkish-mauve bar that is overlaid with cherry-red veins. As the six broad, overlapping tepals mature their margins and blunt tips recurve slightly to make a very round looking flower. The contrasting stamens have creamy-white filaments and yellow anthers. Sadly, in early summer its lower leaves go brown, which is quite unsightly. We would therefore strongly recommend growing this clematis through a host shrub which will disguise this rather unfortunate trait so that its blooms can be admired without distraction. Best suited for planting in the garden.

'Vince Denny'   Tangutica Group

Flowering Period Early summer to mid autumn
Aspect Any, and free-draining
Pruning Hard
Height or Spread 8–10ft (2.6–3.3m)
Flower Size 1½–2in (4–5cm)

Deciduous climber. An excellent cultivar raised in 1992 by, and subsequently named after, the clematarian from Preston, Lancashire. The deep rich reddy-chocolate nodding bell-shaped flowers have yellow margins which taper towards the pointed recurving tips. The inside of the four tepals is shiny like polished mahogany flushed with yellow which merges to golden yellow margins. The stamens are the colour of dark chocolate and the prominent stigma is bright yellow. The cut flowers keep well in water. Best suited for planting in the garden.

'Viola'   Late Large Flowered Group

Flowering Period Mid summer to early autumn
Aspect Any
Pruning Hard
Height or Spread 8–10ft (2.6–3.3m)
Flower Size 4–6in (10–15cm)

Deciduous climber. Raised in 1983 by Uno and Aili Kivistik, Estonia. This truly delightful clematis has the most gorgeous semi-nodding to outward facing blooms that are a rich velvety violet-purple. Their five or six broad, overlapping tepals taper to pointed or blunt tips via crimped and undulating margins. The golden stamens are an excellent contrast to their dark purple background. Best suited for planting in the garden.

'Violet Elizabeth'   Early Large Flowered Group

Flowering Period Late spring to early summer and early autumn
Aspect Any
Pruning Light
Height or Spread 6–8ft (2–2.6m)
Flower Size 5–6in (12.5–15cm)

Deciduous climber. Raised in 1962 by Walter Pennell, Lincoln. The pretty, yet rather irregular shaped double blooms look rather like a ragged 'peasant' skirt. The many layers of tepals vary in depth of colour, from the light mauve-pink of the outer layers through to the very pale mauve-pink of the inner layers. All have a delicate satin sheen. Each tepal tapers to a pointed tip with the margins recurving as the bloom matures. The stamens have white filaments and pale yellow anthers. Single blooms are produced later in the season. Suitable for growing in containers or planting in the garden.

viorna   Viorna Group

Flowering Period Early summer to early autumn
Aspect Any
Pruning Hard
Height or Spread 6–8ft (2–2.6m)
Flower Size 1–1½in (2.5–4cm)

Semi-herbaceous, deciduous climber. A native of eastern USA first documented in 1730, whose common name is 'Leather Flower'. The small nodding bell-shaped flowers have four fleshy tepals that vary in colour from plant to plant. Bluey-violet to light purply-red merges to cream along the margins and at the pointed, strongly recurved tips so that the cream inside and the tips of the pale yellow anthers are visible. Suitable for growing in containers or planting in the garden.

vitalba

Vitalba Group

Flowering Period Mid to late summer
Aspect Sunny, to encourage flowering
Pruning None
Height or Spread 30+ft (10+m)
Flower Size ½in (1cm)

Deciduous climber. The only clematis that is native to the British Isles, *C. vitalba* has clusters of small white flowers that leave an array of silky seedheads which give rise to the common names of this clematis, 'Old Man's Beard' and 'Traveller's Joy'. Only suitable for 'wild' gardens where it can be left unpruned, as nature intended. This is not recommended for the majority of gardens!

viticella

Viticella Group
AGM 2002

Flowering Period Mid summer to early autumn
Aspect Any
Pruning Hard
Height or Spread 8–10ft (2.6–3.3m)
Flower Size 1½–2in (4–5cm)

Deciduous climber. A native of southern Europe. When introduced to Britain in 1569 it was known as 'The Virgin's Bower'. The delightful bluey-purple nodding bell-shaped flowers of this 'wild' clematis are perfect for that 'cottage garden' look that many of us try to achieve in our modern gardens. Their outer surface is deep bluey-purple down the centre of the tepals merging to paler greyish-purple margins. The inner surface is very dark dusky blue towards the crimped margins and has a paler bar. The pointed tips of the four tepals flare out making a very dainty looking flower. Best suited for planting in the garden.

'Vyvyan Pennell'

Early Large Flowered Group

Flowering Period Late spring to early summer and early autumn
Aspect Sheltered
Pruning Light
Height or Spread 8–10ft (2.6–3.3m)
Flower Size 7–8in (17–20cm)

Deciduous climber. Raised, and introduced in 1959, by Walter Pennell, Lincoln, and named after his wife. The early blooms produced from the old ripened wood are double, with single blooms later from the current season's growth. The double blooms open a deep rosy-lavender which matures to a deep lilac-mauve, they have an outer layer of six to eight broad tepals with pronounced reddish-purple tips and undulating margins. The many inner layers of shorter pointed tepals have very wavy, almost twisted margins that show their deep mauve-pink reverse. The later single blooms are deep lilac-mauve. The stamens have white filaments and yellowy-beige anthers. It was 'Vyvyan Pennell' that first stirred our interest in the genus *Clematis* – we saw it shortly after it was introduced and were immediately smitten! Sadly, she can be prone to clematis wilt but is so very beautiful that she is well worth trying and is often more successful when grown in a pot. Suitable for growing in containers or planting in the garden.

'W.E. Gladstone'   Early Large Flowered Group
                                                        FCC 1881

Flowering Period Early to late summer *or* mid summer to early autumn
Aspect Sheltered
Pruning Light *or* Hard
Height or Spread 10–12ft (3.3–4m) *or* 8–10ft (2.6–3.3m)
Flower Size 9–10in (22–25cm)

Deciduous climber. Raised, and introduced in 1881, by Charles Noble, Bagshot. The enormous blooms are mid bluey-mauve with a lovely satin sheen and rose-pink shadings when first open, the pink quickly fades and leaves deep violet veins along the grooves of the bars. The six to eight broad tepals overlap and taper via lightly crimped, gently reflexed margins to pointed tips. The stamens have cream filaments and brownish-red anthers. Hard pruning will keep the plant more compact but will delay the flowering period by a few weeks. Best suited for planting in the garden.

'Wada's Primrose'   Early Large Flowered Group
Synonym: *C. patens* 'Manshuu Ki'

Flowering Period Late spring to early summer and early to mid autumn
Aspect Shaded, to preserve colour
Pruning Light
Height or Spread 8–10ft (2.6–3.3m)
Flower Size 5–7in (12.5–17cm)

Deciduous climber. This 'wild' *Clematis patens* was probably collected in Manchuria and was originally named 'Manshuu Ki' (Manchuria Yellow). The plant was given to K. Wada, a Japanese nurseryman in 1933, who then introduced it to Europe in 1965 under the name 'Wada's Primrose'. The blooms first open a really pretty primrose yellow with a slightly deeper shade along the bars, and matures to pale cream. The eight broad tepals overlap and taper to blunt gently recurved tips. The huge crown of stamens have cream filaments and pale yellow anthers. This lovely clematis keeps its delicate primrose colouring better when grown in a shady position. This grows in our garden where others have failed and every year is a joy to us. Best suited for planting in the garden.

'Walenburg'   Viticella Group

Flowering Period Mid summer to early autumn
Aspect Any
Pruning Hard
Height or Spread 6–8ft (2–2.6m)
Flower Size 1½–2in (4–5cm)

Deciduous climber. A seedling discovered by D.M. van Gelderen, the Netherlands, in the garden of the Walenburg Estate and introduced around 1990. The open, semi-nodding deep purply-red flowers have a textured surface with a creamy-white centre which has purply-red veins running out towards the deeply coloured, crimped margins. The four tepals taper via slightly undulating margins to blunt, gently recurved tips. The stamens have greeny-cream filaments and purply-red anthers. The cut flowers keep well in water. Suitable for growing in containers or planting in the garden.

'Warszawska Nike'
(pronounced Var-sharv-ska Nee-ka)
Synonym: 'Warsaw Nike'

Late Large Flowered Group
AGM 2002

Flowering Period Mid summer to early autumn
Aspect Any
Pruning Hard
Height or Spread 6–8ft (2–2.6m)
Flower Size 5–5½in (12.5–13cm)

Deciduous climber. Raised in 1966 by Brother Stefan Franczak, Poland. Named 'Nike' after the Greek goddess of victory whose image, half-woman, half-fish, is depicted on the Heroes of Warsaw memorial that commemorates the Uprising in 1944. The blooms are a glorious rich velvety reddy-purple, slightly redder along their bars when first open, and they mature to a pleasant bluey-purple. The margins of the six broad tepals incurve slightly and taper to blunt or pointed, gently recurved tips but as the blooms mature the margins become somewhat wavy. The stamens contrast beautifully against the dark tepals having white filaments and butter yellow anthers. We used to grow this in a raised herb garden at the base of a barn wall where it grew up through the pink climbing rose 'Compassion' and looked fantastic. Every year a few stray vines used to wriggle their way down amongst the herbs and 'Warszawska Nike's deep colouring looked wonderful against the foliage of the variegated sage. Suitable for growing in containers or planting in the garden.

'Warszawska Olga'
(pronounced Var-sharv-ska Olga)

Early Large Flowered Group

Flowering Period Late spring to early summer and late summer to early autumn
Aspect Any
Pruning Light
Height or Spread 6–8ft (2–2.6m)
Flower Size 5–6in (12.5–15cm)

Deciduous climber. Raised in Poland by Brother Stefan Franczak and selected by him in 1995. Given to us by Brother Stefan in 2002 when we visited him in Warsaw, it was introduced by Thorncroft Clematis Nursery in 2005. The beautiful star-shaped flowers are deep, slightly dusky, rose-pink with a paler bar, and have a fine line of very deep rosy-pink outlining the crimped margins. This deep colouring is seen on the textured surface of the tepals running through the veins. The six or seven broad tepals overlap and taper to blunt tips. The glorious crown of stamens have deep rosy-pink filaments and butter yellow anthers. Suitable for growing in containers or planting in the garden.

'Warwickshire Rose'

Montana Group

Flowering Period Late spring to early summer
Aspect Any
Pruning Tidy after flowering
Height or Spread 20–30ft (6–10m)
Flower Size 3–3½in (7.5–9cm)

Deciduous climber. A seedling discovered in the garden of John Williams, who named it after his home county and his mother. The pretty, star-like flowers have four narrow tepals whose light pink base has very deep rose-pink running through veins across their satin surface to broad, deeply coloured, undulating margins that taper to blunt, recurved tips. The foliage opens reddy-bronze maturing to purply-bronze through the summer. The stamens have white filaments and cream anthers. A fabulous plant that blooms for a good four to five weeks. The cut flowers keep well in water. Best suited for planting in the garden.

'Wedding Day'   Early Large Flowered Group

Flowering Period Late spring to early summer and late summer to early autumn
Aspect Any
Pruning Light
Height or Spread 8–10ft (2.6–3.3m)
Flower Size 5–7in (12.5–18cm)

Deciduous climber. Raised by New Leaf Plants Ltd., Worcestershire, in 2002. An elegant creamy-white when first open, the early blooms can also exhibit a green bar which quickly fades as the flowers mature to pure white. The eight broad, overlapping tepals taper via lightly crimped, gently undulating margins, to blunt tips. Their glorious crown of contrasting stamens have white filaments and deep red anthers. Best suited for planting in the garden.

'Wesselton'   Atragene Group
Synonym: *C. macropetala* 'Wesselton'   AGM 2005

Flowering Period Mid to late spring
Aspect Any, with free drainage
Pruning Tidy after flowering
Height or Spread 8–10ft (2.6–3.3m)
Flower Size 2–2½in (5–6cm)

Deciduous climber. A form of the species *C. macropetala* selected by Jim Fisk, to which he gave the original spelling of the name of the village now called Westleton, where he lived in Suffolk. The light to mid blue semi-double nodding, bell-shaped flowers are much larger and slightly deeper in colour than the species. We used to have 'Wesselton' growing up into the *Malus* 'Van Eseltine' in our garden. In the spring they would bloom in harmony and be a fabulous sight together. But sadly some years ago, the rabbits destroyed 'Wesselton' and this really is one piece of re-planting that is long overdue! Best suited for planting in the garden.

'Westerplatte'   Early Large Flowered Group

Flowering Period Early summer to early autumn
Aspect Any
Pruning Light
Height or Spread 6–8ft (2–2.6m)
Flower Size 4–5½in (10–13cm)

Deciduous climber. Raised in Poland by Brother Stefan Franczak before 1994. Named after the peninsula at Gdansk Bay which was attacked on 1st September 1939, marking the start of the Second World War. The six to eight rich velvety, slightly purply-red tepals have a brighter red bar, they overlap and taper to blunt, slightly recurved tips. The stamens have white filaments and dark red anthers. Suitable for growing in containers or planting in the garden.

'White Abundance'   Forsteri Group
Synonym: *C.* × *cartmanii* 'White Abundance'

Flowering Period Mid to late spring
Aspect Sheltered, free-draining and winter protection
Pruning Tidy after flowering
Height or Spread 6–8ft (2–2.6m)
Flower Size 1½–2in (4–5cm)

Evergreen climber. Raised in 1994 by Robin White, Blackthorn Nursery, Hampshire. These charming creamy-white, male flowers have six or seven tepals that taper to blunt tips. When first open they are semi-nodding but mature to more outward facing and, as they do so, the tepals gently reflex. They have a beautiful crown of stamens with pale lime-green filaments and pinkish-beige anthers. The finely cut evergreen foliage has a bronze tint when young but matures to dark green. Best grown in containers (*see* Forsteri Group notes on page 130). PBR: Unlicensed propagation prohibited.

'White Columbine'

Atragene Group
AGM 1993

Flowering Period Mid to late spring
Aspect Any, with free drainage
Pruning Tidy after flowering
Height or Spread 6–8ft (2–2.6m)
Flower Size 1½–2in (4–5cm)

Deciduous climber. Introduced by Treasures of Tenbury, Worcestershire, in 1986. 'White Columbine' has single white nodding bell-shaped flowers with a tissue paper-like texture to the tepals. Whilst they look very delicate, they remain undamaged even in the worst weather, unlike the white blooms of some other species. The staminodes are white with butter yellow tips. The cut flowers keep well in water. Suitable for growing in containers or planting in the garden.

'White Magic'

Viticella Group

Flowering Period Mid summer to early autumn
Aspect Any
Pruning Hard
Height or Spread 6–8ft (2–2.6m)
Flower Size 2in (5cm)

Deciduous climber. Discovered in 1999 on the nursery of Marco de Wit, the Netherlands, and introduced in 2006. The semi-nodding flowers are a slightly greeny-cream when first opening, but quickly mature to almost pure white. The four tepals are deeply grooved along their central bars and the crimped margins incurve as they taper to pointed, gently recurved tips. The stamens have greeny-cream filaments and pale yellow anthers. Suitable for growing in containers or planting in the garden. PBR: Unlicensed propagation prohibited.

'White Moth'

Atragene Group

Flowering Period Mid to late spring
Aspect Any, with free drainage
Pruning Tidy after flowering
Height or Spread 6–8ft (2–2.6m)
Flower Size 1½–2in (4–5cm)

Deciduous climber. Raised, and introduced in 1955, by George Jackman and Son, Woking. The pretty semi-double nodding bell-shaped blooms open a creamy-white which clears to pure white as the bloom matures. The cut flowers keep well in water. Suitable for growing in containers or planting in the garden.

'William Kennett'

Early Large Flowered Group

Flowering Period Early to mid summer and early autumn *or* late summer to mid autumn
Aspect Any
Pruning Light *or* Hard
Height or Spread 10–12ft (3.3–4m) *or* 8–10ft (2.6–3.3m)
Flower Size 5–7in (12.5–18cm)

Deciduous climber. Raised, and introduced around 1875, by Jackman's of Woking. This lovely old clematis has mid mauvy-blue star-shaped flowers that have rose-pink shadings when first open. The textured surface of their six or seven broad, overlapping tepals has a pretty satin sheen and their crimped, gently undulating margins taper to pointed tips. The contrasting crown of stamens have white filaments and burgundy-red anthers. Hard pruning will keep the plant more compact but will delay the flowering period by a few weeks. Best suited for planting in the garden.

'Willy'   Atragene Group

Flowering Period Mid to late spring
Aspect Any, with free drainage
Pruning Tidy after flowering
Height or Spread 6–8ft (2–2.6m)
Flower Size 1½–2in (4–5cm)

Deciduous climber. Raised, and introduced in 1971, by Rinus Zwijnenburg, the Netherlands. The pale to light mauvy-pink single nodding bell-shaped flowers have a deeper
pink flush at the base of the tepals which radiates out along the veins towards the tips. The inside of the tepals is pinky-
white and the creamy-white staminodes have greeny-yellow tips. The cut flowers keep well in water. Suitable for growing in containers or planting in the garden.

'Winter Beauty'
Synonyms: *C. anshunensis, C. clarkeana* and *C. urophylla* 'Winter Beauty'

Flowering Period Early to late winter
Aspect Sheltered and free draining
Pruning Tidy after flowering
Height or Spread 12+ft (4+m)
Flower Size 1¼in (3cm)

Evergreen climber. An evergreen species that was given a cultivar name by Wim Snoeijer,
the Netherlands, in 2002. The nodding bell-shaped flowers which are borne from the leaf
axils are pale cream when first open but quickly clear to pure white, they have a deeply textured surface and a wax-like
appearance. The four tepals are broad and taper to pointed, slightly recurved tips. The stamens have creamy-white filaments and butter yellow anthers. The evergreen foliage is a glossy dark green. Best suited for planting in the garden.

WISLEY 'Evipo001'   Late Large Flowered Group

Flowering Period Mid summer to early autumn
Aspect Not north
Pruning Hard
Height or Spread 8–10ft (2.6–3.3m)
Flower Size 3–4in (7.5–10cm)

Deciduous climber. Raised, and introduced in 2004, by Raymond Evison, Guernsey, and
named after the Royal Horticultural Society's garden at Wisley in Surrey. The pretty
semi-nodding violet-blue flowers have a hint of reddy-purple along their central bars and
are enhanced by a crown of yellow stamens. The surface of the six broad, overlapping
tepals is textured and their crimped margins taper to pointed gently reflexed tips. Best
suited for planting in the garden. PBR: Unlicensed propagation prohibited.

'Wisley Cream'   Cirrhosa Group
Synonym: *C. cirrhosa* 'Wisley Cream'   AGM 2002

Flowering Period Mid winter to early spring
Aspect Sunny to encourage flowering, sheltered and free-draining
Pruning Tidy after flowering
Height or Spread 10–12ft (3.3–4m)
Flower Size 1½–2in (4–5cm)

Evergreen climber. Selected from seed collected in south-eastern Europe and named
by Raymond Evison, Guernsey. The cream nodding bell-shaped flowers dangle from
the leaf axils. The small leaves are a glossy dark green. Best suited for planting in the
garden.

'Wyevale'
Synonyms: *C. heracleifolia* var. *davidiana* 'Wyevale' and *C. tubulosa* 'Wyevale'

Heracleifolia Group
AGM 1993

Flowering Period Mid summer to mid autumn
Aspect Sunny to enhance perfume, and free draining
Pruning Hard
Height or Spread 3–4ft (1–1.3m)
Flower Size 1½in (4cm)

Herbaceous, deciduous, clump-forming, erect woody stems. A selection made in the 1950s, 'Wyevale' produces the largest blue, scented, hyacinth shaped flowers in the Heracleifolia Group. We believe that over the years, the plants now sold as 'Wyevale' have become mixed and may not be the 'true' original 'Wyevale', a problem that needs addressing. Suitable for growing in containers or planting in the garden.

'Yukikomachi'

Early Large Flowered Group

Flowering Period Late spring to mid summer and early to mid autumn
Aspect Any
Pruning Light
Height or Spread 6–8ft (2–2.6m)
Flower Size 3½–5in (9–12.5cm)

Deciduous climber. Raised by Chieko Kurasawa, Japan. The broad, pale mauve-blue margins merge towards a yellowy-white bar which clears to pure white as the bloom matures. The six tepals overlap and taper via slightly incurved and undulating margins to pointed tips. The stamens have white filaments and yellowy-beige anthers. Suitable for growing in containers or planting in the garden.

'Yukiokoshi'

Early Large Flowered Group

Synonym: *C. patens* 'Yukiokoshi'

Flowering Period Late spring to early summer and early autumn
Aspect Not north
Pruning Light
Height or Spread 6–8ft (2–2.6m)
Flower Size 3–4in (7.5–10cm)

Deciduous climber. A naturally occurring, double form of *C. patens*, a native of Japan. These unusual irregular shaped double blooms are white and have green mottling on the outer layers of tepals; the inner layers often have pale green bars on the early blooms. The tepals are very narrow at their base giving a rather gappy appearance at the centre of the blooms; they then broaden out before tapering to pointed tips. A few inches below the bloom is a ring of leaf-like bracts around the flower stalk. The stamens have white filaments and cream anthers. Best suited for planting in the garden.

Further Information

BIBLIOGRAPHY

Bean, W.J. Bean, *Trees and Shrubs Hardy in the British Isles* (John Murray, 1914, reprinted 1989).

Gooch, Ruth *Clematis, the Complete Guide* (Crowood, 1996).

Howells, Dr John (Editor) *The Clematis* 1994 (British Clematis Society).

International Clematis Register and Checklist (RHS, 2002).

Johnson, Magnus, *The Genus Clematis* (Magnus Johnson Plantskola A.B. and Bengt Sundström, Södertälje, Sweden, 2001).

Markham, Ernest, *Clematis* (Country Life, 1935, revised 1939, 1951).

Moore, Thomas and Jackman, George, *The Clematis as a Garden Flower* (John Murray, 1872).

The Plant Finder (RHS, annual publication).

Snoeijer, Wim, *Clematis Index* 1991 (Jan Fopma, PO Box13, 2770 AA, Boskoop, The Netherlands, 1991).

Snoeijer, Wim, *Clematis Cultivar Group Classification* (Wim Snoeijer, Vest 162, 2801 TX Gouda, The Netherlands, 2008).

Whitehead, Stanley B., *Garden Clematis* (John Gifford, 1959).

USEFUL ADDRESSES

Clematis Societies

British Clematis Society
www.britishclematis.org.uk

International Clematis Society
www.clematisinternational.com

Suppliers

Clematis Specialists
Thorncroft Clematis
The Lings, Reymerston, Norwich, Norfolk, NR9 4QG.
www.thorncroftclematis.co.uk

Old-fashioned Roses
Peter Beales Roses
London Road, Attleborough, Norfolk, NR17 1AY.
www.classicroses.co.uk

Index